Widows and Orphans First

WOMEN IN AMERICAN HISTORY

Series Editors
Anne Firor Scott
Susan Armitage
Susan K. Cahn
Deborah Gray White

*A list of books in the series appears
at the end of this book.*

Widows and Orphans First

The Family Economy and Social Welfare Policy, 1880–1939

S. J. KLEINBERG

University of Illinois Press

URBANA AND CHICAGO

Library of Congress Cataloging-in-Publication Data
Kleinberg, S. J.
Widows and orphans first : the family economy and social
welfare policy, 1880–1939 / S.J. Kleinberg.
p.   cm. — (Women in American history)
Includes bibliographical references and index.
ISBN-13: 978-0-252-03020-8 (cloth : alk. paper)
ISBN-10: 0-252-03020-6 (cloth : alk. paper)
1. Family services—United States—History.
2. Family policy—United States—History.
3. Widows—Services for—United States—History.
4. Orphans—Services for—United States—History.
I. Title. II. Series.
HV699.K585   2006
362.82'0973'09034—dc22   2005009425

*For my sisters-in-law, Mandy O'Keeffe and
Jean Flemming, and in loving memory of
Richard O'Keeffe, 1945–91, and
John Flemming, 1941–2003*

Contents

Tables

Preface

In this book I reflect on the experiences of widows and orphans in the United States during the Progressive Era and the New Deal. I began the research just before my youngest brother-in-law, the British playwright Richard O'Keeffe, died unexpectedly in his midforties, leaving my sister-in-law Mandy to raise two young children on her own. I finished the writing shortly after my husband's younger brother, John, died following a long illness. John Flemming had a distinguished career as an economist and the head of an Oxford college but succumbed to cancer in his early sixties. I dedicate this book to their memory and to their widows. My brothers-in-law died at different stages in their lives. Richard and Mandy had young children; John and Jean's were adults launched on their own careers. I mention this because matters such as age at death, survivors' education and ability to work, and available social support systems all make a difference to widows' and orphans' prospects, although nothing can possibly replace the love of a spouse or parent. While I draw few comparisons between contemporary Britain and the United States in the late nineteenth and early twentieth centuries, the differences in the countries' welfare policies and the experiences of my sisters-in-law, nieces, and nephews have made me acutely aware of the importance of local values in establishing the welfare state.

Another situation alerted me to the significance of place and the changing nature of single parenthood in the United States. When I taught at a University of California campus in the early 1970s, I had two excellent students who symbolized the American welfare state at that time and women's struggles to rise above their circumstances. One, whom I'll call Jane, was the granddaughter of Jewish immigrants. Social Security Survivors' Benefits, a legacy of the New Deal, funded her college degree because her widowed mother's late husband had worked in an occupation covered by Social Security. The benefits paid to widows enabled Jane to attend university and did not penalize her or her mother for the income Jane earned during summer breaks.

The other woman, whom I'll call Juanita, had Mexican-born parents; at the time in question she was a student in her late thirties. Her marriage had broken down, leaving her to support five children, ages five to fourteen. They depended on Aid to Families with Dependent Children (AFDC, the successor to the Aid to Dependent Children program of the Social Security Act) because her ex-husband made no financial contribution to the family. If Juanita earned any money, the welfare authorities deducted an equal amount from the aid she obtained for her children. Moreover, this program would cease helping to support her children once they left high school, whereas Jane continued to receive aid throughout her college career. Even in the comparatively liberal welfare climate of 1970s California, social workers pressured Juanita to leave the university before she finished her degree. They made midnight inspections to find evidence of illicit relations with men, searching for men's trousers hanging in her closet or shoes under her bed. The caseworkers hoped to catch her with a man in her bed so they could expel her from the welfare rolls.

Both Jane and Juanita accomplished their goals, although it was more difficult for Juanita, whose assistance from the government depended on her "good" behavior, ability to stand up for her rights, and strong determination to make a better life for herself and her family. In terms of per-child support payments, Jane's mother received approximately twice as much as Juanita did. Moreover, neither she nor her daughter endured scrutiny of their personal behavior. Under the Social Security Act, widows and their half-orphaned children enjoyed a considerable advantage over other single mothers and dependent children, although both groups had the same needs. The different approach to children's education followed from the act and its amendments, which distinguished between (mostly white) widows and orphans entitled to benefits and divorced, deserted, or never-married mothers (frequently women of color), whose conduct social workers scrutinized and whose families could be broken up.

Jane and Juanita's stories reflect the importance of race, place, and marital status in understanding the American welfare state and the ways in which it distinguished between different groups of single mothers. At the beginning of the twentieth century, widows constituted the vast majority of single mothers. Some 11 percent of all women over the age of fifteen were widows; fewer than 1 percent were divorced. By 1940 the female population and the number of widows within it had doubled, while the proportion of divorced women had climbed sevenfold. The programs that constructed the American welfare state differentiated between these groups, providing inadequately for the children of divorced or never-married mothers. These interventions had a racial and gendered subtext that privileged some single mothers and penalized others. Widows' pensions originated in the Progressive Era, when public support for widows with young children emerged as part of the contested terrain of industrial society. Issues of family structure and roles then became matters of public debate at the levels of city, state, and federal jurisdictions, a development that continued during the New Deal, when political compromises ensured local control over key aspects of Social Security.

In this book I map the changes in widows' lives, the family economy as it developed in the late nineteenth and early twentieth centuries, and the welfare system that emerged at the state and federal levels. I first investigate widows' employment and family structures and then explore children's employment, a key concern of Progressive reformers. Finally, I analyze charity, widows' pensions, and New Deal measures to tackle the economic cataclysm of the Great Depression. I use census and charity records from three localities to contrast widows and orphans' experiences in the distinctive economic settings of Pittsburgh, Pennsylvania; Baltimore, Maryland; and Fall River, Massachusetts.

A number of individuals and organizations have greatly aided me research and write this work. The sociologist Sara Arber of the University of Surrey, England, helped devise the original sampling frame and made it possible to get the data keypunched. (This project began before machine-readable versions of the census became widely available.) Research assistants Michael Bracken and Charlotte Keeble helped with the coding, computing, and data analysis, while Cheryl Hudson and Natalie Stenson furnished qualitative research support. David Ryden enlightened me about the IPUMS data sets and clarified the data on children's education and employment. Robin Judd and Iain Liddell offered technical computer support. Iain rescued chapter 2 when it persistently froze my computer and I thought I would have to abandon it and start over. Diane Woodhead provided invaluable assistance in producing the final copy.

Librarians and archivists at Brunel University, the London School of Economics, the Library of Congress, the U.S. National Archives, the Maryland Room of the Enoch Pratt Free Library (Baltimore), Baltimore City Archives, Towson University, the Pennsylvania Division of the Carnegie Library of Pittsburgh, the Fall River Library, the Archives of Industrial Society at the University of Pittsburgh (especially Frank Zabrosky), and the Fall River Historical Society all aided my quest for documents and materials. Sister

M. Ludivine of the St. Vincent's Children's Home of Fall River, the Family Service Association of Greater Fall River, the Family Welfare Association of Baltimore, and the Pittsburgh Association for the Improvement of the Poor permitted me to examine their old cupboards, records, and filing cabinets for documents that might shed light on widows and orphans. I am indebted to Donald Emond of the Family Services Association of Fall River and John Weldon of St. Vincent's Home of Fall River for permission to cite material contained in their records.

Eileen Boris, W. Andrew Achenbaum, Susan Armitage, Vivien Hart, Gareth Davies, Tony Badger, Brian Gratton, Trevor Burnard, Inge Dornan, Michael Dostal, and Rachel Cohen have read all or parts of this work. I am especially grateful to Eileen and Andrew, whose helpful and detailed comments helped me to revise the manuscript, and to Susan, whose suggestions sharpened the final draft. Colleagues at the universities of Oxford, Cambridge, Sussex, Warwick, Glasgow, Pittsburgh, Toronto, and London have invited me to address seminars or workshops and have made valuable suggestions, as have commentators at meetings of the Social Science History Association, the European Social Science History Association, the International Economic History Society, the Social History Society, the British Association for American Studies, the Netherlands American Studies Association, the Women's History Network, and the Roosevelt Study Centre in Middelburg, Holland. I can only apologize when my own limitations have prevented me from following their excellent advice.

I have been fortunate to receive sustained funding from Brunel University's Research Committee that permitted me to employ research assistants. The Arts and Humanities Research Board gave me a fellowship so that I had time to write. This support has been very welcome. I am also grateful to Laurie Matheson and Bruce Bethell of the University of Illinois Press for their guidance and helpful suggestions. My thanks also to Gemma Barber for her splendid work on the index.

Last, and of course not least, I would like to thank my immediate and extended families, who have been an immeasurable source of joy and diversion. They have never known a time in my adult life when I was not working on a book and have been supportive through it all. My sisters-in-law have been a source of inspiration and a reminder that this subject is far more about people than about numbers. Nic Flemming, the model academic husband, has read so many permutations of this work that he probably can recite portions of it from memory. Our long and happy partnership has produced two wonderful children, a number of books, and a lot of laughter and fun.

Introduction

The Lord watches over the alien and sustains
the fatherless and the widow.
—Psalm 146

In November 1886 the Reverend T. Grace of St. Mary's Church in Fall River, Massachusetts, recommended the admission of three boys to the St. Vincent's Home, which the Sisters of Mercy ran in that city. Ten-year-old Patrick Cantwell and his two brothers, six-year-old Matthew and two-year-old Michael, were half-orphans living with their widowed mother. Since it was difficult for Mrs. Cantwell to work and look after such young children, she appealed to her priest for help in placing them safely. Within the year Patrick had gone to work in the mills. His mother reclaimed her two younger sons from the orphanage, for she was now able to sustain the family on Patrick's wages and the contributions of other family members.[1]

Several years later visitors for the Associated Charities of Fall River complained that a widow in her middle years was neglecting her elderly mother, also a widow, by leaving her "without fire or care" when she worked. Described simply as "an old woman," Mary Dixon lived with her daughter, Margaret, who supported her and two young nephews by laboring in a local textile mill. The visitors wanted "to have the old lady better cared for" by removing her to the city hospital. Fearing the stigma and misery of relegation to the poorhouse, this family group managed to keep itself intact by sending one young nephew into the mills (a solution that later reformers would reject as sacrificing the young for the old). The Flower Mission helped further by making a comforter to keep the old woman warm during the cold Massachusetts winters.[2]

Both the Cantwells and Dixons faced dilemmas shared by thousands of families: how to balance the needs of the generations, look after young and old, and support the fatherless on the low wages paid to women and children in an industrial economy. Abraham Epstein, a campaigner for the elderly, summarized reformers' anxieties over the family: "The family—the only source which secured sustenance and bare comfort in old age in pre-industrial society—has disappeared for a great many."[3] Charity workers such as Mary Richmond questioned how widows could balance employment, supervision of young children, and care of their own widowed mothers.[4] Epstein may well have overstated families' effectiveness in looking after dependents in some mythic agrarian golden age, and Richmond later opposed widows' pensions; nonetheless, their disquiet illustrates contemporary observers' anxieties about the effectiveness of family support systems and the balance between economic and domestic activity. The problems facing widows and the elderly were intimately bound up with the evolving attitudes toward poverty, child and maternal labor, and the family economy in industrial America.[5]

Widowhood causes major economic and social discontinuities, creating a distinct social role for the bereaved and, in many cultures, restricting them to particular styles of life. Cultures recognize the break in family relations wrought by death, labeling those left behind as widows, widowers, or orphans, yet they take widely divergent approaches to the resulting family status. Traditional Hindu society expected a widow to throw herself on her husband's funeral pyre; indeed, the Sanskrit term for "good woman" gave its name to the practice of suttee (or sati). The Abrahamic tradition regards widows and orphans as dependents needing support, whereas the matrilineal inheritance patterns of many Native American peoples conferred autonomy on widows with little financial penalty on bereavement, whatever the emotional loss.[6]

Widows need not be passive victims, as the sociologist Helena Znaniecki Lopata has demonstrated in her study of widowhood in Chicago during the 1960s and early 1970s. Yet historians have either neglected widowhood or regarded widows principally as the objects of welfare policy.[7] There are of course notable exceptions to this trend, especially among scholars of antebellum America. Lisa Wilson Waciega and Claudia Goldin analyzed widows' economic performance in the early republic, while Anne M. Boylan investigated their participation in women's organizations.[8] Regional studies, such as Arlene Scadron's volume of essays on widowhood in the Southwest, have painted a diverse picture in which widows exercised agency and resourcefulness by undertaking employment, putting children to work, and living in extended households.[9]

The family remained widows' primary means of support in the Gilded Age and Progressive Era, despite a growth in private and public institutions and the development of social provision. The family underwent its own transformations, however, which led to a rearticulation of appropriate roles for women and children. Reformers developed new approaches to welfare that embedded certain age and gender roles within social policy. They rejected widows' own economic strategies precisely because such approaches required the labor of women and children at a time when middle-class and skilled workers had adopted a family wage model that called for a single, preferably male, breadwinner.[10]

A century ago widows constituted a disproportionate share of wage-earning women, yet in terms of lives and labor, we know far less about this group than we do about other groups of women in industrial America.[11] In this book I redress the neglected history of widows with an analysis of social-welfare policy rooted in the changing family economy and divergent needs of local economies. The story I tell transcends that of widows' strategies for coping with the economic hazards of bereavement mainly through their own and their children's employment, for it includes an interpretation of the development of the welfare state that emphasizes the importance of local values. I demonstrate the striking variations in widows' circumstances by race, ethnicity, and geographic location, comparing their experiences in three distinctive urban environments—Pittsburgh, Fall River, and Baltimore—at the height of the industrial era and during the transition from local to federal domination of social-welfare policies.

White widows in industrial societies enjoyed greater financial control over their assets than they had as wives, yet sustaining themselves remained a problem. The assumption that children would reside with and support a widowed mother pervaded many rural cultures. As the ranks of the urban poor swelled in the late nineteenth century, fewer men had property to bequeath. At the same time, family sizes shrank, so there were fewer coresident children to contribute to their mothers' subsistence and more pressure on those still at home to enter the labor force.[12] The end of the nineteenth century saw a sharp increase in the number of orphanages, homes for older people, and charities caring for the widowed and elderly as substitutes for or augmentation to familial resources. Combined with aid to widows and older people in their own homes (widows' pensions in the 1910s and 1920s and Social Security in the 1930s), these developments indicate that American society viewed support for widows and their children as a growing public responsibility.[13]

The complex history of American social welfare has generated a number of parallel tracks of investigation. The pioneering sociologist Sophonisba Breckinridge formulated the problem of "neglected widowhood" in 1910. She observed that, lacking inherited property or children old enough to work, "the unsupported mother undertakes to carry the double burden of earning the support and of performing the domestic duties which, under our present habits of thinking, are inextricably intertwined with her maternal duties."[14] Breckinridge and other social reformers saw an inherent contradiction between motherhood and employment that justified the great distinctions between programs aimed at men as workers and those targeting women as reluctant or incompetent economic actors.[15] These activists held gendered models of agency and dependence in which the supposed contradiction between the role of mother and that of breadwinner warranted public provision for women forced into both.[16]

Early analyses of social welfare incorporated widows as objects of social policy. Roy Lubove established many of the lines of debate when he contrasted the origins and supporters of social insurance, workmen's compensation, and mother's pensions in the late nineteenth and early twentieth centuries. Aid to both sexes reflected gendered understandings of men's and women's roles, although Lubove did not characterize it in quite that fashion.[17] Mark Leff's article "Consensus for Reform: The Mothers'-Pension Movement in the Progressive Era" elaborates on this historical framework. Leff describes a bandwagon onto which "moral reformers and economic-efficiency buffs, women's clubs and labor unions, middle-class do-gooders and relief recipients" all jumped, noting the narrow scope of what he describes as a cheap and morally uplifting program.[18]

Leff traces the tensions between private philanthropy and public provision; the importance of the 1909 Conference on the Care of Dependent Children, opened by President Theodore Roosevelt; and the centrality of women and women's organizations to the passage of pensions. He also notes these programs' shortcomings: the moralizing grip of social workers, the regional variations in coverage, and the urban-rural and North-South differentials. Like Lubove, however, he says nothing of the racial biases contained in mothers' pension programs, a point highlighted by Andrew Billingsley and Jeanne Giovannoni in their study of African American children's welfare and one that I emphasize in this book.[19] The way in which differences in employment and benefit rates correlate with race and ethnicity forms a key component of the story told here.

Scholars interested in aging, old-age pensions, and the Social Security Act have examined older people's employment and social status as a means of understanding why and how retirement (as opposed to soldiers') pensions came into existence. In many cases these analysts have concentrated on the question of whether the United States was slower to provide aid to the less fortunate than its European counterparts had been.[20] They contrasted the fuller development of employment benefits to male workers in Britain and noted that American Civil War veterans were receiving a panoply of benefits by the end of the nineteenth century.[21] The struggle to provide for the elderly took place in an economy that offered less employment to older male workers than it had previously and almost none at all to older women, but not until the Great Depression was there systematic provision for the elderly.[22]

In the following pages I attempt to enrich our understanding of the welfare state by exploring the economic and social conditions that gave rise both to mothers' pensions and to provisions for older widows. I treat widowhood as a continuum from young to old, because the problems of widowhood did not cease once the widows' children left school. Early historical analyses of old age and the welfare of the elderly tended to group all older people together, obliterating distinctions of race, gender, and ethnicity.[23] Subsequent accounts, such as those by W. Andrew Achenbaum, Brian Gratton, and Carole Haber, explicitly contrasted men's and women's experiences.[24] Some historians of old age have focused on the plight of older women, on whom retirement pensions had little direct impact because few had participated in the labor force during their adult lives.[25]

State-formation theorists have analyzed the centrality of the American political structure, especially early universal white male suffrage and restrictions on female suffrage, to the development of old-age and mothers' pensions. Proponents of this "structured-polity" approach have concentrated on the way institutional and political structures gave rise to and transformed systems of social provision. Theda Skocpol's pathbreaking book *Protecting Soldiers and Mothers* examines the role that gendered social policy and "institutionally conditioned political alliances" played in the origins of American public social provision from the Civil War to the Progressive Era.[26] Unlike European nations that had a paternalistic welfare state, with male bureaucrats administering social insurance, the United States forged a "maternalist welfare state, with female-dominated public agencies implementing regulations and benefits for the good of women and their children."[27]

Not all scholars accept this approach. Linda Gordon observes that Skocpol fails to define *maternalist* or *paternalist,* to contextualize the organizations to which she attributes the success of the mothers' pension movement, or to consider the importance of race in the passage and implementation of either pensions or workmen's compensation.[28] Skocpol aligns the passage of widows' pensions with literacy levels, yet educational spending in the early twentieth century reflected states' racial compositions as well. Southern states spent little money on mothers' pensions for the same reason they devoted few resources to education. They restricted public expenditure as a way to keep tax levels low and limit the resources devoted to their large, disfranchised

African American populations.[29] As Charles Noble concludes in his political history of the welfare state, racial cleavages combined with delicate balances of power between political constituencies to depress social-welfare spending in the United States, especially in the South.[30]

Some scholars of social welfare concentrate specifically on the interconnected roles of gender ideology and social structure, locating social-policy developments in class, racial, and gender inequalities.[31] They investigate women's participation in local and national reform campaigns, the politics of difference and separate spheres, and women's economic disadvantages in an urban, industrial society. Peggy Pascoe, for example, scrutinizes female moral authority in the West in her study of cross-race rescue homes.[32] Molly Ladd-Taylor, Robyn Muncy, and Linda Gordon explore maternalism and women's welfare activism, with varying degrees of differentiation between widows and other single mothers.[33] Eileen Boris, Robert C. Lieberman, Rickie Solinger, and Lisa Levenstein, among others, have foregrounded racial issues in their analyses of New Deal and post–World War II social policy.[34] The interaction of race, class, and gender contoured the growth of the welfare state and, in Lieberman's opinion, prevented the "development of a strong, unitary, centralized welfare state in the United States."[35]

Historians of welfare are thus converging on the notion that men received benefits based on employment and as individual citizens, while women saw any aid filtered through their marital status—if they received any assistance at all.[36] This was no less the case when women wrote or had significant input into social-welfare legislation. Although most female social workers and social-policy innovators eschewed marriage for themselves, they valorized it for their clients and potential beneficiaries.[37] The policies they constructed restricted aid to "physically, mentally, and morally fit" mothers in order not to reward "crimes against society" such as desertion or illegitimacy.[38] Miriam Cohen and Michael Hanagan's comparison of welfare-state development in Britain, France, and the United States points to the emphasis on "welfare politics as gender politics," which Cohen and Hanagan attribute to "a lack of tradition of universal entitlement and . . . of constitutional limitations on the power of the state to interfere with the rights of families and individuals."[39] The close link between motherhood and women's citizenship meant that women and men did not receive equal treatment.[40]

The United States has never had a single, unified welfare system, at least as far as women are concerned. Instead, it established a two-track system of social provision in the Progressive Era, with workmen's compensation providing aid to (white) men in industrial occupations and mothers' aid assisting (white) widowed mothers of young children.[41] It has (and had) a plurality of welfare states with distinctive local approaches, a trend that the Social Security Act broke for men, especially older ones, but not for women.[42] Social workers may have hoped this landmark legislation would bring "some measure of coordination and comprehensiveness to the chaotic, varied, and uneven local public expenditure programs" of the early twentieth century, but decades after its implementation, welfare outputs still differed among locales.[43]

To understand distribution patterns for widows' pensions, I investigate local attitudes toward race, women's and children's employment, and the family economy during both the Progressive Era and the New Deal. Some jurisdictions proffered state-funded assistance to widows and orphans, while others did not. Divergent patterns of economic opportunity and racially biased views of who should work and which children needed saving combined to make social-welfare provision a patchwork quilt.[44] Widows' pensions inscribed racial, gender, and marital status into American welfare policy, defined women in ways never applied to men, and differed widely across the country. This variability persisted after the New Deal, because the local-contributions approach enshrined in Social Security legislation for "welfare" but not for retirement programs gave community officials considerable discretion in setting benefit criteria and levels. As Suzanne Mettler observed, the New Deal gave white men national citizenship while women and nonwhite men remained "under the auspices of the states, subject to highly variable forms of citizenship inherently tied to the politics of place."[45]

Dominant cultural values shifted in the late nineteenth and early twentieth century, moving away from a collective approach to family welfare toward an individualistic understanding that one ought not sacrifice a child's prospects to benefit the family.[46] At a time when the number of young workers rose sharply (peaking in 1910),[47] reformers valued mass education as a means of assimilating immigrants' children. They feared that the marginalized—urban poor generally and immigrants specifically—would neglect their children by subordinating young people's best interests to the support of the family. They opposed previous solutions to widows' and orphans' poverty, such as putting children to work, institutionalizing young children so their mothers could work, transporting children to supposedly more wholesome rural families in the West, taking in boarders or washing, accepting live-in domestic service positions, or doubling up with other family members in extended households. They turned instead to the state to avert the negative effects of these approaches: the curtailment of children's education, close contact with strangers, and maternal overwork.[48] These reformers called for increased school attendance to unify the nation, cure social ills, and ensure that young people would become "effective and useful member[s]" of their communities.[49]

Although the twentieth century was supposed to be the "century of the child," many reform innovations failed to improve children's lives, either because they had unintended and perverse consequences or because they did not reach all children.[50] Mothers' pensions rarely permitted women to leave the labor force to look after their children; neither did they reach the most marginalized, including the urban poor, people of color, and rural dwellers. Compulsory education and bans on child labor undermined poorer families' economic strategies because many working-class and widow-headed families survived only through the combined employment of parent(s) and children.[51] The death of the main breadwinner cut family income drastically, since jobs for women paid very poorly, an issue that few reformers addressed but that lay at the heart of widows' financial problems. Paradoxically yet inevitably, when legal changes made it more difficult to send children into the labor force, widows and working-class households generally placed greater dependence on women's earnings.[52]

The paradox emerged with the maternalist reformers' emphasis on mothers' domestic rather than economic roles, which filtered these women's lives through what Alice Kessler-Harris has termed the gendered imagination.[53] The gender-bound society in which they worked led social investigators to declare that "it should always be kept clearly in the woman's mind that the main object in whatever she does is the bringing up of her children."[54] Reformers viewed widows primarily in terms of their family status and responsibilities, problematizing them because they were "widows known to charity," people who seemed unable to make it through life without outside assistance.[55]

When more widowed mothers took jobs outside the home, reformers called for restrictions on maternal wage earning in the interests of their children.[56] Welfare authorities repeatedly said that widows on their own could support themselves but that those with young children needed help to combine their natural maternal role with the supposedly unnatural one of breadwinner.[57] They warned that no woman, "save in exceptional circumstances, can be both the home-maker and the breadwinner of her family." On this view, the state has an obligation to intervene because "normal family life" is "the foundation of the state and its conservation an inherent duty of government."[58] This version of the family economy depicts women as economic dependents while recognizing the difficulty of combining homemaking and income production. It swept aside the high proportion of widowed mothers who had jobs (up to 80 percent among young African American widows),[59] as well as the problems encountered by lone fathers with young children, while lodging social policy within a restricted view of the family economy.

Female reformers transposed their domestic concerns into the public arena, with widows' pensions constituting one of the cornerstones of the twentieth-century welfare state. Also known as mothers' pensions or mothers' assistance programs, these programs spread rapidly through the northern and western United States in the 1910s, providing material help to some women bringing up children on their own. Although a handful of divorcees, deserted women, or women of color obtained assistance, almost all such funds went to white widows. Despite pensions' real limitations, however, this relief reflected the growing importance of the state in sustaining the poor and a collective willingness to use the state to enforce a particular value system.[60]

Widows' pension programs had three purposes, two of which conflicted with each other. First, these measures attempted to stem the tide of families ruptured when mothers placed their children in institutions so that they could take jobs as live-in domestic servants or factory workers. Second, pensions were child-conservation measures and part of a general legislative effort to keep children out of the labor force until they were old enough to work without damaging themselves or the state. This laudable goal clashed with the third objective, to keep mothers at home and looking after their young children. If children did not support the family, then either the mother (or other relatives) must work or someone else must provide funds on which the family could live. In theory pensions subsidized poor families, permitted children under the age of fourteen to attend school, and allowed mothers to concentrate on domesticity. In practice, as I show in this book, inadequate funding and restrictive acceptance criteria accelerated the trend toward younger mothers' participation in the labor force and the substitution of maternal for child labor.[61]

Progressive reformers linked the welfare of widows to that of orphans. While it is possible to claim that mothers' pensions expanded women's rights, they were designed as child-welfare measures and justified in terms of protecting children from demographic and economic misfortune, as were the later Aid to Dependent Children (ADC) provisions of the Social Security Act.[62] Widows (and to a greater extent other lone mothers) benefited from such aid only when their children were quite young. Those without children or with children in their teens rarely received public assistance, yet they still suffered a disadvantage in the labor market. Because widowhood is analyzed here as a separate phase in the life cycle, this book includes those in their middle years, later labeled "displaced homemakers," whom historians have neglected.[63] The prospect of trudging "over the hill" to the poorhouse clouded the existence of childless middle-aged and elderly widows who could not work because of age, illness, disability, or a lack of appropriate jobs.[64]

Public assistance levels depended on the local economy and racial composition, with northern and western cities much more likely than southern or rural areas to tender either private charity or public assistance. Although white reformers offered state aid to those deemed worthy of support, they evinced little concern over the welfare of people of color. Welfare systems in the early twentieth century reproduced economically stratified racial and gender hierarchies that assumed white men should support their families and the state should intervene if death or long-term illness prevented this. Policy makers viewed family stability as being in the interest of the state, but their opposition to maternal employment did not extend to African Americans or other people of color. As Joanne Goodwin observed in her study of welfare in Chicago, "race problematizes maternalism's universalist assumptions and feminism's focus on sex equity."[65] The prevailing ethos took for granted that all people of color, including women and children, should be economically active, so the absence of a paternal wage earner in their households did not provoke much public concern among white reformers.[66] Nor did socially supported motherhood extend to the textile districts of New England or the South, where local elites depended on women's and children's nimble fingers to tend machines at low wages.

The influence of race and region on the development of public welfare in the United States makes it particularly important to contrast African American widows and white widows in terms of their divergent employment and household experiences.[67] While the proportion of extended families remained essentially static among European Americans between 1880 and 1910, complex households became more prevalent in the African American community.[68] Self-help efforts assisted widows, single mothers, dependent children, and the elderly from all races and ethnic groups, but prevailing racial prejudices frequently denied blacks access to public aid. Reliance on extended kin networks enabled them to manage the transition from country to city and served as a bulwark against racial prejudice in housing and social services.[69]

As I emphasize in this book, the uneven geographical distribution of pensions reveals another major contradiction in mothers' assistance legislation: although purportedly child-conservation measures, such laws conserved only certain childhoods. They incorporated a series of value judgments that favored some groups of children over others. Help depended on race and maternal conformity to the ethos of the dominant society, whether through wedlock, postwidowhood sexual restraint, or docility. Social Security benefits initially followed a similar pattern, allocating provision according to maternal status and the late husband's or father's occupation while excluding the predominant occupations for African American and Mexican American women—namely, domestic service and agricultural labor.[70] The children of never-married mothers and those with fathers outside favored employments (primarily industrial and skilled manual trades) received lesser benefits. In the program's early phases deliberate prejudice and political expediency meant that Social Security served people of color poorly, structuring coverage to exclude them. The Social Security Act left in place local governments' control over welfare (in the Aid to Dependent Children and Old Age Assistance programs) but not over entitlement programs (unemployment compensation, old-age pensions, and survivors' benefits), which went primarily to white men.[71]

Since cities and regions differed in their racial and ethnic compositions and willingness to assist poor people from diverse backgrounds, much of the ensuing discussion focuses on racial and ethnic divisions in employment, household structure, and public assistance. I explore these complex patterns by comparing the family economies and welfare structures of three eastern cities with differing economic, ethnic, and racial bases; setting them in their national context; and then examining the evolution of welfare systems in the Progressive Era and the New Deal. The early chapters deal primarily with widows, who at first formed the overwhelming majority of single mothers. By 1940 divorced, never-married, and separated women constituted the bulk of young single mothers, a fact that had serious consequences for their children yet was overlooked by contemporary social-policy makers.[72]

Social reformers left plentiful records of their actions and motives, and beginning in 1873 lawmakers's activities were documented in the *Congressional Record* and published accounts of legislative inquiries. But the behavior of families from different classes, races, and regions must be built up from statistical material, charity reports, and government documents, primarily the U.S. census. Few poor widows or orphans inscribed diaries or other qualitative documents; indeed, many were illiterate or preliterate.[73] By using the manuscript census schedules of these three industrial cities, however, it is possible to ascertain the lived experiences of widows and orphans. I then contrast their living situations with couple-headed households and analyze the variations that race and ethnicity wrought in their lives before investigating the social-welfare facilities and programs that developed during the Progressive Era and the New Deal.

The Three Cities

As sites for investigation, Baltimore, Pittsburgh, and Fall River have much to offer historians of social welfare and the family. I use them to show the diversity of women's and children's experiences in industrial America and the development of distinctive welfare regimes. Among the nation's fifty largest cities in the late nineteenth and early twentieth centuries, they exhibited quite different economic structures, employment prospects for women and children, and attitudes toward social assistance. The study of widowhood in these cities demonstrates the complex interaction of gender, race, region, and economic structure on evolving social-welfare programs.[74] It reveals the wide range of problems facing widows and their children and the diverse responses to them. All three had manufacturing bases, yet they differed greatly in what they produced and whom they employed. Their economic opportunities made them attractive to migrants and immigrants alike. In 1900 nearly half of Fall River's inhabitants had been born abroad, as had more than one-quarter of Pittsburgh's but only one-eighth of Baltimore's. Baltimore also had a large African American population, among the most numerous to be found in any American city in 1900. Blacks made up 16 percent of its population, whereas they constituted only 5 percent in Pittsburgh and almost none in Fall River. The proportion of widows in the three cities (16 percent in Baltimore, 13 percent in Fall River, and 12 percent in Pittsburgh in 1900) was slightly higher than the national average (11 percent).[75]

Cities with plentiful employment opportunities for women and children, such as Fall River, or with large African American populations, such as Baltimore, tended to be less generous to the poor than were those such as Pittsburgh, which offered few jobs for women or children. Fall River, the center of America's cotton-milling industry throughout the late nineteenth and early twentieth centuries, was the nation's thirty-third largest city in 1900 and produced 20 percent of all cotton cloth manufactured in the United States. The Spindle City, as it was known, drew immigrants of both sexes into its mills: the British and Irish during the 1830s and 1840s, French Canadians from the 1870s until the early 1900s, and southern and eastern Europeans in the twentieth century.[76] It had one of the highest employment levels for urban women; 45 percent of women worked in 1900, and 5 percent of the labor force was under sixteen.[77]

After World War I pressure from southern competitors threatened the preeminence of Fall River as a manufacturing center, driving manufacturers to further mechanize and vigorously cut wages as a means of sustaining market share. Its narrow industrial base meant that operatives in Fall River endured low wages, unsanitary working and domestic conditions, and a meager standard of living. Some of the largest mills closed completely in the 1920s, and others moved south. The Great Depression further undermined manufacturing; three-quarters of all mills shut, and the number of cotton operatives dropped to less than one-third of the 1900 level.[78] Although Fall River shared the Massachusetts tradition of public "outdoor relief" (aid given to the poor in their own homes), the city's small elite gave charity reluctantly and made few concessions to domesticity or education as ideals appropriate for poor women and children. Since the affluent in Fall River regarded employment as the solution to widows' poverty, they attempted to restrict public charity in order to force women into the labor market.[79]

Pittsburgh's employment and charity dynamics contrasted sharply with Fall River's. The expansion of heavy industry after the Civil War caused Pittsburgh to jump from sixteenth to eighth place among large cities by 1910. The Steel City, as it came to be known, produced one-quarter of the iron and steel manufactured in the United States at the turn of the century, and one-third of its male labor force toiled in its mills and metalworking establishments. Although strong men could easily find employment, there were relatively few jobs for women or young people. The city's small textile industry disappeared in the 1870s, leaving an overwhelmingly masculine employment base. Pittsburgh had the lowest proportion of employed women of the three cities: 20 percent in 1900, when other urban areas averaged 30 percent. The women who found jobs tended to work as domestic servants or dressmakers or (infrequently) in white-collar occupations.[80]

Pittsburgh is particularly interesting to historians of widowhood because its industries were "widow makers," even though Baltimore and Fall River had a greater proportion of widowed women.[81] The plethora of industrial accidents in iron, steel, and railroading affected mostly men in their prime working years with young families. Their widows found it difficult to obtain jobs in Pittsburgh's less than female-friendly employment environment, and there was relatively little industrial work for young children. Only 2 percent of workers were under the age of sixteen. Inspired both by the horrific nature of the industrial accidents and by the dearth of jobs available to widows and orphans, the city's charitable establishment looked more sympathetically on their plight than did similar organizations in Fall River.[82]

The North-South border city of Baltimore was a port with a productive fishing industry and a rich agricultural hinterland, whose staple crops it processed. Possessed of an excellent natural harbor, it derived its wealth from trade and manufacturing. By 1910 it was just barely bigger than Pittsburgh, yet it had a much more diversified economy. Baltimore's broad array of industries included food processing, railroad manufacturing, production of men's and women's clothing, shipbuilding, broom making, timber working, tobacco processing, and umbrella making. The consequent range of occupations made it attractive to women, who constituted three out of every ten workers.[83]

As in Fall River, over 5 percent of the labor force in Baltimore was under the age of sixteen; children as young as six or seven toiled alongside their mothers in the canneries and packing sheds. Much of women's and children's employment in and around Baltimore was seasonal. The jobs—picking over crab meat, shelling shrimp, shucking oysters, and processing peas—had to be done within narrow windows of opportunity. In addition, children prepared vegetables, operated machinery in the canning plants, helped in the woodworking industry, tended looms in the cotton mills, did hand sewing, and made hats. Many moved with their mothers from city to country during the crop picking and processing season, shortening their schooling as families sought to maximize income.[84]

Public parsimony and racism limited the funds devoted to public provision in the South and border states. Services of all kinds came later to Baltimore than to the more northerly cities, for that city's politicians wished to keep taxes low and ensure a ready supply of cheap labor.[85] Education, for example, became mandatory at a much later date there than in Fall River or Pittsburgh. Racism suffused public services even though the African American community succeeded in keeping the vote for black men and defeated the segregation of public transportation early in the twentieth century. The white middle class took an active interest in charity and welfare activities but gave little assistance to blacks. African American women in that city, as elsewhere, established a parallel set of institutions, including orphanages, service clubs, and day nurseries, to serve their community.[86]

The structure of this book reflects my belief that responses to the family and local economy governed the development of social-welfare policy. The first part establishes the demographic and economic parameters against which welfare institutions and services for dependent children and widows emerged. In it I pay particular attention to family structure, the family economy, and the role of children in society, probing widows' and orphans' employment and residential patterns. Wherever possible and appropriate I draw contrasts among the experiences of widows and orphans in the three cities and nationally. Since this is essentially an urban study, the complex issues of rural widowhood can be only alluded to and await further investigation.[87]

In chapter 1 I investigate the factors that defined widows' situations in the three cities: demography and family structure, residential patterns, age, race, and employment. In chapter 2 I probe the changing place of children in American society and the development of the family economy in the industrial era. I review national and local trends in children's employment and education, setting widows' and couples' children in the three cities into their national context. This chapter focuses on variations in activities in these two areas, specifically those based on race, ethnicity, and age. I conclude that the distortions that widowhood wrought on children's life chances were as acute for adolescent children, whom policy makers largely ignored, as they were for younger ones.

This chapter also relates the uses to which widows put public institutions. Especially in Fall River, where there were close ties between deeply religious Roman Catholic families and church-run children's homes, orphanages served as a form of extended family and provided a safe haven for children while their mothers worked or fathers sought alternative means of child care. Such institutions were, as Timothy A. Hacsi tellingly describes them, "second homes" that sheltered many half-orphans. Although they fell out of favor in the early twentieth century, with reformers and policy makers preferring to keep families intact, they were an important part of widows' and working-class strategies for coping with economic crises.[88]

Having established the outlines of widows' family economy in the first two chapters, in the rest of the book I explore the development of social-welfare policy for widows, beginning with widows and welfare before widows' pensions. Social reformers evinced growing concern over widows in the nineteenth century as they responded to the problems of urban poverty and to the divergence of widows' lives from the dominant middle-class pattern of domestic wife and dependent children. Widows came to be regarded as a uniquely needy group once the urban economy grew more hostile to their wage-earning efforts and society rejected female economic activity in favor of domesticity.[89] Chapter 3 provides an overview of the changes in charity in the late nineteenth century, enmeshing the growth in provision both in middle-class women's increased public roles and in municipal efforts to cut the costs of supporting a growing number of poor people. It traces the development of charitable aid for widows in each city, the emphasis in Fall River and Baltimore on women's employment as the solution to their poverty, and the battles for widows' pensions fought in each state.

In chapter 4 I examine the implementation of widows' welfare in the Progressive Era. Much of this discussion reflects state rather than local policy, because state law provided the mandate for pensions and the framework for their distribution. Even so, events at the city level make clear that local interpretations played a crucial role in determining who actually received help. Baltimore, for example, refused to fund widows' pensions in 1916 despite statewide enabling legislation.[90] The distribution pattern in the more northerly cities demonstrated the inadequacy of pension funding, despite maternalist rhetoric, and the continued need for additional workers in widow-headed households.

In the last chapter I scrutinize the transition to federal social-welfare policy through a consideration of widows' and children's experiences during the Great Depression and the New Deal. I reflect on the values incorporated into the Social Security Act, the limited prospects it held out for single mothers, and the blatant prejudice against African Americans at its heart. The Social Security Act followed the example of widows' pensions in restricting the labor force to certain age and social groups. The New Deal "aged" and "gendered" economic participation, curtailing the labor of children and older people while devaluing women's work.[91] New Deal legislation accepted distinctive regional approaches to public responsibility for the poor. That, too, had a long-term impact on widows and orphans, other single mothers and their children, and people of color.

This book links the origins of American welfare policy to anxiety over maternal and child labor. It demonstrates the diversity of the widowed population and the neglect of certain members of that group. In addition, it provides an exploration of the role race and gender played in welfare-state development through a comparison of race, gender, and economic systems in the United States during the Progressive Era and the New Deal. Ultimately, I locate the American welfare state in cities and states and emphasize the consequences of locally based public and private assistance during this period.[92] Paying attention to the divergent models of welfare systems illuminates the impact of race and gender constructs on social-welfare policy. The book thus focuses on the differences in single mothers' and children's chances for assistance during the Progressive Era and the New Deal. Above all, it shows the persistence of inequality and the inadequacy of local solutions to the problems of gender- and race-based poverty in the United States.

1 Widows: A Demographic and Economic Overview

> There came a time when *Grossmutter* felt that there was no
> real home for her in any of the crowded houses of her children.
> —*Fifty Years of the General German Aged People's Home*
> (Baltimore, 1931)

Marie Besonet, a middle-aged widow, moved to Fall River from Quebec in the late 1870s so that her four oldest children could take jobs in the cotton mills. Her twelve-year-old daughter stayed home to help with the two youngest children, while one son toiled as a farm laborer. Despite being unemployed for three months in the previous year, the children earned enough among them to support a family of nine. They sacrificed their education for the good of the entire family. None of the children could read or write, though probably the four and five year olds would go to school in conformity with state requirements.[1]

Forty years later Katy Perkins, age forty-five, supported her family as a bookkeeper while her three children (ages fourteen, ten, and six) attended school. Mrs. Perkins, born in Pennsylvania and resident in Pittsburgh, had received sufficient education to sustain her family.[2] Whatever domestic assistance fourteen-year-old Grace gave her mother, contemporary household technology and the smaller family size meant that she could go to high school rather than enter a factory, scrub floors, or stay "at home" to help with the housework and younger children.[3]

In the 1920s Maisie Ward, an elderly African American widow, lived with her daughter and son-in-law in their Baltimore home. She looked after one grandchild and helped around the house, while her daughter did day work and her son-in-law worked as a teamster. Mrs. Ward could neither read nor write, although the younger generation could, and her nine-year-old grandson attended school.[4] Her daughter relied on Mrs. Ward to care for her son while she scrubbed and cleaned, demonstrating both the ways the two generations depended on each other and the contributions coresident relatives made to their families.

These vignettes reveal the multiple solutions that widows crafted to their common problems. Most turned to their families for support, although their particular strategies depended on age, race, place, personal attributes, and preferences. Widows without living children faced difficult prospects in old age, and a number ended their days in institutions for the elderly or destitute. The Allegheny City Home housed many widows and a few never-married women, including among the former Barbara Doultner, an ex-housewife from Germany. Neither of her two children survived into her old age, so sometime before she reached seventy she entered the home. There she joined, among others, Mary Gordon, who was childless, and Scottish-born Margaret Day, whose one surviving child offered her no help.[5] Mrs. Day's sad situation was uncommon but not unheard of. In 1916, 3 percent of the charity cases in Baltimore arose because children failed to provide for their parents. For example, the Charity Organization Society of Baltimore consulted "Mrs. L's" minister when neither her children nor more distant relations would take her in. The minister facilitated her placement in the Aged Women's Home.[6] The lack of family or of help therefrom led a number of widows to enter the poorhouse they so feared.

In this chapter I map the basic demographic and economic shifts occurring in the late nineteenth and early twentieth centuries as a means of understanding how women responded to the financial challenges of widowhood, how family structures changed, and how local economic configurations affected widows' strategies. I first consider the demography of widowhood before examining with whom widows lived and how they supported themselves and their families. Finally, I contrast widows' experiences in Baltimore, Pittsburgh, and Fall River in the light of the cities' distinctive employment prospects for widows and children.

Evolving family structures, residential patterns, and widows' efforts to find solutions to their problems provided, in effect, the aggregate demand side of social-welfare policy, the objective conditions to which reformers and government officials responded. The issues taken into account—household composition; widows' employment; and variations across races, ethnicities, and cities—provided the context in which those policies evolved and signified the diversity of widows' experiences even within broad national trends. Where the patterns differ greatly among the cities, the data are disaggregated; otherwise they are presented for the three cities together to give a portrait of urban widowhood.

The way that widows used their families as economic and social resources altered in response to industrialization.[7] The balance between women's and children's economic contributions shifted with the transition to a commercial and industrial economy. In the early nineteenth century, when the separation of home and workplace began to impede women with family responsibilities from combining income production and domestic management, widows experienced a downward employment trend. The greater amount of capital needed to sustain businesses in the late nineteenth and twentieth centuries meant that women, especially those who had been out of the labor market for many years, found it difficult to engage in the forms of petty entrepreneurial activities that had sustained their counterparts in the colonial or early national eras. In addition, few women could take over their late husbands' jobs or enterprises, as had been commonplace in the smaller-scale economy of the late eighteenth and early nineteenth centuries. Instead, they turned to their children as economic actors since industrialization provided plentiful opportunities for young people to earn a cash wage.[8]

Age and stage in the family life cycle complicated widows' abilities to fashion solutions to the issues widowhood engendered. By the early twentieth century increasing numbers of young widows were entering the labor force and achieving a stable economic situation through their own efforts. At the same time, however, the situation for older widows, who lived longer and had fewer children than their counterparts of previous generations, grew financially more precarious. They were less able or willing to preserve independent households, and they increasingly took up residence in the homes of married daughters and sons or with members of their extended families. Once widows moved into their children's households instead of heading their own, they came to be viewed as dependents, which contributed to social concern about their well-being.[9]

The Demography of Widowhood

The problems facing widows represented a potential breakdown in the social order and undermined the belief that men should support their families both during their lifetimes and thereafter.[10] Indeed, social-welfare initiatives for widows and orphans arose during the Progressive Era despite, not because of, the substantial proportion of the population they constituted. This proportion was not a new phenomenon, however; widows made up approximately 10 percent of the adult female population in the colonial and early national eras and 11 percent between 1890 and 1940. The overall stability of these figures nevertheless masks a shift in the composition of this group. Between 1890 and 1940 the proportion of widows who were under the age of forty-five declined from 24 to 11 percent, while that of widows over sixty-five rose from 32 to 45 percent. Nor was widowhood distributed evenly across geographic, racial, and ethnic divisions. Although fewer than 10 percent of all native-born white adult females were widows, 15 percent of African American and foreign-born women were. There was also a slight urban bias, with 12 percent of urban and 10 percent of rural women suffering bereavement.[11]

Urban areas had a special allure for some groups of widowed women. White widows spread evenly throughout urban and rural districts, yet African American widows clustered in cities both to find employment and to escape the stifling racial regime of the rural South.[12] In 1920, 18 percent of all urban African American women were widows. The urban migration occurred because, as one former South Carolina Sea Islander observed, there was "no way for women to make money" in the rural South.[13] The city offered possibilities not to be found in the country, a fact understood by widows such as Ellen Calloway; sometime between 1895 and 1900, when she was forty-one, Calloway left South Carolina and moved herself and four of her surviving six children to Pittsburgh. Mrs. Calloway and her fifteen-year-old daughter took jobs as day servants so that the younger children could attend school. Lacking entrepreneurial opportunities, Mrs. Calloway deployed her domestic talents, along with those of an older daughter, to support her family.[14]

Southern farming practices posed particular problems for African American widows. Blacks rarely owned the land they farmed. They depended on whites' willingness to accept them as tenants, which was unlikely in the case of widows with young children.[15] It was a common perception that women were not strong enough to farm on their own. "When you live on the farm, the man is the strength. Must be a man to till the land." Even when they owned land, their relatively small holdings left them vulnerable to human and natural disasters. Hannah Pinkney, a wife at the age of eighteen and a widow with three children to support by twenty-three, held on to her farm for a few years, but successive storms saturated the land and destroyed her crops. She "despondently left her three children" with their paternal grandparents and moved to the city to find work in 1896.[16] Some exceptional widows managed to till the soil, especially if they had adolescent children, but many migrated to urban centers.[17]

Widowhood pervaded the lives of black women. Among widows between the ages of twenty-five and thirty-four, the proportion of African American women exceeded that of white women four to one; among those thirty-five to forty-four years old, the ratio was two to one. As a result, a greater proportion of African American women had sole support of young children than did native- or foreign-born white women, a fact that mainstream charities and government overlooked but that the black community recognized clearly.[18] Not all single mothers were widows, of course. Divorce levels accelerated in post–Civil War America, while out-of-wedlock births also created mother-child families. Some black women reported themselves to census takers as widowed even though they were separated or never married, as did some white women.[19] Nevertheless, the declared levels of young widowhood increased among urban black women during the period studied here. In 1880 nearly one-third of the African American widows in Baltimore and Pittsburgh were under the age of forty-five, while about one-fourth of all white widows were. This disparity broadened in the early twentieth century, when the younger age group contributed over two-fifths of the African American widows in these cities but just over one-fourth of native-born whites and less than one-fifth of those born abroad (see table 1).[20]

Increased longevity and decreased family size prolonged widowhood as a solitary state in the twentieth century, when female life expectancy rose and birth rates fell.[21] In 1900, for example, only 4 percent of the entire American population over the age of fifty-five lived alone, while 29 percent lived with their spouses only. By 1920 the proportion of single-person households had risen to 9 percent.[22] Many more urban widows were on their own; in 1880 one in eight widows in the three cities investigated here lived alone, whereas one in four did so by 1920.[23]

Three widows in their fifties can serve to typify these changes. The Irish immigrant Bridget Docherty represented the older-style urban family economy. In 1880 she kept house for her six children; the eldest four worked in Fall River's cotton mills, and the two youngest (ten and thirteen) attended school. Mrs. Docherty could have expected her children to remain at home and support her for at least another fifteen years.[24] Like many women of her generation, she would see her nest empty entirely (if it ever did) only in her

Table 1. Age Distribution of Widows by Race/Nativity, 1880 and 1920, in Baltimore, Fall River, and Pittsburgh

Age	1880			1920		
	NBW[a] (*n* = 347)	FBW[a] (*n* = 493)	AA[a] (*n* = 97)	NBW[a] (*n* = 312)	FBW[a] (*n* = 442)	AA[a] (*n* = 163)
15–44	29.7%	23.9%	31.3%	26.7%	17.8%	42.8%
45–64	38.9	52.1	46.9	45.0	46.2	42.9
≥ 65	31.4	24.0	21.9	28.3	36.0	14.3

Source: Data from manuscript census, Pittsburgh, Fall River, and Baltimore.
Note: Not all columns total 100 percent because of rounding error.
[a]NBW = native-born whites; FBW = foreign-born whites; AA = African Americans.

last years of life. Her prolonged child-bearing career meant that she would remain the head of the household with several children at home to support her through much of her old age.

Anna Butler, residing in Baltimore with two sons in their early twenties, faced different economic prospects in 1920. Even though widows' children married later than those from two-parent families, when her boys married (probably a few years later), Mrs. Butler would be hard-pressed to maintain an independent household. Hannah Burton, who moved to Pittsburgh as part of the Great Migration, epitomized the growing number of "singleton" households. She lived in her own rented room and worked as a domestic. Whether she ever had children or left them behind in Tennessee the census did not reveal.[25] Perhaps, when she found washing and cleaning for others too arduous, she resolved the problems of supporting herself by turning to her extended family, as did many African American widows; otherwise the city asylum seems to have been her likely fate.[26]

Widows' households had a distinctive age structure, with fewer young children and more older ones residing in the family home than was the case for two-parent families. In 1880, 3 percent of the children who lived with their widowed mothers were under the age of six, whereas 18 percent of children residing with married couples were. By 1920, 8 percent of widows' and 25 percent of couples' coresident children in the three cities were of preschool age, reflecting smaller family sizes and earlier ages of marriage among the next generation. The growing availability of nonresidential employment (live-out domestic service, for example) enabled more widowed mothers to keep their young children at home, particularly in the black community. By 1920 African American widows' households had proportionately more young children at home than did those of white widows.[27]

Although the age of marriage decreased in the general population during the early twentieth century, half-orphaned children continued to marry later because their widowed mothers needed financial assistance and their widower fathers required domestic support.[28] In 1880, 17 percent of couples' coresident adult children were over the age of twenty-five, while 28 percent of widows' children were. By 1920 the proportion of coresident children who were adults had fallen somewhat for couples but had risen to 38 percent for widows. Numerous widows' children accepted prolonged coresidence with their mothers as their duty, but others felt it a hard price to pay for a situation beyond their control. Some neither wanted nor felt able to maintain their mothers and younger siblings. In 1918 desperation prompted twenty-three-year-old Hermione Rondeau and her brother to ask the Children's Bureau for assistance because they wanted to establish homes of their own. The siblings complained, "In the condition mother and the babies are in, we will simply spend our lives supporting this family unless a pension is provided."[29] Family obligations conflicted with individual desires; these young adults urgently desired someone else to assume financial responsibility for their mother and siblings so they could lead their own lives.

For a small group of widows and rather more widowers, remarriage resolved their need for economic and emotional support, household assistance, and help in bringing up the family. Linda Gordon stated that widowers "either remarried quickly or found a female relative to take charge of the children."[30] This ignores the large number of widowers who could do neither and instead institutionalized their children.[31] Widowers and younger widows were most likely to marry again, but it was never a common occurrence. Older widows generally experienced difficulty in finding suitable partners. Data for Pittsburgh indicate that among newlyweds in 1885 and 1900, 10 percent of the men but only 2 percent of the women had been married previously.[32] Certain ethnic or racial groups and certain regions of the country had higher remarriage rates than others. For example, African Americans (especially those enmeshed in sharecropping) remarried more frequently than whites did.[33] Elman and London's study of remarriage based on the 1910 census discovered that ethnic groups tended to have similar remarriage levels for both sexes until the age of forty or forty-four, but older widowers, especially African Americans, had much higher remarriage levels than did their female counterparts.[34] As a result, most widows carried the problems of widowhood with them to their own graves, since the older the widow, the less likely she was to remarry.

Widows without children were much more likely than other widows to live in residential institutions, with unrelated individuals, or on their own.[35] The situation was not uncommon. An elderly Fall River woman expressed the belief that "among three or four children there'll be one that will be good to you," but all her children had predeceased her, so she had no means of support.[36] Another widow, Frances White, wrote to the mayor of Baltimore, saying she had no one to help her: "[I have] only myself, and that's very little." Mrs. White's children had died young. Her failing health meant she could no longer scrub and clean for others, so she turned to charity and the public authorities for assistance.[37] Her experience mirrored that of elderly almshouse residents in Pennsylvania, two-thirds of whom had no living children. A similar proportion of those resident in the community had at least two offspring still alive, indicative of the significance of children's contributions to widowed parents.[38]

Coresidential patterns clearly demonstrate the importance of the family

economy and children and near relatives as the providers of shelter and subsistence for widows. They underscore the precarious position of those without
relations. Few widows without living children headed their own households.
Most widowed mothers and mothers-in-law residing in their children's homes
had successfully completed their families or suffered the death of only one
child, but comparatively few widows living in extended families as other relations (e.g., sisters, aunts, or cousins) had been so fortunate. In 1900 three-fifths
of widows who shared a dwelling with members of their extended families
and two-fifths of widowed residential domestic servants had no surviving
children, whereas just one-tenth of widowed household heads fell into that
group. High child-mortality rates within the African American community
meant that one-fifth of African American widows had no surviving children,
while fewer than one-tenth of white widows had none.[39]

Widows' Residential and Family Patterns

The African American community relied on coresidence with extended relations or in augmented households (those with boarders or servants) as a
self-help strategy. Although the historian Steven Ruggles has maintained
that "before 1940, the presence of single parents or parentless children can
account entirely for the higher percentage of extended households among
blacks," limited housing opportunities and sequential urban migration also
contributed to the growth of extended and augmented households for this
group.[40] Simultaneously, affluent whites retreated from strangers. New tech-
nologies and lower birth rates made it physically easier for middle-class
women to undertake household management with less assistance.[41] These
families rejected live-in servants and boarders but welcomed their widowed
relations.[42]

Widows and widowers were less likely to head a household than their
married counterparts were. (See table 2 for coresidence patterns.) In 1900
the proportion of widows in the three cities who headed their own homes
(67 percent) closely approximated the national average for widows, while
the figure for those living in extended households was somewhat higher (25
percent in the sample and 17 percent nationally). The proportion of couples
heading their own households in these three cities was 88 percent. The 1920
census described three-fifths of widows and fewer than half of widowers
in the three cities as household heads, with age determining where widows
resided. More older widows moved in with children or other relatives as this
era progressed, even though younger ones increasingly maintained their
own households.[43]

Table 2. Widows' and Widowers' Relations to Head of Household in Three Cities

	Widows			Widowers		
Relation[a]	1880 (n = 937)	1900 (n = 1,118)	1920 (n = 917)	1880 (n = 216)	1900 (n = 308)	1920 (n = 243)
Head	65.5%	66.6%	60.7%	57.9%	49.4%	49.0%
Child	5.6	5.1	4.1	8.3	9.7	6.3
Parent/in-law	14.8	16.4	20.8	13.6	14.3	19.5
Other relative	3.0	3.1	6.0	2.8	6.2	11.2
Boarder	6.6	5.5	5.8	16.2	20.1	14.0
Servant	4.5	3.1	2.6	0.9	0.3	—

Source: Data from manuscript census, Pittsburgh, Fall River, and Baltimore.
Note: Not all columns total 100 percent because of rounding error.
[a]As defined by the census taker.

In 1880 approximately one-third of widows under thirty-five headed their own households (see table 3), and a similar proportion returned to their parents' home following bereavement.[44] By 1920 over half maintained independent households following their husbands' deaths, benefiting from social and financial support for their mothering, while many fewer moved back in with their parents. Charities pointed with pride to the widows they assisted in maintaining their own homes.[45]

While many widows obtained private or public aid, however, even more depended on their own efforts to maintain their households. In 1890 just over one-half of all widows under the age of forty-five had jobs (see table 4). By 1930 more than three-fifths of widows aged twenty and forty-four were in the labor force (see table 5). Employment fostered independence for widows; for large cities in 1900, 56 percent of employed widows headed their own households, although only 12 percent of other working women did so, and there were clear ethnocultural variations. Foreign-born white working widows were more likely to head their own households (62 percent did in 1900) than either African American or native-born white widows (55 and 52 percent, respectively).[46]

Although this study focuses on widows, a comparison with widowers can highlight the impact of gender constraints on the bereaved. In the late nineteenth century young widowers between twenty-five and thirty-four had been relatively successful in maintaining independent households; over two-fifths were household heads (see table 3). While a growing fraction of younger widows managed on their own, however, household headship among young widowers declined in the early twentieth century to 29 percent.[47] The lack of public support and changing family roles led many widowed fathers to put their children into care. Gender-stereotyping, maternalist-oriented

Table 3. Percentage of Widows and Widowers Analyzed by Age and Relation to the Head of Household in Three Cities

Widows

Age	Head		Child		Parent/in-law		Other relative		Boarder		Servant	
	1880 (n=613)	1920 (n=556)	1880 (n=53)	1920 (n=38)	1880 (n=139)	1920 (n=191)	1880 (n=28)	1920 (n=55)	1880 (n=62)	1920 (n=53)	1880 (n=42)	1920 (n=24)
25–34	32.9%	55.9%	34.2%	15.3%	—	—	8.5%	6.8%	19.2%	16.9%	5.5%	3.4%
35–44	78.7	70.7	7.3	9.8	1.1%	1.1%	3.4	9.8	4.5	3.3	5.1	5.4
45–54	73.4	72.5	4.8	3.6	7.2	10.8	3.6	6.5	4.8	5.1	6.0	1.4
55–64	69.9	65.2	—	0.7	17.3	24.8	1.6	2.8	6.5	5.0	4.8	1.4
≥65	54.8	45.7	—	—	35.0	40.8	1.6	6.0	6.5	4.9	2.0	2.7

Widowers

Age	Head		Child		Parent/in-law		Other relative		Boarder		Servant	
	1880 (n=125)	1920 (n=119)	1880 (n=18)	1920 (n=15)	1880 (n=29)	1920 (n=47)	1880 (n=62)	1920 (n=7)	1880 (n=35)	1920 (n=34)	1880 (n=2)	1920
25–34	42.1%	28.6%	42.1%	42.9%	—	—	5.3%	14.3%	10.5%	14.3%	—	—
35–44	58.1	42.8	20.9	14.3	—	—	2.3	21.4	18.6	21.4	—	—
45–54	75.6	58.3	2.4	4.2	4.8%	4.2%	2.4	12.5	14.3	20.8	—	—
55–64	57.1	60.0	—	—	12.2	16.0	2.0	16.0	24.5	8.0	4.1	—
≥65	51.6	49.2	—	—	35.5	33.8	1.6	4.6	11.3	12.3	—	—

Source: Data from manuscript census, Pittsburgh, Fall River, and Baltimore.

Table 4. Percentage of Breadwinners among Widows, 1890

Nativity/race	Ages						All ages
	15–24	25–34	35–44	45–54	55–64	≥ 65	
NBWNP[a]	32.6%	42.2%	42.4%	33.4%	22.6%	9.3%	23.7%
NBWFP[a]	40.5	46.1	40.6	28.7	20.4	8.9	30.3
FBW[a]	51.3	53.6	42.4	27.8	18.0	7.9	21.3
AA[a]	77.2	81.8	80.0	69.5	55.2	29.7	62.6
All races/ nativities	53.5	55.0	50.1	37.0	24.5	11.0	29.3

Sources: Adapted from U.S. Bureau of the Census, *Statistics of Women at Work . . . , 1900* (Washington, D.C.: GPO, 1907), 16.
[a]NBWNP = native-born whites with native-born parents; NBWFP = native-born whites with foreign-born parents; FBW = foreign-born whites; AA = African Americans.

Table 5. Percentage of Breadwinners among Widows, 1930

Nativity/race	Ages			All ages
	15–24	25–44	≥ 45	
NBW[a]	56.4%	64.6%	22.4%	31.9%
FBW[a]	65.7	59.5	16.0	21.1
AA[a]	71.0	81.6	52.5	65.0
All races/ nativities	61.5	68.2	23.9	34.4

Source: Data from U.S. Bureau of the Census, *Fifteenth Census: Population,* vol. 5, *General Report on Occupations* (Washington, D.C.: GPO, 1933), 275.
[a]NBW = native-born whites; FBW = foreign-born whites; AA = African Americans.

charitable organizations urged widowed fathers to give up their children. There were no "widowers' pension" schemes to sustain these families at home, nor could men of modest means afford to hire housekeepers. Patrick Reynolds, a laborer, struggled against all odds to keep his children with him in the late 1880s, despite concerted pressure from the Associated Charities of Fall River to place his children in the Sisters of Mercy orphanage.[48] Children's homes of all denominations contained a disproportionate number of children from motherless households.[49]

The proportion of middle-aged (thirty-five to fifty-four years old) widowers heading households declined in the twentieth century. Progressive legislation required girls to be in school, not at home looking after younger siblings. This deprived widowed fathers of their domestic assistance even as it enhanced daughters' educational and occupational choices. Consequently, many more widowers began living with other relatives or moved into boarding houses. As was typical of this group in 1920, the widowed Baltimorean Roy Harrison, then forty-four years old, took his family to live in the home of Laura McCarthy, an older widow. Mr. Harrison worked as a pressman, as did his sixteen-year-old son. His other three children—Brenda, fourteen; Roy Jr., twelve; and Selma, eight—attended school. A generation or two earlier, Brenda's counterpart would have been at home, looking after her younger brothers and keeping house. Now the landlady provided cooked meals and supervised the children after school.[50]

Only widowers aged fifty-five to sixty-four increased (slightly) the rate at which they headed households. They had sufficient older children, specifically daughters, to maintain the domestic circle. The Irish-born widower John Gill headed a household of six people, including two sons and three daughters. Father and sons had jobs in Baltimore's shipyards and railroads. Two of the daughters were clerks, and the third, Mary, had no occupation and presumably kept house for the rest of the family.[51] Mary's housekeeping skills enabled the family to stay together in their own home.

Widows and widowers in their midsixties found it more burdensome to maintain independent households as the twentieth century progressed. In 1880, as table 3 shows, 55 percent of widows over the age of sixty-five were household heads, as were 52 percent of widowers. By 1920, however, fewer than half in each group headed households. The percentage of household heads among the oldest group of widowers declined slightly, with these men turning to more distant relations and boarding houses if their adult sons or daughters would not take them in. Older widows moved into their children's homes in greater numbers and also went to live with more distant relations. Of those between the ages of fifty-five and sixty-four, 25 percent now resided in the homes of their adult children, as did 41 percent of those sixty-five and older. These women lived longer but lost their independence.

More widows lived in extended households by 1920. This trend was especially marked among skilled working-class families, which had less need of the income garnered from boarders and thus could house widowed relatives in some of the space previous generations had devoted to lodgers. Unskilled and retired households still sustained comparatively high levels of augmentation, taking in widowed boarders, among others, as a means of increasing income. The other social classes housed fewer outsiders and more relations. The proportion of home-owning families that took in widowed relations rose from 9 to 12 percent between 1900 and 1920.[52]

Home ownership offers one guide to relative affluence and poverty in this era. Although not all well-to-do people owned homes, it was a key material goal for most Americans.[53] The proportion of widowed homeowners among the entire widowed population remained static at about 15 percent during the first decades of the twentieth century. This overall stability notwithstanding, those widows who maintained their independence (as indicated by their status as household heads) also increased their proportion of home owner-ship. By 1920 the percentage of widowed household heads owning their own homes paralleled that of couples and widowers, indicating that those able to continue in their own homes had achieved a more comfortable lifestyle than had their turn-of-the-century counterparts. In 1900 about one-third of both married and widower household heads in the three cities had purchased their homes, with one-fourth of widowed heads of household having done so. By 1920 there was little difference between the three groups, although there were strong ethnic variations in home ownership. German and native-born white widows had the highest incidence of property ownership, while African Americans and French Canadians had the lowest.[54]

The Economics of Widowhood

Although a distinct minority, some widows inherited sufficient property and wealth to maintain elaborate establishments without entering the labor force, having their children work, or taking in boarders. Such was the case with Lucy Carnegie, the widow of Andrew Carnegie's brother Thomas. In 1900 she and her eight adult children, none of whom held jobs, shared a large house in Pittsburgh; nine servants lived there as well. Such establishments, of course, were as atypical as the Carnegies' affluence was.[55]

Lacking inherited wealth, many other widows moved in search of work, using their extended families as a base. In the 1910s, during the Great Migra-tion, two widowed sisters traveled from the South to board with a cousin in Baltimore. The sisters, a cook and a laundress both in their forties, depended on their own hands and extended families to sustain them. At the same time their contributions to the household finances enabled the married cousin with whom they lived to leave the labor force and her children to attend school.[56] Such complex households provided a home and companionship to migrants attracted by urban economic opportunities and reveal the strategies urban widows utilized to sustain themselves.[57]

Women of all marital statuses entered the labor force in growing numbers during the late nineteenth and early twentieth centuries. The greatest pro-portionate increase occurred among white married women, who had been poorly represented in the waged economy. Widows, whose overall employ-ment levels were already high, seemingly experienced a small rise in work rates outside the home. In 1890 three out of every ten widows had jobs, a rate exceeded only by that of single women (four-tenths of whom worked) and vastly greater than that of married women (one in twenty was economically active.) By 1930, 50 percent of single women and 34 percent of widows worked, as did 13 percent of married women.[58]

Age, ethnicity, race, and place strongly influenced widows' employment. Younger widows (under the age of forty-five) were far more likely to work than were their older counterparts; their employment leapfrogged from 52 percent in 1890 to 64 percent in 1930, while that of widows over forty-five edged up only slightly (see tables 4 and 5). Those born abroad were better represented in the labor force than their native-born white counterparts were.[59] They had fewer resources on which to draw since in many instances their families were overseas, while foreign citizenship and language barriers limited their access to charity or public assistance. Birthplace had little effect on middle-aged or elderly white widows' employment levels; these women withdrew from the labor force once their children were old enough to take jobs.[60]

African American widows had by far the highest levels of labor force participation. In 1890, four out of five African American widows ages twenty-five to forty-four worked. Although the level of economic activity decreased among those past the age of forty-five, even by sixty-five, an age when virtually no married and fewer than one in ten widowed white women held jobs, three-tenths of African American widows still toiled in kitchens or fields. This disparity widened during the Great Depression, when economic activity declined sharply for older white widows who were more likely to receive relief and Social Security payments of all sorts (cf. tables 4 and 5).[61]

Widowhood amplified the already distinctive economic pattern of black women, who had high rates of economic activity regardless of marital status. Bereaved at a younger age, they had less chance to accumulate property or possessions, especially given the poor wages and limited occupations open to black men and women. The relative youth of African American widows also meant they had younger children, who were less likely to find places in the labor market than were the somewhat older children of European-born widows. In addition, black families tried to protect their children through education; mothers such as Bessie Langston took jobs so their children could stay in school. Mrs. Langston and her daughter moved from Virginia to Baltimore sometime in the 1910s. She cleaned for a family and took in a lodger so that her eleven year-old-daughter could go to school.[62]

Striving to make a better world for their children led other African American widows to leave them with relatives while they migrated in search of employment.[63] These widows stayed in the labor force longer than white widows did both because they wanted to educate their children and because the limited job prospects and low wages facing black children meant they had little to share with the rest of the family. Children who lived with their parents tended to make larger contributions to the family income. French Canadian textile mill families, for example, assumed that children would go to work in the mills and delay marriage, all to help support the family. Children with jobs as live-in domestic servants tended to keep their meager pay packets rather than turn them over to their parents, so their mothers remained in the labor force longer than did those with offspring in the mills.[64]

In 1900 widows worked primarily in three occupational areas: agriculture, domestic and personal service, and manufacturing and mechanical pursuits (see table 6).[65] Some widows ran small shops as a means of combining child care with economic activity, but few of them made a living since competition from larger stores increasingly undercut profit margins. The occupational profile of Mrs. Neil of Spring Gardens, Pittsburgh, encapsulates the problems encountered by widowed petty proprietors. When her husband died and left her with a four-year-old daughter to support, she invested the insurance money in a small shop. This failed, so she returned to the work she had done before marriage, making vests. Each week she sewed a dozen, earning only three dollars for the lot, because the oversupply of skilled needlewomen drove down wages for hand and machine sewers and marginalized widows with no other occupational experience.[66]

In the first decades of the twentieth century some young and middle-aged widows used their educations to obtain white-collar jobs.[67] Business positions

Table 6. Occupations, Widows vs. All Women, 1900 and 1930

	1900		1930	
Occupation	All Women ($n = 4,843,155$)	Widows ($n = 857,922$)	All Women ($n = 10,632,227$)	Widows ($n = 1,826,100$)
Agriculture	16.0%	33.0%	7.7%	14.4%
Professional	8.9	2.3	14.5	6.6
Domestic	40.4	46.1	29.8	48.0
TT&C[a]	6.5	3.5	11.7	10.2
Clerical	3.4	0.6	17.7	6.9
Manu./mech.	24.8	14.5	18.7	13.9

Sources: Data from U.S. Bureau of the Census, *Statistics of Women at Work . . . , 1900* (Washington, DC: Government Printing Office, 1907), 170; idem, *Fifteenth Census: Population,* vol. 5, *General Report on Occupations* (Washington, D.C.: GPO, 1933), 275.

[a]TT&C = Trade, Transportation, and Communication. Almost no women worked in the transportation sector, but they did serve as telegraph and telephone operators. Clerical workers (clerks, copyists, stenographers, and typewriters) were included as part of the trade, transportation, and communication category in the 1900 census. I have disaggregated this category to make it more directly comparable with the 1930 data.

enabled them to sustain their families on their own and keep their children in school longer. Lavinia Fleming had lived with her twin son and daughter in California before moving to Baltimore in the 1910s. The fifty-one-year-old native-born white widow represented a new breed of working mother. Her earnings as a typist for the Baltimore and Ohio Railroad enabled her to keep the twins in high school without recourse to housing strangers. As more mothers such as Mrs. Fleming worked outside the home, however, commentators complained that "the woman who begrudges her own children a few years of her undivided attention perhaps cannot be suppressed, but she need not be admired."[68]

Although white widows expanded their occupational horizons, African American widows encountered significant discrimination in professional pursuits. Fewer than 1 percent held white-collar or professional jobs in 1900, with a scant increase by 1930. Even if they managed to obtain nursing or teaching credentials, general hospitals and schools refused to hire them, limiting their prospects to low-wage segregated institutions. Clerical employment, except in black-owned businesses and a few government departments, was effectively closed to them until well into the twentieth century.[69] In contrast, the first decades of the twentieth century saw increasing diversity in employment for white widows, particularly the native born. In 1900, 9 percent of native-born white widows held clerical or professional positions, a proportion that doubled by 1930. Fewer foreign-born white widows worked in sales or clerical jobs or as telephone operators because, as a group, they were less fluent in English and had lower educational levels. Even so, by 1930 8 percent of foreign-born widows had such jobs. African American widows, however, experienced little career advancement. Almost none held clerical jobs in 1900 or 1930, while a few worked as teachers.[70]

Constrained by their dependents' needs, women with young children had a different perspective on economic activity than single or childless women did. They considered remuneration, of course, but also evaluated a job's child-friendliness. Numerous widows left their children with friends, relatives, or in an orphanage to earn enough money to support the family, but others recoiled at the prospect of separation. Mary Brewer, a white widow in North Carolina, wrote to the Children's Bureau for advice on avoiding the prospect outlined by her state's superintendent of public welfare. He wanted to place her two older children in a home and board the baby with relatives so she could live in as a domestic servant. The thought of putting her children in an orphanage and possibly losing all contact with them drove her to despair.[71]

Other options, such as industrial work at home, might have enabled mothers to look after young children, but low piecework rates meant few could survive on it for long. Some jobs, such as laundressing, could be done at home or part-time. Washerwomen either picked up dirty clothes and delivered clean ones or washed clothes in other families' basements, kitchens, and yards. Washing clothes for a living suited only those strong enough to carry buckets of water and wring out sodden clothes and linen. It frequently left women with health problems, including rheumatic pains, tired legs, and swollen muscles.[72]

Washerwomen had considerable independence because they lived outside their places of employment and worked for a number of employers. Unlike other domestic servants, they could draw firm distinctions between working and leisure time and were not at the beck and call of one mistress all day long.[73] Yet independence exacted a price. Clients paid washerwomen between seventy-five cents and one dollar for a week's wash; the rate varied little between 1900 and 1930 and was even lower in the South. Remuneration in commercial laundries in 1911 ranged from five to twelve dollars per week, a subsistence wage that barely allowed women to pay the rent and feed the family.[74]

Household service typically required the worker to reside at her employer's premises, making it difficult for her to care for her own children. Although charity workers sought situations where children could stay with their mothers, these remained the exception. Live-in domestic service usually entailed separation from the servant's family, which made it unappealing to those with young children.[75] One African American widow lamented that to keep her job, she had to leave her three young children in the care of her oldest daughter. She saw her children only every other Sunday afternoon, since her employers would not permit her to stay at her own home overnight. She caught glimpses of her children when they came to the "yard," yet they visited her infrequently because, she said, "white folks don't like to see their servants' children hanging about their premises." Her position paid ten dollars a month.[76] Where possible, African American widows preferred day work, washing, or cooking to live-in domestic service because such occupations conferred some autonomy and time to be with their families.[77]

Widows in Divergent Economies

The distinctive local economies of Pittsburgh, Baltimore, and Fall River offered widows contrasting employment prospects (see table 7). In 1880, for example, Pittsburgh's heavy industries remained resolutely closed to women—relegating them to domestic service, home sewing, and washing—and depressed female employment levels generally. In terms of gainful employment in the Steel City, that year saw little difference between widows and women generally, with 15 percent of widows working outside the home and an additional 10 percent monetizing their domestic labor by taking in boarders. In contrast, Fall River's textile economy provided ample employment for widows. Still, they were less likely than women as a whole to be in the labor force in 1880, although 11 percent had lodgers. In Baltimore, with its mixed industrial economy and large black population, widows sustained high employment levels throughout the late nineteenth and early twentieth centuries; in 1880, 36 percent worked for wages, while 8 percent had lodgers.[78] By 1920 widows' employment levels in the three cities had converged: between 33 and 38 percent of the widows were economically active, for young widows were entering the labor force in increasing numbers.

Overall female employment levels in Fall River grew to be among the highest in the country at this time as women flocked to the mills. Instead of working, however, many Spindle City widows used their children as breadwinners. They relied on children over the age of ten or twelve to earn wages while they looked after the younger ones and the home.[79] With jobs plentiful for young workers, mothers chose to provide domestic comfort and supervision for the entire family, staying at home while their sons and daughters worked. Widows' employment in Fall River rose in the early twentieth century after child-labor legislation banished young adolescents from the cotton mills. By 1920 one out of every three widows had a job.

Children's ages, the laws governing their activities, and local occupational structures were all factors determining whether widows worked.[80] In 1880, when she was thirty years old, the widow Bridget Wallace labored in one of Fall River's cotton mills while her landlady and neighbors looked after her two infant children. Since Mrs. Wallace's children were too young to reach the looms, this Irish-born widow became a cotton operative. A Fall River widow

Table 7. All Women's and Widows' Employment Levels, by City

City	1880		1900		1920	
	All women	Widows	All women[a]	Widows	All Women[b]	Widows
Pittsburgh	14%	15%	24%	29%	28%	33%
Baltimore	23	36	34	36	33	38
Fall River	34	23	50	29	46	34

Sources: Data from U.S. Bureau of the Census, *Social Statistics of Cities* (Washington, D.C.: GPO, 1885–86), vols. 1 and 2.; idem, *Statistics of Women at Work . . . , 1900* (Washington, D.C.: GPO, 1907), 220, 244, 286; manuscript census, Pittsburgh, Fall River, and Baltimore, 1920.
[a]Women ages sixteen and over.
[b]Women ages fifteen and over.

of French Canadian origin took a boarder to supplement her children's wages. This woman removed her youngest child from school before she was thirteen to work in the mill; a twenty-five-year-old daughter lived at home as well and turned over her pay packet to her mother. The local economy provided plenty of work for young laborers, while demand for cheap housing enabled a great many widows to take in one or two boarders and hence use their domestic talents to supplement the household income.[81]

Although the area's overall employment rates for widows were lower than Baltimore's, a great many younger widows worked in Fall River. In 1880 nearly half the widows younger than forty-five had jobs, almost all in the textile mills (see table 8). Only three in ten younger widows in Pittsburgh had jobs, however, mostly in domestic service. Baltimore had the highest proportion of economically active younger widows (53 percent), evenly divided between domestic service and other manual work.

Economic activity for young widows climbed to even greater levels by 1920, for shrinking family sizes, educational requirements, and child-labor laws meant there were fewer children available for work. In 1880 younger Baltimore widows had the highest employment levels, but by 1920 an even greater proportion of Fall River widows under the age of forty-five were working. Pittsburgh widows more nearly resembled their counterparts in other cities in the early twentieth century, for the city's economy had diversified somewhat. More widows worked in the textile and garment factories that proliferated in the tenement districts; they sewed jeans, overalls, and baby clothes, as well as rolling cigars.[82] Middle-aged and older widows' employment levels rose slightly between 1880 and 1920 as well, but they remained much lower than that of younger widows in all three cities.

Race and nativity interacted with local economic structures to shape widows' employment (see table 9). Pittsburgh's marginalization of women workers meant that African American widows experienced lower levels of economic activity, even though they were far more likely to work than na-

Table 8. Widows' Labor-Force Participation Rates by Age in Three Cities, 1880 and 1920

	1880			1920		
Age	Pittsburgh ($n = 325$)	Fall River ($n = 304$)	Baltimore ($n = 308$)	Pittsburgh ($n = 312$)	Fall River ($n = 276$)	Baltimore ($n = 329$)
15–44	29.9%	46.7%	52.8%	64.4%	84.4%	70.0%
45–64	14.4	20.7	37.4	22.9	29.0	38.5
≥ 65	1.2	4.8	13.9	4.2	7.5	14.5

Source: Data from manuscript census, Pittsburgh, Fall River, and Baltimore.

Table 9. Percentage of Widows in the Labor Force by Race/Nativity in Three Cities, 1880 and 1920

	1880			1920		
Age	Pittsburgh ($n = 325$)	Fall River ($n = 304$)	Baltimore ($n = 308$)	Pittsburgh ($n = 312$)	Fall River ($n = 276$)	Baltimore ($n = 329$)
NBW[a]	9.8%	19.3%	22.3%	31.3%	35.9%	25.8%
FBW[a]	16.3	24.7	30.9	23.8	25.4	36.1
AA[a]	38.9	—	66.7	43.3	—	81.3

Source: Data from manuscript census, Pittsburgh, Fall River, and Baltimore.
[a]NBW = native-born whites; FBW = foreign-born whites; AA = African Americans

tive-born white widows were in 1880. By 1920 the rising tide of female economic activity had lifted the level of native- and foreign-born white widows' employment closer to that of African American widows. Employment rates for white widows in Pittsburgh were now similar to those in the other cities. Baltimore's percentage of working African American widows, however, was twice that of Pittsburgh. Four-fifths of African American widows in Baltimore were economically active, while just over two-fifths were in Pittsburgh.

Typical of widows trying to make a living for themselves and their families in Baltimore in the early twentieth century, thirty-eight-year-old Alberta Chase participated in a complex family economy. She moved from Virginia sometime after the birth of her youngest child in 1912, possibly soon after her husband died. Restricted by racial prejudice to domestic work, she chose to wash clothes at home to help support her four children. Her two young teenage daughters began working as laborers in a nearby factory, while her eight- and ten-year-old sons stayed in school. A single female cousin boarded with the family and worked as a servant in a private household. This family's economic strategy encompassed working from home for the widowed mother, low-level factory labor for the older children, school for the younger ones, and board money and possibly help with the children from a relative.[83]

Baltimore's garment factories and canneries provided jobs primarily for adult white women. Racial prejudice largely excluded African American widows from industrial work and relegated them to domestic and personal service, where even experienced workers received low pay. A black Baltimore cook earned between $5 and $7 per week in 1916. Live-in maids typically received between $2.50 and $5.00 for working from 7 A.M. until 9 P.M., with free time limited to one afternoon per week and alternate Sundays. Domestic workers did not tolerate these poor conditions passively. Throughout the late nineteenth and early twentieth centuries, they changed jobs in search of a better working environment and sometimes struck against employers for higher wages.[84]

The narrow compass of occupations open to African American widows, especially in southern and border states, meant that nearly nine out of ten economically active African American widows in Baltimore worked as domestic servants, laundresses, or waitresses. In 1880 only about six in ten of their Pittsburgh counterparts labored in these occupations, suggesting the African American widows who migrated farther north after the Civil War initially enjoyed a wider range of opportunities.[85] Native-born white widows, especially in Baltimore, eschewed domestic service to an even greater extent than did German-, British-, and Irish-born widows. In contrast, Pittsburgh's restrictive economy meant that the proportion of white women working as servants was higher there than in the other cities. African American widows in Pittsburgh endured even less occupational diversity by 1920, when four-fifths were employed in domestic and personal service. Conversely, the proportion of native-born and immigrant white women in these jobs had declined by 1920.[86]

The increased predominance of African American women in domestic service helped alter its character from live-in to live-out work in the first decades of the twentieth century.[87] Unlike white women, African American women frequently remained as domestic servants throughout their married lives and into widowhood. They wished to return to their own families and communities at night and create a world apart from their jobs by resisting the all-encompassing life of the live-in servant. Penny-saver clubs and church groups encouraged women to make the transition from live-in to live-out servants.[88] Many day workers took rooms in boarding houses run by older African American women, frequently widows themselves. They created a new community in the city and helped each other in work and social relations. The need for cheap housing within the African American community explains why keeping boarders continued to feature in African American widows' economic strategies long after white widows abandoned it.[89]

This form of ancillary income production declined in the early twentieth century for widows of both races, although one in eight African American widows still looked after boarders in 1920. In 1880 over one-fifth of black and French Canadian widows took in boarders, as did one-sixth of northern European and one-tenth of native-born white widows. Levels of boarding-house keeping remained high at the turn of the century but had declined by 1920. In that year about 4 percent of white widows, whether native or foreign born, took in boarders; the proportion of African American widows who did so was approximately three times higher.[90]

Most widowed Pittsburgh, Baltimore, and Fall River landladies were middle-aged or older widows, not the younger ones about whom reformers expressed most concern. In 1880 northern European widows with boarders tended to be older than other landladies, while African American widows were the youngest.[91] The average age of native-born white, African American, or northern European landladies changed little between 1880 and the turn of the century, but it increased among French Canadians. Younger and middle-aged French Canadian widows relied on their own labor or that of their children for support, waiting until their sons and daughters left home before taking in boarders. Southern and eastern European widows became landladies at a relatively young age, illustrating the constricted options they faced, especially in Pittsburgh, where numerous immigrants endured the aftermath of industrial accidents.[92] By 1920 the age at which southern and eastern European widows took boarders into their homes had come to approximate the average for widows generally. That of French Canadian widows continued to be higher, signifying that they continued to view boarders as a viable means of support after their children formed their own households. The overall increase in the age of landladies indicates that many younger women found alternative forms of economic activity. Fewer older ones did, so they continued to transmute domestic labor into sustenance.

Levels of boarding increased during the Great Depression, when desperate economic circumstances once again forced families to trade privacy for income.[93] Northern social-service agencies actively discouraged widows from taking lodgers, prohibiting widows in receipt of state pensions from housing unrelated men. They believed these women were, in the words of Pennsylvania's mothers' assistance manual, "often depressed and tired, physically below normal." Nor was that all: "The presence of a man in the same house, with a full pay envelope, may offer an overwhelming temptation" for improper behavior.[94] While this may have been the case, the quantitative evidence suggests that middle-aged rather than young women tended to take in boarders because they had room in their homes and used it as a means of converting their domestic skills into cash. Younger widows, unless tied to the home by very young children, preferred to enter the labor market, where they could earn more money.

The authorities' disapproval of strangers in the household displays the extent to which reformers perceived the home and the women and children within it as needing protection from interlopers.[95] In the twentieth century many Americans came to regard the home as the preserve of the nuclear family, with younger widows relying increasingly on their own extrahousehold labor for support. When they could not make ends meet, they turned to charities and the state for assistance. Eastern and southern European immigrants and African American widows, less likely to receive public funds than native-born whites and confined to the most menial end of the job market, continued to take in boarders for several generations after native-born whites and the middle class had abandoned the practice.[96]

Helping Widows to Earn

In the late nineteenth century local charities in some areas tried to devise means of aiding widows to be economically active and so shift the burden of support away from public authorities.[97] Fall River in particular displayed little or no emphasis on poor widows' domesticity. The "Cult of True Womanhood" had little salience in a city where jobs for women were plentiful and the small middle class had no desire to raise taxes or charitable funds to protect working-class, immigrant women's domesticity. Fall River's Associated Charities sought work for widows in the mills and would not countenance a household orientation for poor women. If widows were physically able to tend the looms and spindles, they were advised to find alternative methods of caring for young children among neighbors, friends, or the local children's homes. The charity might help clothe a family, but it rejected housewifery for women such as Mrs. Margaret Feeny, an Irish immigrant, even though she had five children ranging from eight weeks to eight years. She earned $6.60 per week in the mill, which left the family destitute. Rather than seek municipal aid for the family, the Associated Charities referred them to the Flower Mission charity for provisions. Under no circumstances was Mrs. Feeny to stay at home; the charity people adjured her to wean her baby and take a job in the mills.[98]

In Pittsburgh, where few nondomestic jobs for widows existed, local philanthropic organizations tried to create family-friendly employment. The Pittsburgh Association for the Improvement of the Poor (PAIP) opened a charity laundry in 1898 to furnish jobs to the many widows on its caseload. The PAIP arranged the working day so that mothers with young children washed clothes while the children were at school. Although the laundry paid less than commercial wages, it enabled widowed mothers to dovetail economic activity with domestic responsibilities. Unlike the Associated Charities of Fall River, the PAIP recognized that women needed help to combine their jobs inside and outside the home. Given the paucity of work for widows in Pittsburgh, such ventures enabled a few to be self-supporting. Nevertheless, widows remained the largest single category of needy on the PAIP caseload.[99]

While not specifically aimed at widows, the Urban League of Pittsburgh launched a home-economics project to improve the domestic skills of post–World War I migrants to the city. It acted as a clearinghouse for African American workers and endeavored to help newcomers adjust to city life. It shared the concerns expressed in the *Pittsburgh Courier,* Pittsburgh's African American newspaper, that the newcomers from the rural South needed to be acculturated to big-city ways and working practices in order not to embarrass the more established members of the black community.[100]

Baltimore charities also tried to train or retrain widows for employment. The Electric Sewing Machine Society purchased sewing machines for widows and other worthy women who needed financial assistance. It taught them how to operate the machines prior to finding them work in the city's garment industry. "Their earnings, although small, enable them to live without alms," its annual report concluded in 1896. The society manifested more sympathy for the child-care dilemmas facing its clientele than did the Associated Charities of Fall River. It provided a day nursery to look after the young children while mothers learned their trade and practiced it in the society's workrooms. These women machine stitched shirts, overalls, aprons, and plain household goods that the society took in at commercial rates from a local factory. Many of its clients subsequently went off to work in the city's garment industry. Others remained in the society's workrooms. These tended to be older women who could not work rapidly, those in poor health, or women with family responsibilities. In keeping with the prevailing racial norms of the period, this charity assisted only white women, although it did make some efforts to instruct "foreigners ignorant of our language."[101]

Like many large cities, Baltimore had numerous small garment factories honeycombing its tenement district. The profits from the "cheap clothing trade," as Maryland's Bureau of Industrial Statistics stigmatized it, depended on the underpaid home and sweatshop labor of widows. One thirty-seven-year-old widow reported to the bureau that she earned about three to five dollars per week in 1886, sewing pantaloons eighteen hours a day. She had five children to tend, and working at home enabled her to combine wage earning and nurturing, albeit at the cost of exhaustion. Women in her situation worked in the "dense, close atmosphere of small tenements," in homes with "poor light, bad air, long hours, and indifferent food," the bureau concluded. They toiled longer hours than men did, and for lower wages, but homework enabled them to blend domesticity and wage labor.[102]

Widows in Baltimore's fruit and vegetable packinghouses, too, cared for their children while earning an income. The documentary photographer and social reformer Lewis Hine took pictures of women nursing their babies as they hulled peas and taught older children to do repetitive processing tasks to contribute their share of the family labor. Mothers brought the entire family, leaving the babies to "slumber in the pea hulls" while the rest of the family worked. The majority of these women were foreign-born widows, others were African American, and there were also a few native-born whites. In return for a convenient and informal workplace, however, the women had to make do with only modest wages. Earnings averaged $4.50 a week during the packing season. A woman would have to fill twenty measures with hulled peas to earn $1.00, something only the most accomplished managed to do in a day.[103]

Manufacturers demanded a relentless pace from their workers by setting low piecework rates. Reformers objected to domestic piecework because they believed the household should be a place of emotional rather than economic life. Doing industrial homework, such as sewing jeans or vests, led to the neglect of housework and children, the social investigator Elizabeth Butler concluded in 1907. She condemned outwork, believing it to be "no wonder that the bare floors seem never to have been cleaned; that the children are ragged, ignorant, uncared for." Butler and other Progressive reformers believed that mothers should not combine family care and employment; doing piecework in the home violated the sanctity of the dwelling place.[104]

Worried about the physical burden carried by working mothers, reformers and labor leaders alike acted from a set of cultural assumptions about the family economy, the place of the home in society, and the gendering of work.[105] The battle against homework assumed that home and workplace should be segregated—that "real" work takes place outside the home, that domestic life occurs within it, and the two should not mix. The home, which at the turn of the nineteenth century had been a place of production, was by the turn of the twentieth an emotional space from which economic activity should be banned. Part of a general industrial health and safety movement, the campaign against homework attempted to harness the power of the state to regulate who worked and under what conditions. The judiciary accepted that men had the right to contract their labor freely but that women's right to contract (if it existed at all) could be curtailed on the grounds of their maternal functions and the good of the state.[106]

The rising levels of employment for young widows troubled reformers who favored enhanced domestic roles for women. The uneasiness over young working mothers intersected with another cause for concern, the increase in waged labor for young children around the turn of the century.[107] Reformers also worried about the welfare of older widows, who were living longer but had fewer children to sustain them in their last years. Ultimately the Social

Security Act provided at least a partial answer to these economic dilemmas.[108] Not unexpectedly in a country so divided by race, ethnicity, class, and region, African American widows differed from their white counterparts by being younger and more highly urbanized and having greater levels of economic activity. They also were limited to a narrower range of occupations. Their experiences remained distinctive in the twentieth century as white widows, especially those born in the United States, began edging into white-collar jobs. The need or willingness to work varied by age and race; older African American widows remained economically active longer than whites since their poorly paying jobs prevented them from saving money toward their own departure from the labor force.

A number of social-welfare changes resulted from the demographic, economic, and cultural shifts of these decades. The rising number of elderly widows and declining family sizes led to more institutions for older women. A greater proportion lived as dependents in their children's households, which sparked fears that they would drain resources from their own grandchildren. Younger widows responded to increased employment opportunities and restrictions on child labor by working in greater numbers, although the percentage of economically active widows differed among the three cities. Widows in Baltimore and Fall River found it easier to locate work than did those in Pittsburgh, but they all suffered the constraints of trying to mix waged labor with child and household responsibilities. Reformers in many cities reacted against the economic strategies of poor widows who attempted to combine motherhood with employment or who used their children as breadwinners. In the next chapter I explore the growing disquiet about the presence of certain children in the labor force (white urban youths, not black or rural ones). The combined anxiety over women's and children's wage earning in turn set the stage for widows' pensions as a means of facilitating a particular form of family economy in which neither mothers nor children worked outside the home.

2 Widows' Children and the Cult of True Childhood

Fifteen years ago there were instances of children of ten being
placed at work to help widowed mothers keep their home together.
We know better now.
—Charity Organization Society of Baltimore, *Twenty-Fourth
Annual Report* (1905)

The preceding epigraph attests to a changed attitude toward child labor, even
for the poorest families. Only a few decades earlier social commentators had
lauded young people's efforts to support their families. *McGuffey Eclectic
Readers,* popular midcentury school texts, celebrated religiosity, honesty, and
hard work. Featuring young lads, often with widowed mothers, the stories
rewarded their heroes' honesty with jobs in stores, shops, and offices. They
ignored the realities of child labor, however; few of these fictional protago-
nists worked in mills or factories or undertook the unremitting agricultural
toil that characterized most young people's employment.[1] Once education
became more important for getting ahead, *McGuffey*'s depictions of youthful toil as the route to success had less salience, especially for middle-class
children. This widened the gap between poor and affluent children's activities; at the same time children's work grew ever more arduous as conditions
in mills and factories deteriorated, leading to protests against premature
economic activity.[2]

The rise of manufacturing extended the value of children into the financial
realm. The separation of home and workplace that accompanied industrialization engendered new modes of behavior for fathers, mothers, and children.[3] Whereas previously the family had functioned as a unit of production,
or family members scrambled between occupations depending on the seasons
and economic cycles, nineteenth-century urban families became units of
consumption and reproduction.[4] This was especially true in the middle and
upper classes, where families could manage on paternal income while moth-

ers devoted their energies to caring for the family, and children remained in school until their mid- to late teens and sometimes thereafter.[5] Until the twentieth century, however, when state and federal legislation intervened, poor and widow-headed households relied heavily on children's labor to sustain them since they were more concerned with immediate survival than with the enhancement of individual children's long-term prospects.[6]

As traced by Viviana Zelizer in *Pricing the Priceless Child,* the transformation in the cultural meaning of childhood (at least for some children) paralleled a similar transformation in that of womanhood, whose result Barbara Welter labeled the "Cult of True Womanhood." Welter describes the woman's sphere in antebellum America as being separate from the man's and located within the domestic realm. The burgeoning women's press assiduously promulgated domesticity, piety, purity, and submissiveness as defining female characteristics, urging women to immerse themselves in their homes and families.[7] Always of considerable concern to women, these areas were to be their primary interests and the basis for participation in events outside the domestic sphere. Nineteenth-century bourgeois society set children apart from adults, emphasizing their vulnerability and impressionability at the same time that affluent women turned from the production of commodities at home to more intensive mothering and a greater participation in public affairs.[8] In the early twentieth century a supposedly scientific approach to mothering based on innovations in child psychology fostered an expanded and more intensive approach to childrearing. Social pundits expected mothers to be domestic "professionals" who undertook the systematic study of their children. They placed great stress on the intense emotional tie between parent and child, making the family a haven from chaotic urban society yet more subject to external advice and regulation.[9]

The interdependent paradigms of "true womanhood" and "true childhood" exhibited similar racial and class shortcomings. They encompassed the white, urban middle class but excluded the majority of Americans. Many working-class, immigrant, and one-parent families depended on the pennies earned by young workers.[10] Widows' children tended to be enmeshed in wage labor from an earlier age than were those from two-parent families, as were children in certain settings, whether the rural South or the industrial North. Technological innovations made it feasible to employ young people in industrial processes, while the immiseration among large segments of the population, especially recent migrants, made such employment a vital component of working-class economic strategies.[11] Children constituted a particularly useful source of cheap labor in the food-processing and textile industries of Baltimore and Fall River. The loss of a parent clearly played a role in impelling young people into economic activity. Yet they were far more likely to work if they lived in Fall River, which had a history of child labor, than if they lived in Pittsburgh, where jobs in the iron and steel mills required physical strength beyond their capacities. Widowhood, in effect, exacerbated a situation in which children were already well represented in the labor market.[12]

Once an individualistic family economy oriented toward personal achievement had replaced the more collective agricultural and preindustrial one, public sentiment condemned the use of child labor. In 1903 the founder of Chicago's Hull-House settlement, Jane Addams, told the National Conference of Charities and Correction that "children subject to premature labor are handed over to the future in an abnormal condition." Addams highlighted the nature of employment under the industrial system, where machines simplified complex tasks and reduced the amount of physical strength required. For the first time in history, "the labor of the little children [had] become as valuable as that of a man or a woman."[13] Young workers toiled alongside adults, both tied to the brutal pace of machines and factory discipline. Writing of his "long and busy life" in 1890, Benjamin W. Pearce of Fall River disapprovingly recalled that during his boyhood, children as young as eight worked twelve to fourteen hours a day in the textile mills for fifty cents per week. These girls and boys had their ears boxed by the overseer if they nodded off from exhaustion. Some supervisors punished the children with yard-long knotted leather straps. They blacklisted parents who dared to protest, making abusive child labor commonplace in mill towns. Such intolerable behavior led to widespread demands to improve conditions for young workers, if not to abolish child labor altogether.[14]

A wide variety of organizations opposed child labor.[15] Labor unions sought to restrict employment to adults: in the 1870s the Knights of Labor called on states to ban the employment of children, as did the American Federation of Labor from the 1880s onward. Women's organizations, including the General Federation of Women's Clubs and the National Consumers' League, battled against child labor, as did the residents of Hull-House and the Henry Street Settlement House in New York City. The campaign acquired further impetus with the founding of anti-child-labor societies, such as the National Child Labor Committee, formed in 1904. Their disapproval of industrial work for children reflected changes in the nature of employment, the burgeoning class disparity in rates of employment, and despair at the vast number of children who toiled under appalling conditions.[16] The tension over who should work and who should go to school was also part of the national debate on the assimilation of the large number of immigrants moving to American cities in the nineteenth and early twentieth centuries.[17] Fearing the newcomers' distinctive cultural values, reformers wished to have children immersed in the American way of life through compulsory education to the age of fourteen.[18]

Progressive reformers, epitomized by the Children's Bureau (established in 1912), believed that children have "a right to childhood." Theodore Roosevelt, a strong supporter of the bureau, believed that it would strengthen the family and individual children's rights by exposing child-labor abuses. Like many reformers, he felt that the sacrifice of a child's welfare for that of the entire family was intolerable, and he asserted a vision of family life in which men support women and children in domesticity and education.[19] This set the stage for conflict over child labor, which had continued to be essential for the economic survival of widowed and working-class families through the turn of the century and thereafter. The articulation of social-welfare policy aimed specifically at widows' children (in the form of indoor relief such as orphanages and outdoor relief through widows' pensions) testified to spreading anxiety over children's welfare.[20]

These reformers defined childhood as the crucial stage in the development not only of the individual but also of the body politic. Fearing, along with Jane Addams, that "the development of industry had outrun all the educational and social arrangements," they sought to delay children's entrance into the labor force and educate them in the democratic political traditions and social values of an earlier era.[21] Reformers viewed children as innocents to be nurtured and the salvation of a rapidly changing and uncertain society, not as economic actors. The social analyst Charlotte Perkins Gilman maintained that children needed recognition as a class, as "citizens with rights to be guaranteed only by the state."[22] The influential writings of the Clark University psychologist G. Stanley Hall in the 1890s stressed that childhood is the critical phase in an individual's development. During these years adolescence came to be defined as a separate stage in the life cycle, with the business of young people (at least among affluent Americans) being preparation for adulthood rather than contribution to the family's economic well-being.[23] "True children," the youthful counterparts of "true women," had a prolonged period of economic dependence in which they received training for adulthood and were forcibly removed from the temptations of city life through immersion in education.

The regulation of children's employment in northern states became a matter of heated public debate, although few in the southern states exhibited qualms about young people's economic activities.[24] In 1832 New York passed legislation requiring poor children to attend school.[25] A decade later

Massachusetts forbade the employment of children under the age of ten for more than ten hours a day.[26] Such laws substituted state direction for parental preference but ignored the poverty that forced many working-class families to rely on their children's employment for survival.[27] Unstable working-class incomes and high rates of un- and underemployment made children's earnings an essential component of the family economy. Children under the age of fifteen accounted for about one-fifth of Massachusetts laboring families' incomes in 1875, with one in ten textile operatives being under the age of sixteen.[28]

The collection of more reliable statistics in the late nineteenth century made young people's economic activities highly visible and fueled reformers' concerns about the treatment of children.[29] From the 1880s onward anticruelty organizations such as the Western Pennsylvania Humane Society and the Society for the Protection of Children from Cruelty and Immorality of Baltimore City tried to curtail the employment of children and ensure they were "properly trained" so they became a blessing instead of "a menace to the nation's welfare."[30] Their annual reports contain brief case notes and statistics designed to awaken the conscience of their readers. The Pittsburgh Survey (1907) investigated children's and women's lives as well as those of the men working in the mills, while reformist inquiries such as John Spargo's *Bitter Cry of the Children* (1906) and Lewis Hine's documentary photographs graphically depicted the poverty that propelled working-class children into the labor force.[31]

Such publications dramatized the statistics on children's employment, first tabulated by the U.S. Census Office in 1870, when it discovered that 13 percent of all children between the ages of ten and fifteen had jobs. Textile centers had especially high rates of youth employment. In many New England mill towns 40 percent of the operatives were younger than twenty-one; in Fall River a staggering 55 percent of the workers were minors in 1870.[32] These statistics focused the National Child Labor Committee (NCLC) and other reformist groups on rescuing children from premature labor in "the sweatshop, the coal mine, the glass factory, the silk mill, the cotton mill, the cigar shop, and the whiskey bottling works."[33]

Many southern states still had no child-labor laws in the early twentieth century, and four (South Carolina, Georgia, Virginia, and North Carolina) specifically permitted the employment of widows' children under the age of twelve. As a result, employment of ten- to thirteen-year-old children was highest in that region. When child labor peaked in 1910, 26 to 33 percent of young children had jobs in the South Atlantic, East, and West South Central census regions, with the figure rising to between 40 and 50 percent for fourteen and fifteen year olds. Child-labor levels were about half as high in the North.[34]

Although overall rates of youthful economic activity were lower in the North than in the South, some northern areas experienced a surge in child labor at the beginning of the twentieth century. The Massachusetts Child Labor Committee documented a doubling in the number of child workers between 1899 and 1912.[35] Across the nation the proportion of employed ten to fifteen year olds had risen to 18 percent by the turn of the century, falling only in 1920, when a combination of child-labor legislation, mandatory education, increased parental incomes, and a modest expansion in wives' employment shifted younger adolescents out of the labor market.[36] The decreased demand for unskilled workers and a greater pool of adults available for work also contributed to declining levels of underage workers, so that by 1930 a mere 2.4 percent of children had jobs.[37]

Parents deployed complex household strategies to maximize family well-being in these years. Many opted to enhance domestic comfort by keeping mothers at home, even though adult women earned more than children did. The census estimated that in 1899 a child working full time earned $242 a year, while women earned $429, and men, $793.[38] Very few married white women held full-time paid employment outside the home, even in cities with large working-class populations, because of the skilled tasks performed by housewives. They preferred "to save money by good housekeeping [rather] than earn a little more and neglect the home," as Margaret Byington wrote of steelworkers' wives in Pittsburgh.[39] Those married women in Pittsburgh, Fall River, and Baltimore who had jobs outside the home tended to be young (with an average age of 36.5 years in 1900), while those who remained outside the labor force were older (with an average age of 44.6).[40] Reflecting this, working wives and mothers tended to be those with younger children, for whom there were no jobs or whose labor was poorly recompensed. When restrictions on child labor reduced potential income, however, more women entered the labor force. In the same interval when children's economic activity declined from 18 to 2 percent, that of wives nearly trebled (from 4.6 to 11.7 percent), and that of widows grew from 29.9 percent in 1890 to 34.4 percent by 1930.[41]

Widow- or widower-headed families were more likely to include multiple wage earners than were their two-parent counterparts, although working mothers in all families tended to leave the labor force as their children grew older and could earn more. In one typical multiple-wage-earner household, Mary Hosbuch, a thirty-two-year-old German widow, worked as a washerwoman while her fourteen-year-old son labored in a nearby bolt factory.

Their combined earnings, along with income from a boarder whom Mrs. Hosbuch tended, supported them and the three younger children.[42] In Baltimore, Pittsburgh, and Fall River 41 percent of employed half-orphans under the age of fifteen had working mothers, whereas only 8 percent of young workers from two-parent families did. Among fatherless workers between fifteen and twenty-four years old, 29 percent had mothers who worked; among those living with both parents, the figure was about 5 percent.[43]

Declining demand for some forms of labor within the home significantly affected child labor by releasing girls into the labor force. Preindustrial mothers had required their daughters' assistance in running the household, but this became less necessary as family sizes constricted and households purchased rather than made goods. Between 1870 and 1910 girls' employment rates doubled, although great disparities emerged along lines of race and nativity. Employment levels were much higher among young African Americans of either sex than among whites of the same age. Nearly 40 percent of African American girls between ten and fifteen had jobs in 1910, while only 13 percent of foreign-born white girls and 8 percent of native-born white girls did. For boys the corresponding figures were 54, 17, and 20 percent, respectively. The disparity in employment levels between the sexes was greatest among native-born whites, with boys outnumbering girls in the workplace five to two, and lowest among the foreign born and African Americans, with boys outnumbering girls by only four to three in both cases.[44]

In addition, age, ethnicity, race, and gender often determined job opportunities. Early employment for native-born children of any color was overwhelmingly agricultural. Nearly nine out of every ten African American child workers toiled in the fields, with little difference between the sexes. Native-born white boys and, to a lesser extent, their sisters were also farmhands, although few foreign-born boys or girls were. The latter clustered in manufacturing and mechanical pursuits, with foreign-born girls being especially well represented among machine operatives. By contrast, not many native-born white girls with native-born parents were factory workers in 1910, and almost no young African American women had such jobs. Few of the youngest black females worked as servants, possibly because their parents preferred to keep them on the farm, insulated from the corrosive racial relations and abuse that accompanied domestic service in the South.[45]

Job opportunities influenced where child workers lived. Between 1880 and 1920 the sex ratio of widows' children living at home altered: in 1880, 52 percent of coresident children were boys and 48 percent were girls. Domestic service as an occupation for young females accounted for this imbalance; maternal poverty meant that a greater proportion of widows' daughters went into live-in domestic service and thus were not counted by the census as members of their mothers' households. This ratio reversed in the early twentieth century, because new employment prospects for girls permitted them to work and live at home. In 1900 forty-seven boys resided in widows' homes for every fifty-three girls who did so, and by 1920 the proportions were 45 and 55 percent, respectively. Couples, less in need of their daughters' labor, had a balanced sex ratio in 1880 and 1900. By 1920, however, married couples had slightly more sons at home, with fifty-two boys for every forty-eight girls. While widows increasingly held on to their daughters, couples more often let them move away from home (typically into marriage, but also to live on their own) in the early twentieth century.[46]

The African American community presented an extreme form of these sex ratios. In 1880 only 39 percent of the children residing in their widowed mother's homes were girls. As opportunities for live-out domestic service and other forms of employment increased, however, this proportion swelled; in 1900 African American girls made up 52 percent of the half-orphans living at home, and the proportion had risen to 55 percent by 1920. This pattern mirrored a trend in black families generally; in 1880, 44 percent of the co-resident children of African American couples were female, but by 1920, 56 percent were.

Young Children in Three Economic Settings

Contrasting the education and employment of six to fourteen year olds underscores the impact of widowhood on these children's prospects in three distinctive social and economic settings. The economic structures, educational requirements, and child-labor laws of Pennsylvania, Massachusetts, and Maryland differed sharply from one another. Along with gender, race, and ethnicity, these factors influenced the disposition of children's time in Pittsburgh, Fall River, and Baltimore. Both Pennsylvania and Massachusetts had strict educational requirements for children under the age of fourteen (albeit with inconsistent enforcement), but school remained optional in Maryland until the twentieth century. Massachusetts had a long history of child-labor regulation, Pennsylvania had an ineffective system of factory inspection, and Maryland had none at all in 1900.[47] For these reasons, overall school enrollments were higher in Fall River and Pittsburgh, despite the prevalence of young workers in the textile city. Even within these constraints, however, there were discrepancies between one- and two-parent families. Regardless of the city, in 1880 couples' children attended school in greater proportions than did widows', although there was little distinction between the groups in Baltimore (see table 10). Widows' younger children had lower school attendance rates, indicative of their families' desperate need for income.

By 1900 the school-attendance rates of Fall River's half-orphans had come into line with those of their two-parent counterparts, largely because of an 1894 law that forbade the employment of children under the age of fourteen. This effectively encouraged the substitution of maternal for child labor in widow-headed households.[48] Pittsburgh underwent a similar convergence in children's educational levels in one- and two-parent families and a similar increase in maternal employment.

Legislation, parental poverty, and employment opportunities pulled families in different directions. Pennsylvania passed a compulsory education statute in 1894, effectively forcing widows to keep children in school longer. At the same time, the extreme poverty of recent immigrants and expanded openings for young workers in the glass, food-processing, and tenement industries led some parents in the Pittsburgh area to remove their daughters and sons from school as soon as they could. In Sharpsburg, an industrial suburb of Pittsburgh, school attendance dropped by 19 percent at the age of fourteen, when a child might work legally under a 1904 Pennsylvania statute—this following another "drop of 21 percent at the age of twelve."[49] The desperately poor southern and eastern European immigrant children had attendance levels about 20 percent lower than those of native-born whites. The Pittsburgh Survey concluded that insofar as the decrease was "caused by racial elements," the culprits were "recent foreigners and . . . native Negroes."[50] Such statements reflected the surveyors' prejudices rather than enrollment figures. Census enumerations indicate that young African Americans and second-generation whites had almost identical attendance rates in 1900, although foreign-born children were less likely to be in school after the age of ten, and native-born whites had significantly better representation at the high school level.[51]

Southern and border cities lagged behind northern ones in effective education and employment legislation, resulting in high levels of employment for young people there. Maryland had been home to sporadic efforts at

Table 10. Percentage of Coresident Six to Fourteen Year Olds Attending School

	1880		1900		1920	
City	Widows ($n = 379$)	Couples ($n = 318$)	Widows ($n = 390$)	Couples ($n = 370$)	Widows ($n = 397$)	Couples ($n = 373$)
Pittsburgh	69%	84%	77%	81%	96%	93%
Fall River	68	79	81	82	84	88
Baltimore	64	65	66	67	91	94

Source: Data from manuscript census, Pittsburgh, Fall River, and Baltimore.

developing schools for white children in the early and middle decades of the nineteenth century, but no public provision for African American children existed until after the Civil War, when Baltimore opened segregated schools.[52] Prior to that, the black community maintained denominationally sponsored schools for Protestant and Catholic children. The Oblate Sisters of Providence, an order of black nuns founded in Baltimore in 1828, established its School for Colored Girls in its first years and ran four schools by the time of the Civil War.[53] Thus some black children managed to obtain an education, despite the lack of public support.

In the 1880s dissatisfaction at the number of child workers led to an expanded provision of public education, but because attendance was not compulsory, Baltimore's children still received little schooling at the end of the century, with scant distinction between widows' and couples' children in this respect (see table 10). School attendance in Baltimore finally came into line with that in northern cities after Maryland enacted a compulsory-education law in 1902.[54] By 1920 over 90 percent of Baltimore children between the ages of six and fourteen attended school, although couples had a slightly greater tendency to send their children to school than widows did.

Table 11 indicates two factors that influenced employment levels for children living at home: location and parents' marital status. Encouraged by an employment structure that welcomed young workers, 45 percent of Fall River's half-orphaned ten to fourteen year olds worked in 1880, a far greater proportion than in either Baltimore or Pittsburgh. Even couples' children in the Spindle City had higher rates of economic activity than did children elsewhere. The Godains, a Canadian family, participated in this trend. The family immigrated to Fall River in the 1870s so that the ten- and twelve-year-old sons might join their older siblings in the mills. They sought what they perceived to be the "optimum good" for the entire family by putting the children to work in the textile mills as soon as possible.[55] In 1882 the superintendent of schools for Fall River complained that such "avaricious parents" attempted to get their children certified as being over fourteen so

Table 11. Percentage of Coresident Ten to Fourteen Year Olds in the Labor Force

	1880		1900		1920	
City	Widows ($n = 211$)	Couples ($n = 177$)	Widows ($n = 217$)	Couples ($n = 206$)	Widows ($n = 198$)	Couples ($n = 187$)
Pittsburgh	25%	20%	32%	22%	1%	2%
Fall River	45	36	28	30	7	8
Baltimore	28	24	36	24	3	1

Source: Data from manuscript census, Pittsburgh, Fall River, and Baltimore.

they could leave school and work in the mills full time. He claimed the falsified documents came mostly from French Canadian families, who migrated to Fall River to monetize the labor of the entire family.[56]

Once the 1894 child-labor law banned children under the age of fourteen from the workplace, employment levels dropped sharply for all young children in Fall River. While some families resorted to lying about their children's ages to get them into the mills at the beginning of the twentieth century, legislation, technological developments, and vigorous competition from southern textile mills made openings for young workers dwindle.[57] Family strategies altered to accommodate the new climate: mothers, whether married or widowed, began to substitute for their children in the mills. The mill towns also lost some of their allure to migrants; immigration abated once employment opportunities for young children diminished in the early twentieth century.[58]

In 1900 half-orphans in Fall River had slightly lower rates of economic activity than did their counterparts from two-parent families. Both the city and private charities assisted widows' families but were reluctant to help poor couples.[59] The perception of widows as a particularly needy group led some factory owners and state legislators and even some charitable societies to justify employment for young half-orphans. A Virginia mill official asserted that one-third of the families in his village contained widows attracted there by the employment opportunities for their children. In his view the poor renters of the South faced severe hardship when the breadwinner died; the cotton mill was the "best place for them." Jane Addams, however, "believed that the widowed mothers' argument [had] been seriously overworked" as a defense against the regulation of child labor and pressed hard to curtail employment of young adolescents.[60]

In 1902 Maryland legislators created a special category of labor legislation applicable only to widows' children. Its child-labor statute forbade the employment of persons under the age of fourteen "unless said person is the only support of a widowed mother, invalid father, or is solely dependent upon such employment for self support." This legislation applied to mills and factories but did not cover farmworkers or the many young workers who labored in canneries processing perishable agricultural produce.[61] Local charities opposed this law, believing that widowhood did not release the community from its obligation to "give such a child a fair chance and the same opportunity as its more fortunate comrades for physical growth and mental education."[62] By 1912 pressure from Baltimore's Charity Organization Society, among other groups, led authorities to end the exemption for children of widows. Nevertheless, the law still permitted the employment of children under the age of fourteen if they had "fulfilled [school] attendance requirements."[63]

Legal structures, then, had an important role in determining whether young children worked.[64] The introduction of even more stringent child-labor legislation in Massachusetts in 1912 forced younger children out of the labor force. Tightening legal requirements reflected the public sentiment that children should be in school until their midteens and resulted in much higher attendance levels for all children by 1920. Parents in the Spindle City continued to resist state efforts to control their children's time but also substituted adult women for young workers to make up the shortfall in the family budget. Some youngsters not in school helped at home, either looking after younger brothers and sisters or doing housework while their mothers worked.[65] Despite this anomaly, the legal framework restricting younger children's employment and requiring longer periods of education meant that over 90 percent of six to fourteen year olds were in school in Baltimore and Pittsburgh in 1920, as were 88 percent of couples' children in Fall River. Widows' young children in Fall River still lagged behind somewhat; in 1920 only 84 percent were in school, despite charitable support and legislative requirements. The rest had unskilled jobs in the mills (usually obtained late in their fourteenth year) or helped at home.

Enrollment and employment rates do not tell the entire story of children's labor. One of the big shifts in the deployment of children's time was the collapse of the "at home" category, the census designation used for those neither at work nor in school. In all cities this group shrank dramatically over the forty years under examination here as families chose to educate children or send them to work rather than have them help out at home. As household sizes shrank, store-bought goods substituted for homemade ones, and households acquired labor-saving devices, daughters' labor could be released from the home into the wider economy. By the early years of the twentieth century, few young girls took on the role of unpaid domestic assistants once they left school. Either they remained in school for a few more years or they went to work and contributed to the family's income.

Enrollment and employment rates could be misleading for other reasons as well. A 1923 study of child labor on Maryland truck farms found some Polish and African American crop pickers as young as twelve. Many illegally skipped school to do farm work. Indeed, according to one African American father, "Negro schools had to close during May and June, that is, during strawberry picking season." The African American schools kept shorter school years to accommodate farmers' desire for cheap labor, and in some parts of the South, such as Maryland's eastern shore, educational authorities concluded that "education is not a reality for Negro children." These children (many of them with widowed mothers) came from Baltimore to perform field labor.[66] The census listed these children as being in school, but actually they received little education. Nevertheless, the disposition of children's time changed significantly as the state exercised greater control over it.

Education and Employment Patterns of Older Children

Most of the rhetorical attention paid to child labor and widows' children focused on those under the age of fifteen, whom reformers regarded as especially vulnerable, yet widowhood affected life chances and choices throughout adolescence and young adulthood. At the turn of the century, the Pittsburgh-born Ellen and Robert Powell, a telephone operator and printer, respectively, continued to live with their widowed mother in their midtwenties, an age when the majority of their peers had married and formed homes of their own.[67] They had received sufficient education to undertake skilled employment, but their mother's widowhood delayed their embarkation on the next stage of their life journeys.[68] No welfare programs abated widowhood's impact on young adult children in the Gilded Age and Progressive Era, although such individuals did benefit from the general increase in educational standards during these years.

In 1880, when few teenagers received an education, twice as many couples' children stayed in school after the age of fourteen. By the turn of the century even families of modest means began sending their children to high school to improve their life chances.[69] Couples, able to tap the higher wages paid to men (and, in a growing number of instances, to substitute wives' labor for young people's), sustained longer periods of economic inactivity for their offspring, so that 10 percent benefited from high school or college education in 1900, when only 6 percent of widows' children enjoyed this opportunity. By 1920 educational levels had increased significantly for both groups, yet education rates among couples' children were still twice that of widows' (see table 12).

In the late nineteenth century Pittsburgh youths stayed in school longest, both because authorities in the area emphasized education as a means of getting ahead and because the employment climate did not encourage young workers of either sex. Although widows' adolescent children had higher employment rates than did those with two parents, the rates in Pittsburgh were still much lower than in Fall River (where almost all widows' children worked) or Baltimore (where three-fourths were economically active; see table 13).[70] During the same interval the textile-factory culture in Fall River

Table 12. Occupational Distribution of Widows' and Couples' Coresident Young Adult Children, Ages Fifteen to Twenty-Four

	1880		1900		1920	
Child's occupation	Widows (*n* = 637)	Couples (*n* = 479)	Widows (*n* = 736)	Couples (*n* = 549)	Widows (*n* = 710)	Couples (*n* = 506)
Manual	69%	54%	62%	56%	59%	47%
Clerical	7	11	14	14	21	20
Professional/ managerial	1	1	3	2	2	2
Student	3	7	6	10	12	23
None	20	27	15	18	6	8
Total	100	100	100	100	100	100

Source: Data from manuscript census, Pittsburgh, Fall River, and Baltimore.

Table 13. Percentage of Coresident Fifteen to Twenty-four Year Olds in the Labor Force

	1880		1900		1920	
City	Widows (*n* = 637)	Couples (*n* = 479)	Widows (*n* = 736)	Couples (*n* = 549)	Widows (*n* = 710)	Couples (*n* = 506)
Pittsburgh	64%	54%	77%	69%	80%	66%
Fall River	93	87	90	86	87	77
Baltimore	75	52	81	67	81	60

Source: Data from manuscript census, Pittsburgh, Fall River, and Baltimore.

and poor public provision and racial politics in Baltimore depressed education levels and encouraged the employment of widows' sons and daughters. By 1900 employment levels for widows' and couples' children in Pittsburgh had risen, with more daughters entering the labor force and white-collar jobs proliferating. By 1920 the employment rates of couples' children had decreased, an indication of the growing importance of education and the substitution of maternal for adolescent labor in some of these households.

In the late nineteenth century the typical female college graduate came from a family with an income about three times the national average. Some widowed mothers could sustain their daughters' advanced education from savings; others made valiant efforts to provide their daughters with the education they valued or wished they had. The historian Barbara Solomon concludes that "many of these widows, living on fixed or declining incomes, realized the economic value of an education."[71] Most widows, however, could not or would not sustain comparable rates of education for sons and daughters. Although roughly the same quite low proportion of both genders went to high school or college in 1880, by 1920 widows seemed to be investing more in their sons' education, with 14 percent of their sons aged fifteen to twenty-four enrolled but only 10 percent of their daughters (see table 14). Couples' adolescent children, in contrast, had higher education rates distributed equally between the sexes (22 percent of daughters and 23 percent of sons were still in school.)

In some cities widows and couples relied heavily on both their sons and their daughters to help support the household; few older children went to school in Fall River at the end of the nineteenth century, and almost all were economically active. Parents responded to the ban on labor for younger children by keeping their older ones in the mills, a pattern that began to break down only in the 1920s. Widows in particular depended on the income brought in by their older sons and daughters, with this group seeing a smaller decrease in employment between 1880 and 1920 than did other groups. By 1920 Fall River couples had begun sending a greater proportion of their sons and daughters to high school and college than widows did, although they still lagged behind their counterparts in either Pittsburgh or Baltimore.

Early entrance into the labor force disadvantaged widows' children. They had high levels of manual labor, especially in 1880, when nearly seven out of every ten widows' children held such jobs but only five out of ten children from two-parent families did. By 1920 the levels of manual labor had declined for both groups, but such occupations still dominated the working lives of widows' children. The proportion engaged in clerical, professional, and managerial occupations expanded, with little difference between the two groups after the turn of the century.[72] The major distinction between young adults from one- and two-parent families was the continued investment by couples in their children's education, although other aspects of economic

Table 14. Occupational Distribution of Widows' and Couples' Coresident Children, Ages Fifteen to Twenty-four, by Gender

Child's occupation	1880				1920			
	Daughters		Sons		Daughters		Sons	
	Widows (n = 317)	Couples (n = 229)	Widows (n = 320)	Couples (n = 250)	Widows (n = 381)	Couples (n = 234)	Widows (n = 329)	Couples (n = 272)
Manual	54%	41%	83%	68%	53%	41%	64%	52%
Clerical	2	4	11	19	22	22	19	19
Professional/ managerial	2	1	1	1	3	3	2	1
Student	3	6	3	8	10	22	14	23
None	39	48	2	4	12	12	1	5
Total	100	100	100	100	100	100	100	100

Source: Data from manuscript census, Pittsburgh, Fall River, and Baltimore

inactivity declined. By 1920 few adolescents helped their mothers at home; as these pursuits had done for their younger siblings, education and work squeezed the "at home" category down to 12 percent for widows' and couples' daughters, 5 percent for couples' sons, but only 1 percent for widows' boys.

Comparisons between the employment patterns of different racial and ethnic groups demonstrate another aspect of widowhood's distorting impact on adolescent children. Widows' children from most racial or ethnic groups had higher levels of employment than their peers from two-parent families did (see table 15). In keeping with their parents' reasons for moving to Fall River, French Canadian adolescents had the highest rate of employment throughout this era. Initially widows' children had slightly lower levels of employment than did their peers from two-parent families, possibly because their mothers needed them to stay home to look after younger children in these large households. The Duvalls, who lived in Fall River during the 1880s, exemplify such families: one daughter stayed home to help her mother keep house and care for her six brothers and sisters.[73] By 1920 smaller family sizes and improved domestic technology had released these girls to the labor market, so that 96 percent of widows' adolescent children had jobs. Surprisingly, perhaps, the disparity between the employment levels of black adolescents from one-parent families and of those from two-parent homes narrowed in this era, for more black couples' children entered the labor force once nonresidential jobs opened to them.[74]

By 1920 the greatest employment-level difference caused by parental marital status occurred among native-born whites, where over four-fifths of widows' children were economically active but only three-fifths of those living with both parents were. In no other ethnic group did widowhood impose such a sustained heavy penalty on the offspring, if only because native-born white

Table 15. Percentage of Coresident Fifteen to Twenty-four Year Olds in the Labor Force, by Race/Nativity

Race/ nativity	1880		1900		1920	
	Widows ($n = 637$)	Couples ($n = 479$)	Widows ($n = 736$)	Couples ($n = 549$)	Widows ($n = 710$)	Couples ($n = 506$)
NBW[a]	61%	50%	76%	55%	84%	61%
AA[a]	89	53	82	67	84	77
NE[a]	79	70	75	76	83	84
CN[a]	96	100	90	96	96	83
SEE[a]	—	—	87	80	89	74

Source: Data from manuscript census, Pittsburgh, Fall River, and Baltimore.

[a]NBW = native-born whites; AA = African Americans; NE = northern Europeans; CN = Canadians; SEE = southern or eastern Europeans.

children tended to start from a position of relative advantage. Hilda Eric's father had planned to give her a good education, but his untimely death meant she needed to find work as soon as possible. Girls or boys like her might use their schooling to obtain a clerical or sales position, but they still left school to seek employment years before they would otherwise have done.[75] While 23 percent of native-born white couples' children over the age of fourteen were still in school in the 1920s, only 7 percent of widows' children of this age group were. Early entry to the labor force meant that 35 percent of widows' native-born white adolescent children had unskilled and other manual jobs, while the figure for those with two parents alive was 26 percent.[76]

Despite gains in education for widows' younger sons, in 1920 parental poverty caused by their fathers' untimely demise still curtailed their career opportunities. In 1880 over four-fifths of fifteen- to twenty-four-year-old widows' sons were engaged in skilled or unskilled manual occupations, while only two-thirds of boys from two-parent families were similarly occupied; they also had lower levels of white-collar employment (see table 14). By 1920 the two groups had similar levels of representation in white-collar jobs, but the widows' offspring remained far more likely to be manual workers. Losing their fathers also distorted the occupational profile of widows' daughters; over half had been unskilled workers in 1880 (when two-fifths of couples' daughters were), a proportion that still obtained in 1920.

The lives of adolescent women altered fundamentally during these years as the proportion of those neither in school nor at work declined sharply. In 1880 nearly half of couples' fifteen- to twenty-four-year-old daughters helped at home, working under their mothers' close supervision on domestic and family-care tasks, as did two-fifths of widows' daughters. By 1920 the "at home" category had declined to 12 percent for both groups (see table 14). Couples now sent their adolescent daughters to school in greater numbers, enabling them to take jobs in the economy's expanding white-collar sector once they finished their educations (increasingly with a high school diploma). Widows' daughters resembled their peers in the proportion with white-collar jobs, but their lower levels of education and higher proportion in unskilled occupations indicate that widowhood still circumscribed their prospects.

Children's Institutions

So far I have limited my discussion of children's life chances to those who lived with their parent(s). The growing number of children's homes and orphanages in the late nineteenth and early twentieth centuries, however, signifies that despite widows' and older children's efforts, not all families remained intact. In the early twentieth century, charities maintained, "Where once families would have been broken up because funds were not at hand to keep them together, we now take it as a matter of course that where family conditions are normal and the mother is a proper guardian the children should be kept with her."[77] Notwithstanding these intentions, the three states examined here spent considerable amounts on institutions for "dependent, delinquent, and defective" children, with Maryland having more institutionalized children per 100,000 inhabitants (339) than either Pennsylvania (285) or Massachusetts (236) in the early twentieth century.[78]

The rising number of children "placed out" (fostered) or housed in residential establishments made manifest the difficulties encountered by urban families trying to combine employment and child care. Baltimore's Society for the Protection of Children from Cruelty (SPCC) investigated between 300 and 500 cases of purported neglect annually. In most instances it removed children from their families, placing them in orphanages or private homes. Some had been poorly treated, but others, like William T——, an African American boy of thirteen, were institutionalized because their families sent them out begging to help support the household. The society removed Alice M——, aged nine (race unspecified and therefore probably white), from her family because she asked for alms on street corners.[79] Urban anticruelty societies disapproved of begging and attempted to remove children from homes when their contributions took this form.

This interventionist approach went hand in hand with a proliferation of institutions for poor children throughout the nineteenth century. Earlier practices of auctioning paupers to local farmers as cheap labor or placing them in poorhouses or asylums with the old, feeble, and deranged seemed inappropriate for the swelling numbers of urban children in need of assistance. Well-intentioned individuals and organizations founded orphanages and reform schools in the antebellum era, as did some cities and states. Many of these children's homes housed poor children from distressed families where one or both parents might be alive but incapable of supporting their offspring. By prohibiting contact between children and their relatives, these institutions replaced parental guidance with institutional authority.[80]

The Civil War marked a turning point in American children's history. The loss of national innocence that the war's dreadful bloodshed engendered led many to project an aura of virtue and purity onto the young. At the same time the war created more orphans and drew additional young people into the labor force. It also prompted the federal government to provide pensions to the children and widows of Union soldiers who died in service. Unfortunately, not all war orphans found succor through such pensions. Many were still treated as paupers and lived in insalubrious almshouses.[81]

The number of orphanages expanded rapidly in the post–Civil War era. At the start of the Civil War there were about 75 children's homes in the United States. The number of orphan asylums had grown to 208 by 1877 and triple that number by 1890. A decade later more than 92,000 children resided in any of 1,000 orphanages. Some of these institutions were small family-style homes, such as Coit House in Concord, New Hampshire. Founded by a ministerial couple in 1866 to help children left destitute by the Civil War, this cottage home cared for children who had lost one or both parents or were otherwise impoverished. Other homes were considerably larger, dressed their children in uniforms, and operated along highly regimented lines. Pennsylvania had more small homes than New York, but it nevertheless averaged about 92 children per institution, while New York's average was 249.[82]

Fall River, with its large number of working children, had the fewest number in public facilities. In 1910, 554 children resided in the city's three children's homes. Baltimore and Pittsburgh each housed over 2,000 children in literally dozens of establishments. These discrepancies may stem from the continued, albeit lessened, economic utility of Fall River children, as well as the plethora of orphanages in the other cities.[83] Records of the St. Vincent's Home in Fall River contain many entries for boys such as John Harrington. In 1890, when he was ten, his parish priest placed John there following the death of his mother. Three years later a Mr. Hughes removed John from the home and gave him a job.[84] Boys stayed until they were old enough to work and then returned to their families or were sent to prospective employers. As the twentieth century wore on, the proportion of older boys still in the home rose noticeably, reinforcing from yet another perspective the point that the family economy had shifted and sometimes marginalized family members who could not contribute financially.

Highly urbanized, industrial states had more children's institutions than did rural ones, even on a per-capita basis.[85] Middle-class children may have become "emotionally priceless," but a segment of poor families, especially those with only a single parent, could not afford to support their children and so put them into care. Impelled by the inability of many single parents and some couples to look after their children and earn a living, institutional facilities proliferated during the Progressive Era. In 1910 more than 111,000 children resided in institutions. At the height of the Great Depression there were 144,000 young people living in orphanages and children's homes, many of whom were half- rather than full orphans, and some with both parents living but unable to care for them.[86]

As the number of children in orphanages increased, reformers sought alternative solutions to the problems of social child care. Their desire to remove poor children from the potential contamination of the cities (and supposedly feckless urban parents) led a number of charities to propose transporting them to rural areas where they could be housed with families in what proved to be an uneasy cross between indentures and adoption. Many fostered children traveled on the orphan trains to supposedly "real" families out west. By 1929 the New York Children's Aid Society (NYCAS) had placed 150,000 children, mostly boys, in rural western homes.[87] These placements could and did break down, sometimes stranding children thousands of miles from home or turning them into unpaid drudges. One sixteen year old recalled her foster home in 1928 thus: "My new 'mother' met me with an apron in her hand and left no doubts in my mind as to what my relation was to be to the rest of the family. They took me to save a maid's wages."[88]

Societies in other cities and states emulated the NYCAS example, though they placed fewer children. In 1883 the Children's Aid Society of Philadelphia urged the state legislature to limit almshouse stays for children between two and sixteen to sixty days. Instead the state referred dependent children to the Children's Aid Society, which supervised their placement in family homes.[89] This system met with less favor in Pittsburgh, where the city's large Catholic population preferred to keep their children in asylums run by nuns rather than risk adoption by Protestant families in the West. The Children's Home Society of Pennsylvania, the Western Pennsylvania Humane Society, and the Children's Aid Society of Pittsburgh, among other Pittsburgh-based agencies, fostered a total of 457 children in 1912, mostly within the local community.[90]

Roman Catholics generally opposed placing out, except when the parish priest vouched for the receiving family. This distinguished Catholic homes from secular or Protestant ones, which readily gave children to any well-dressed prospective adoptive parent or foster parent who called at their premises. Between 1886 and 1900 the Sisters of Mercy, who ran St. Vincent's Home in Fall River, released almost no children except to the children's own relatives, another Catholic institution, or a parish priest. After the turn of the century, the number going to a named, unrelated individual increased slightly, with all being placed in Irish Roman Catholic homes. When Catholic parents consented for their children to be placed out, they stipulated that it should be in Catholic homes.[91] For Catholics, placing children with their coreligionists took primacy, although as Linda Gordon has discovered, transracial adoption provoked extreme anxiety when "white" Catholic children were placed in Mexican American homes in Arizona.[92] The Roman Catholic communities in these three cities looked after their own: Pittsburgh's community supported five orphanages; there were two in Fall River; and twelve were run in and around Baltimore, with separate facilities for black and white children, in conformity to local racial norms.[93]

Baltimore's orphanages maintained active placing-out programs. The Henry Watson Children's Aid Society (HWCAS), founded in 1860, fostered four out of every five children in its care in "carefully selected" country homes, employing a trained teacher to carry out home visits. Although Maryland lacked compulsory education laws through the turn of the century, the society informed foster parents that children should attend school for four months a year. The HWCAS maintained that it did not place out children as cheap labor, stating in its annual reports that it would not "permit children to be ill-treated or neglected" or "place them out as servants or drudges." Moreover, it differed from a number of child-placing societies in that it gave "worthy" parents the addresses of their children. It respected parental rights, except where the parents forfeited control through "immorality or neglect."[94]

The HWCAS kept careful records of its charges, followed up their placements, and set guidelines for foster parents. Yet boarding out and fostering could be problematic. Foster homes rejected between one-quarter and one-half of all children placed in them. Agencies, popular journals, and private individuals entered into the child-placing business without proper safeguards. Even those involved in the home-placement movement worried that they had been too interventionist and had broken up homes that might have been kept intact.[95] Some societies were less scrupulous than the HWCAS, which tried to maintain family links, if not coresidence. The Boston charity worker C. C. Carstens told the 1909 meeting of the National Conference of Charities and Correction that it was a great wrong to remove "children from a reputable and industrious widow and scatter them among various foster homes." Many of the children so placed had living parents, so that it was better to keep them nearby, and city children did not necessarily want to live in country homes.[96]

Placing out put more pressure on bonds already strained by family bereavement and poverty. For African American children in Baltimore, it sometimes resembled the postbellum judicial proceedings that enforced the apprenticeship of former slave children despite their parents' objections.[97] Baltimore's supervisor of city charities had the power to remove children from their homes for neglect as well as destitution and give them to institutions for placing out. This practice continued in Maryland through the 1930s, with a disproportionate number of the children (about three-fifths) coming from the African American community. Some black children were "virtually indentured" in a shabby example of racially inflected social-welfare policies.[98] All the white children had been placed in white families, yet only 5 percent of the African American children lived with black families. Families of both races preferred younger children for same-race fostering or adoption; the average age of African American children taken in by black families was six, and that for white children fostered by white families was nine. Yet virtually all black children placed in white families were over the age of twelve.[99]

Black and white families put foster children to widely varied uses, depending on the child's age and race. According to a survey of fostering in Baltimore conducted by the Family Welfare Association of America, the white families who took in black children exploited them as unpaid help and certainly did not regard them as cherished adopted sons or daughters. When people wrote to the supervisor of city charities or an orphanage requesting a child, the supervisor's office concerned itself with "supplying [a child] which will meet the applicant's requirements as to age, sex, race, and ability to do the work expected." An investigator for the Family Welfare Association reported the underlying racism: "This applies particularly to the placement of Negro children in white homes. The needs of children are generally given only secondary consideration."[100]

Same-race homes generally accorded children the privileges of family members, giving them their own bedrooms and sharing meals, living rooms, and social activities with them. African American children placed in white homes endured servant status with no remuneration. They generally ate alone, and many slept in a room "up the kitchen stairs," meagerly furnished with a bed and a few hooks for clothing. Sometimes the child had no room at all but slept on a mattress in the kitchen, hall, or shed. These young people needed homes and families; they got a job that paid no wages and over which they had no choice or control.

The racial politics of the era pervaded these children's lives. Regardless of their age or sex, Baltimore's African American children placed with white families did their own laundry, even washing their bedding by hand. Not a single white family with a black foster child answered yes when asked whether the child ate with the family. Because these white families regarded African American children as servants rather than family members, they refused to send them to school and provided no medical or dental care. They also deprived their "foster" children of contact with the African American community. Baltimore's supervisor of city charities concurred in the policy of not allowing black children placed with whites to associate with people of their own race, for fear that they might become dissatisfied and not properly attend to their work. The contrast with children placed in city homes or with people of their own race could not have been sharper. All these attended school; they had toys; they were part of the family, even if not formally adopted. Black children placed in white farm families received little protection from the agencies charged with their well-being. Instead, they endured state-sponsored neglect.[101]

In states and cities with complex ethno-religious patterns, mutual suspicion fueled tendencies toward separate sectarian institutions. A few northern states had public, integrated facilities in this era, but religious and racial separation obtained in most children's homes. Protestants founded institutions for their own orphans, as did Roman Catholics, Jews, African Americans, and various immigrant groups.[102] Pittsburgh, Fall River, and Baltimore witnessed a rapid growth in children's homes structured along racial and religious fault lines. Immigrant communities established their own language- or faith-based institutions to avoid placements across religions. Separate ethno-religious orphanages in Fall River served the Irish and French Canadian Catholic communities. Pittsburgh's German Protestants, Methodist Episcopalians, Protestant Episcopalians, Jews, United Presbyterians, and members of the Reformed Church also established orphan asylums in Pittsburgh to serve their congregants. Baltimore's ethnically diverse population supported the Christ Church Asylum, the General German Orphan Asylum, the Hebrew Orphan Asylum, St. Anthony's German Orphan Asylum, St. Elizabeth's Home for Colored Children, and St. Mary's Home for Little Colored Boys, among others.[103]

Each of the three cities exhibited the separatist ethos of nineteenth- and early twentieth-century American welfare systems. In Fall River the Children's Home, founded by members of the city's manufacturing elite in 1873, admitted only Protestant orphans. Subsequently the Sisters of Jesus-Mary (later called the Sisters of Charity) started the St. Joseph's Orphan Asylum, which took French Canadian children. In 1885 the Sisters of Mercy opened the St. Vincent's Home; almost all its charges had Irish immigrant parents.[104] Baltimore's large German community sustained both secular and religious children's homes. The General German Orphan Asylum started in 1863, funded through the efforts of the entire German community. The Sisters of Notre Dame later established St. Anthony's German Orphan Asylum to serve the German Catholic community. In 1872 the Hebrew Orphan Asylum provided shelter for Baltimore's Jewish children. This institution atypically accepted orphans of its coreligionists abroad. In 1905 the Hebrew Ladies' Orphans' Aid Society raised nearly $2,000 to bring children orphaned during the Russian pogroms to Baltimore. By 1910 there were twenty-eight orphanages in Baltimore, divided along racial, ethnic, and religious lines.[105]

After emancipation Protestant African American churches, the Johns Hopkins hospital, the Franciscan Sisters, All Saints Sisters of the Poor, and the Oblate Sisters of Providence all opened facilities in Baltimore to care for African American children. In addition, compassionate black women opened their homes to parentless boys and girls. Church and club women began others, a common practice in both black and white communities, with group-supported homes being more likely to survive than were those with a single progenitor. A number of children's homes took orphans referred through their churches and the city charity authorities, with the city subsidizing both religious and secular orphanages.[106]

Nondenominational Protestant groups ran the early orphanages in Pittsburgh; in 1833 the Protestant Orphan Asylum opened its doors. A German Protestant orphanage began a few years later, as did a number of Roman Catholic institutions. The white Women's Christian Association set up a home for African American children, while atypically even for a northern city, the Pittsburgh City Home at Marshalsea (the city's almshouse) accommodated both black and white orphans. Marshalsea housed young children openly, albeit illegally, in order not to separate them from mothers ill in the almshouse hospital. By 1907 Allegheny County had three nonsectarian almshouses, the Protestant orphan's home, and a home for widows and orphans maintained by the Independent Order of Odd Fellows. There were four homes each for boys and girls (five Protestant and three Catholic) and twenty-one coeducational institutions, mostly Protestant, with four for Catholics and one for Jewish children. The Franciscan Brothers ran St. Joseph's Protectory for Boys, while the School Sisters of Notre Dame and the Sisters of St. Francis ran orphanages for English- and German-speaking children, respectively. The African American community supported several of these homes, including a temporary home for children from infancy to twelve years.[107]

Widows, widowers, and sometimes couples used orphanages to shelter their children temporarily so they could earn enough money to support their families. The institutionalization of half-orphans was commonplace, with remarkable fluidity within the institutional population. Although the proportion varied between children's homes, a significant number of orphanage residents had one or both parents still alive. The Boys' Register of St. Vincent's Home, in Fall River, reveals that two-fifths of the residents from the 1880s until the 1920s had two living parents, while only one in ten had suffered the demise of both. As was characteristic of many orphanages elsewhere, sons of widowers outnumbered sons of widows, a reflection of the difficulties fathers encountered trying to do both parents' work. The proportion of fatherless orphans dropped slightly (from 24 to 19 percent) when widows' pensions became available, but there is no way to know whether this was a coincidence or the pensions enabled more mothers to keep their children. A noticeable increase in the number of children institutionalized at a young age occurred during World War I, suggesting that mothers took advantage of the increased demand for workers to take jobs in the mills. They used St.

Vincent's as a form of child care until the children were old enough to enter the labor market or care for themselves after school.[108]

Many other institutions boarded children whose families experienced temporary financial or other distress. Half-orphans constituted about two-thirds of the children in the Baltimore Orphan Asylum in the late 1880s and early 1890s, while the rest had lost both parents. This asylum returned about half its residents to relatives, indicating a population as shifting as that of St. Vincent's. Pittsburgh's children's homes showed a similar pattern. There were few full orphans (fewer than 8 percent) but many half-orphans and some children whose parents simply could not cope with their child-care responsibilities. While fewer than 25 percent were widows' children, about one-third lived with both parents, and a similar fraction had widowed fathers.[109]

The welfare institutions and practices that emerged in the late nineteenth and early twentieth centuries were intended to ameliorate the ill effects of urban life and family disruption, even if they sometimes ran roughshod over the households they were designed to help. Families themselves had diverse self-help strategies. Mothers took jobs outside the home; they placed their children in institutions, put them to work, and later delayed their marriages to retain their wages and companionship. Families took in extended family members or boarded children with relatives. Each family carved its own route through the crises provoked by single parenthood and poverty, as widows, especially those from immigrant and African American backgrounds, found it difficult to conform to emerging standards of education and employment. Their children had higher levels of economic activity and were more likely to spend at least part of their childhoods in institutions, foster care, or relatives' homes.

In this chapter I have analyzed the U.S. manuscript census for three eastern cities to explore how and to what extent the death of one parent led to divergence from the norms manifested by two-parent families. I have shown that labor-force participation peaked for children in the 1910s. White-collar employment grew in significance both for widows' and couples' children, as did education. Widows' young offspring (ages six to fourteen) had lower rates of education in 1880, but changing legal requirements led one- and two-parent families to exhibit comparable levels by the early twentieth century. While all older children's educational levels rose in the Gilded Age and Progressive Era, couples' offspring were about twice as likely as widows' to attend school after the age of fourteen both in 1880 and 1920.

In the confrontation between models of the family economy, the United States consolidated on the middle-class pattern in which children stayed in education for longer periods and mothers had a household focus. This transformed the way some widows supported their households, as the public purse opened wider to facilitate domesticity and education, initially for native-born white and naturalized widows. Over the long term, mothers replaced children as ancillary wage earners, emulating the model of African American families, in which women had high rates of economic activity.

There was some convergence of occupational patterns between native- and foreign-born white children, but African Americans continued to have distinctive educational and occupational profiles through 1920. They remained largely excluded from the sheltered childhood envisioned for white children. While a racially stratified society disadvantaged all African Americans, the children of African American widows fared poorly indeed. They had higher rates of unskilled and domestic employment and fewer opportunities to use their schooling in the shops and offices of early twentieth-century society. Their families had a smaller number of older children at home to share the burdens of support. It is thus all the more ironic that widows' pensions and other public-welfare measures excluded African Americans in this era. The development of charitable and public assistance for widows reveals the gulf between the strategies widows' families adopted to provide for themselves and the emergence of new household models in which women and children were supposed to depend on men or the state for economic support.

3 The Transition from Charity to Widows' Pensions

> It scarcely needs saying that the destitution of widows does not necessarily arise from moral defect in the widow, but is first of all economic.
>
> —Massachusetts Commission on the Support of Dependent Minor Children of Widowed Mothers, *Report* (1913)

Local economies produced distinctive charitable regimes.[1] Maternalism—the belief that women's presumed virtues of caring and nurturing endow them with needs and perspectives that transcend class, racial, and ethnic differences—was an important factor in the development of social-welfare policies in the late nineteenth and early twentieth centuries.[2] Even so, charities in Pittsburgh, Baltimore, and Fall River pursued widely different public-provision strategies as they responded to racial, social, and employment structures that either hindered or promoted the acceptance of maternalist values. The Fall River charity elite rejected the maternalist ethos as the basis of social-welfare policy. In Baltimore racism and the vigorous Charity Organization Society delayed the implementation of widows' pensions until the Great Depression. Pittsburgh charities, however, based their generosity toward widows on the belief that society should help mothers look after their young children, a presumption fostered by an economy that offered few jobs to women or young children. Tracing the divergent charitable structures and battles for widows' pensions in the three cities clarifies the limits of maternalism as the basis for the development of social-welfare policy during the Gilded Age and Progressive Era.[3]

Within the world of middle-class white reformers, women were either dependent wives who looked after their homes and children or, much less likely, single, career-oriented women. Maternalist social policies incorporated the belief that women should not combine marriage with employment. This conviction ignored the reality in many African American and white working-class communities, where mothers' employment was an integral and growing component of family economic strategies.[4] Believing that child rearing constitutes a service to the state—albeit one categorically different from those undertaken by, say, firefighters or soldiers—maternalists sought to compensate for the absence of an adult male breadwinner by marshaling the state's collective resources to support certain poor families. Even so, maternalism did not overcome the gaping social and economic divisions that marred American life in this era.[5]

Charity in Fall River

Again, the development of charitable societies in the three cities elucidates the correlation between social policy and divergent economies. Fall River, the smallest of the three cities, had the fewest institutions and organizations dedicated to self-help and the welfare of the poor. Its 1854 charter provided municipal assistance to the impoverished through the overseers of the poor—town-appointed officials charged with aiding the poor from public funds—and an almshouse for those unable to support themselves. Protestant and Catholic churches ran their own relief societies, with different Catholic ethnocultural groups maintaining separate organizations, as did the Jewish, British, and other immigrant communities. Charity for widows and orphans, especially those among the largely Catholic immigrants who worked in the textile mills, did not seem to be a major concern for Fall River's Protestant elite.[6]

Whereas groups in other cities built orphanages in the 1830s and 1840s, the recognition that children have special needs took much longer in Fall River, a factory town that regarded them as cheap labor. In the 1880s Protestant women expanded their child-welfare work somewhat, opening the Women's Union Day Nursery for the children of working mothers and participating in the Associated Charities, the largest welfare organization in the city. At the behest of the vicar general of the Fall River Diocese, who was "moved to sympathy at the sad plight of those good mothers who were forced by economic conditions to work in the mills and still rear their families," the Sisters of Jesus-Mary and Sisters of Mercy established orphanages in the 1880s and a day nursery in 1910.[7]

The Associated Charities of Fall River (ACFR), formed in 1877, had a female volunteer staff, although its officers were men from the local elite—doctors, ministers, and mill owners. It adopted the sentiments and organizing principles of the Charity Organization Society, lobbying the overseers of the poor to withdraw public assistance from the "lazy, dirty, and drunken."

Members of the ACFR believed that cash assistance demoralized the poor and undermined the work ethic. Hence, they provided limited material assistance to their impoverished clientele, and that only after so-called friendly visitors determined their worthiness through a home visit.[8] Coming from middle- and upper-class Yankee backgrounds, the visitors were genuinely concerned for the less fortunate but also wanted to ensure that their money was well spent. While charity workers generally regarded widows and orphans as belonging to the worthy poor, this status could not be assumed, so each case needed individual scrutiny.[9]

In a city with a small middle and upper class and a large working class, outdoor relief was generally popular. Nevertheless, it led to higher taxes and garnered a limited number of votes for politicians in this largely immigrant city. Ironically, outdoor relief enabled factory owners to underpay their workers, for it sustained the working poor in hard times.[10] At the same time, keeping relief to a minimum served the elite by ensuring a ready labor supply without burdening the taxpayers unduly.

Fall River philanthropists believed that wage labor, not public or private aid, best solved poor widows' problems and thus rejected a maternalist ethos for poor women. Even during the economic depression of the 1890s, the ACFR tried to curtail city largesse by instituting work tests for relief applicants. As skeptical of impoverished women as other charities were of men, it favored a work test for women who applied for aid, a female equivalent of the wood yard where unemployed men chopped logs in return for food or a night's lodging. Zilpha D. Smith, the secretary of the Associated Charities of Boston, urged the ACFR to concentrate on securing work for male tramps and worthy men out of work. Nevertheless, the ACFR both tried to find jobs for women and petitioned the overseers to terminate city aid, no matter how modest the recipient's income, if the applicant or her family could work at all. Ann Boyle, a Union veteran's widow, took in washing, earning between $2.00 and $2.50 a week. She had two daughters, the elder making $3.25 to $4.00 per week in a mill. The ACFR asked the city to end her assistance in 1888, when her younger daughter got a job. There was no question of the twelve year old staying on in school to better her chances. Instead, she went into the mills and contributed her mite to sustaining the household.[11]

The ACFR remedies for widows' poverty sometimes entailed the manipulation or destruction of family life. In the case of a widow with five children, the organization asked the overseers to place the three older ones in the municipal children's home so that her outdoor relief would end; the woman would then "be forced upon her own resources and become more industrious." Public assistance could be granted legitimately to the incapacitated, but giving it to the able-bodied, whether male or female, married or widowed, would undermine the work ethic.[12]

Maternal responsibilities justified domesticity for poor mothers only if they had very young or sick children. Thus Ellen Casey was "in every way worthy" of support, since she had a nursing child who prevented her from working, but the ACFR expected her to return to work once she weaned the baby. Friendly visitors labeled Margaret Dooley "very trying" for refusing to leave her infant son in the day nursery and take a job in the mills. They complained about another woman who they thought should have been at work for at least six weeks, because her baby was four months old. They added that an "old woman" who was living with the family (presumably the woman's mother or mother-in-law) could care for the children, freeing the mother to work outside the home. Believing her "inclined to be lazy and shiftless," they wished her city aid withdrawn. Poor mothers, however, preferred to stay home with their infants rather than risk their own and their babies' health by returning to work too soon. Their fears were well founded: cotton-mill workers who combined maternity with employment had elevated mortality levels, while the insistent pressure for early weaning contributed to the extremely high rates of infant mortality in Fall River.[13]

Although children's homes opened in the 1870s and 1880s, the almshouse remained the city's only facility for the elderly until the end of the century. The small middle class and its deep division from other Fall River inhabitants limited provision for the elderly. Not until 1898 did a group of church women launch the first Protestant old-age home. Class and ethnicity, not gender or marital status, defined admission criteria. The institution housed both men and women, showing that the concern for the welfare of the elderly was not sex specific, as it was elsewhere, possibly because of the restricted population the home served. It provided "a haven in old age for the Fall River Gentlefolk of reduced circumstances." Prospective residents had to be at least seventy years old and have lived in Fall River for ten years prior to entrance. The home charged a $150 entrance fee (quickly raised to $200) to maintain its exclusive clientele. Its administrators wished to help the genteel elderly avoid the poor farm, "where everyone—beggars, drunkards, orphans, truants, vagabonds, the insane—found shelter." The managers of the home refused to admit applicants who could not pay the entrance fee.[14]

There was no Catholic provision for the elderly in Fall River in this era, even though the Catholic Church ran over 10 percent of the nation's 753 permanent homes for adults in the late nineteenth century. This lack of facilities in Fall River may have resulted from the way in which groups within the Catholic population used family members as a form of old-age assistance. The high levels of children's employment in the French Canadian community and prolonged residence of adult offspring in the family home supported older men and women within the household context through the early twentieth century.[15]

Ethnicity, religion, and class thus determined assistance in Fall River, with little regard for domestic constraints on female employment. Single-parent families (whether headed by widows, widowers, or divorced or deserted spouses) all encountered the same problem: how could one parent provide the support and supervision usually given by two? Fall River philanthropists believed that the surviving spouse should either work and pay for child care if the children were very young or put them to work if they were slightly older. In a city where children's and women's employment sustained the main industries, neither motherhood nor childhood had sacred status. The charity records do not imply a belief that working-class women should stay at home. Rather, they indicate the opposite: a woman who did not help her family by working in the mills or taking in washing was remiss and should not receive aid from either the city or private charities unless there were other, compelling factors.

Despite a theoretical acceptance of public responsibility for the impoverished through a well-established system of local poor relief, relatively few people benefited, and many widows' families endured dreadful poverty. Outdoor relief in Fall River constituted only 20 percent of the city's expenditure on health and welfare at the turn of the nineteenth century. In 1912 the overseers of the poor supported fifty-three widow-headed families in Fall River, whereas other municipalities across the state supported a higher proportion of such families. Even then, the price of assistance was the public acknowledgment of destitution. The groceries selected by the overseers arrived in a wagon marked "Overseers of the Poor," informing the entire neighborhood about the family's economic inadequacy.[16]

The ACFR's opposition to outdoor relief kept it to a minimum. Fall River's overseers of the poor claimed to allow widows' families as much as $2.50 per week for groceries, fuel, shoes, and medical costs. The Fall River authorities, however, gave much less per person than did other jurisdictions. Nearly half the relief families in Fall River received less than $1 per week per person in 1912, although only one-fifth of widow-headed households across the state received such a paltry sum. Hectored by an elite determined to keep taxes down, charity firmly under control, and a large pool of applicants available for jobs in the mills, Fall River provided relatively little assistance to widows.[17]

This approach differentiated Fall River from other cities, both inside the state and across the nation, that extended aid to widows on a more generous basis. In Chicago, for example, mothers headed 5 percent of the families, but such families accounted for 42 percent of all those receiving relief in 1910. Fall River's overseers of the poor bolstered the incomes of the working poor but provided little support to those who lacked an income altogether.[18] As a result, some widowed mothers placed their children in institutions while they worked, and others sent them into the mills until education and labor laws restricted that approach to family survival. The matron of the Fall River Children's Home explained to the Massachusetts Commission on the Support of Dependent Minor Children of Widowed Mothers that demand for places at her facility remained high because many widowed mothers believed there was no way to keep young children at home and work to support them.[19] Even after the institution of widows' pensions in the 1910s, widows and other poor mothers relied on children's homes to look after their children so they could work.[20]

Sensitive to the demeaning nature of charity, one of the largest children's homes in Fall River, the St. Vincent's Home, noted that even mothers in need of assistance would not allow themselves and their children "to become the object of private charity."[21] Placing the children in an orphanage, contributing a small sum for their keep, and raising money for the home enabled mothers to retain their self-respect. These widows viewed church children's homes as halfway houses, places free from the stigma of charity that would not only care for their children but also transmit the family's sociocultural values.[22] When family finances improved or the children grew old enough to work, mothers took them home again. Some mothers resorted to day nurseries, but there were few such organizations; about one-tenth of turn-of-the-century children's institutions offered short-term care for the children of working mothers. Half of these were in Massachusetts and New York, which both had a high proportion of employed women with children.[23] Many working-class mothers distrusted these facilities, fearing they would try to convert their children to an alien religion or way of life.[24]

The paucity of day nurseries and working-class suspicions about them meant widowed mothers relied on schools, neighbors, or family members to watch their children during working hours. Day nurseries cared for only 5 percent of the children of working mothers who received poor relief in Massachusetts in 1912. In addition, 44 percent of such children went to school, extended families looked after 15 percent, and "other brothers and sisters" watched over 19 percent (since only 7 percent of these families had extended kin living with them, relatives likely assisted widowed mothers even when they had separate residences). Neighbors kept an eye on 10 percent. Mothers made no child-care arrangements for about 6 percent of the children and were vulnerable to anticruelty societies' accusations of neglect.[25]

Massachusetts child-placing societies and children's homes itemized the reasons children came under their jurisdiction. Maternal employment and poverty were the most common causes, with most institutionalization produced by a multiplicity of factors. Insufficient income caused 27 percent of family breakups, followed by mother's absence from home due to work (21 percent). In addition, 16 percent of the mothers were deemed unfit, and 15 percent had been labeled immoral. Maternal illness accounted for another 10 percent of the cases. Social investigators concluded that children's bad conduct or, "much oftener, the immorality or other unfitness of the mother" accounted for the institutionalization of about two-fifths of the residents of children's homes in 1912.[26] Despite general concern over children's welfare, several factors limited the expansion of aid to widows in Fall River during the Progressive Era, including the availability of employment for women; large families that could share the burden of supporting widows, orphans, and the elderly; and the continued existence of general outdoor relief.

Charity in Pittsburgh

Pittsburgh's economy presented fewer employment opportunities for women and children than did Fall River's, leading its large philanthropic community to devote more attention to them. Some of the impetus for private charity in Pittsburgh came from the sort of public reluctance to support the poor via taxes that was manifest in Fall River. In Pittsburgh, however, this took the form of enhanced private provision and concern for the widows and orphans excluded from the city's main industries. Pittsburgh abandoned outdoor relief after the Civil War era, leaving poor widows and orphans dependent on self-help and private charity. Through various governmental reorganizations in the late nineteenth and early twentieth centuries, public support retained its institutional focus in the city almshouse and hospitals. There were modest amounts of outdoor relief in kind—deliveries of provisions, coal, and shoes to destitute families, primarily during the winter—but outdoor relief amounted to less than 10 percent of the welfare budget. Even during the 1890s depression, the city spent a minuscule amount (less than $4,000 annually) on cash assistance.[27]

Pittsburgh's public philanthropy helped all ages and sexes, yet its private charity centered on women. Widows suffered severe economic disadvantage in Pittsburgh because of the paucity of nonresidential jobs for women and lack of employment suitable for young children. Rising accident rates in the iron, steel, railroad, and mining industries focused public attention on the plight of widows and orphans. In 1870 accidents and violence accounted for 200 deaths per 100,000 men in the Steel City. The rate had risen to 350 per

100,000 in 1900, for the mills were taking on more unskilled workers, who suffered disproportionately. In particular, industrial accidents cut a broad swath through Pittsburgh's immigrant community. Accidents and violence caused two-fifths of the deaths among southern and eastern European male immigrants, twice the rate for all adult men. The horrific nature of these accidents made them a staple feature of Pittsburgh's daily and labor newspapers and a cause for concern throughout the entire community.[28]

Other factors contributed to the philanthropic focus on women, especially widows. The family wage ethos and dearth of female-friendly jobs made them an object of concern. Even when men found work easily, "the women who battle[d] for bread [did] not share equally in this prosperity," concluded Pittsburgh charity workers.[29] Moreover, those women who did find work endured significant gender-based discrepancies in income. Skilled iron- and steelworkers earned $1,000 to $1,500 a year in 1899; male glassworkers averaged $638, while female glassworkers typically received around $250. Teachers, the best paid women, earned between $545 and 600 per year, which was still less than what their male counterparts received. The annual income of women working in the city's cigar, canning, and laundry industries ranged between $150 to $350. Domestic servants, at the bottom of the employment hierarchy, averaged around $150 to $200 a year.[30] Such low wages made losing a husband a serious financial crisis for women, especially those with young children.

Pittsburgh's large and diverse population sustained a broad range of institutions and charities. Women there had a long tradition of helping one another through separate charity groups, such as the Female Benevolent Society (established in the 1820s) and the Ladies' Society for the Encouragement of Indigent Industrious Females (founded in the 1840s). The Pittsburgh Women's Christian Association, founded in 1868 during a "wonderful revival of religion" in the city's evangelical Protestant churches, articulated the concerns of affluent Pittsburgh women for the less fortunate of their sex. It proclaimed, "The great work of an Association like ours, must ever be the rescue and relief of women and children."[31]

In the decades following the Civil War, Pittsburgh's female elite established the Home for Aged Protestant Women, the Home for Destitute Women, the Boarding Home for Working Women, the Children's Temporary Home and Day Nursery, the Colored Orphan Asylum, Widows' Home and Tenement House, the Episcopal Church Home for Orphan Children and Aged Women, the Home for Aged Colored Women, and the Home for Aged Protestant Men and Aged Couples in Pittsburgh and Allegheny City. They opened homes for girls, boys, and the aged of various denominations. By the turn of the century there were about twenty orphanages and other institutions that boarded children and thirteen homes for aged, widowed, or destitute women, significantly more than Fall River's three children's homes and one home for the elderly.[32]

Women set up what became the largest outdoor relief association in Pittsburgh, the Pittsburgh Association for the Improvement of the Poor (PAIP). Founded during the depression of the 1870s by Protestant women meeting in "fashionable Fourth Ward Parlours," it expressed concern for poorer women's economic disadvantages. In contrast to Fall River, where men and women were equally likely to receive aid and where married couples were well represented, Pittsburgh's female-headed households constituted a large portion of those aided by the PAIP. Between one-half and three-fifths of those assisted were either widows or families supported by women and children. The elderly also fared badly in Pittsburgh's economy, with its demands for physical strength. An additional 5 percent of the PAIP's caseload were "aged."[33]

The PAIP subscribed to the family wage ideology fostered by Pittsburgh's economic structure. Steel City widows, it said, endured "the unnatural responsibility of the wage-earner. Mothers are designed by nature to care for their own children, nor do they wish to place them in homes or other institutions." Its charity laundry provided employment in a familiar, if arduous, occupation. The appeal of laundry work as a means of support for widowed women manifested itself in other cities, too, for charities elsewhere opened similar laundries with child-care facilities and flexible hours allowing mothers to be at home after school.[34]

As in Fall River, population diversity impeded communication between charities and potential clients in Pittsburgh. The "friendly visitor" system depended on interaction between the visitor and the visited, but there was a wide gulf between classes and ethnic groups. The caseloads of the Associated Charities of Fall River and the PAIP consisted largely, if not entirely, of English-speaking people. Baltimore's Charity Organization Society also encountered difficulties communicating with families who spoke little English. In 1903 it lamented that the Polish "people are very clannish and keep their affairs to themselves." Excluded by language barriers, few non-English-speaking foreign-born women and children received aid from mainstream charities, although their own communities established religious and secular philanthropic societies. Nevertheless, the PAIP gave sustained aid to the one impoverished migrant community with whom it could communicate. African Americans made up about 10 percent of its caseload at the turn of the century, receiving groceries, coal, and clothing.[35]

Widows figured prominently among those assisted by Pittsburgh's fraternal and ethnic organizations. The female Rebekah Lodges, affiliated with the Odd Fellows, operated a home for widows and orphans a short railway ride from the city. The Masons, too, maintained homes for widows and orphans of their members and were one of the largest secular providers of such assistance. The "Ladies' District" of the German Beneficial Union, which had thirty branches in Pittsburgh in the 1890s, helped their countrywomen. Similarly, the Society of St. Vincent de Paul, the Catholic Mutual Benefit Association, and the Ladies' Catholic Benevolent Association gave a helping hand to their coreligionists.[36]

Private indoor relief for orphans in Pittsburgh dated from the 1830s. During the Civil War charitably minded women realized the need to shelter children whose fathers were off at war or whose mothers were the sole providers. They opened the Pittsburgh and Allegheny Home for the Friendless in 1862. Organized by benevolent women from various Protestant denominations, it assisted children in distress, especially those whose mothers worked and were "unable to extend to their children that care which their tender years require." The Home for the Friendless helped widows to sustain their families by offering inexpensive accommodations to them and their children.[37]

Prompted by high Civil War mortality rates, the "lady managers" of the Allegheny Widows' Home Association bought properties to provide rent-free housing to widows and orphans. The managers came from the nucleus of elite women who raised funds for the city's sanitary commission and founded the Women's Christian Association and the Pittsburgh Association for the Improvement of the Poor. This home also accommodated aged women as an "incentive and encouragement to their efforts for self-support."[38] By the 1890s it housed over one hundred women and children in four rows of houses and one large central building with a chapel. Widowed mothers "wearing out their lives in miserable cellars or crowded houses striving to maintain their families" had an acute need for such housing. The widows' home meant they could avoid "the landlord's monthly claims which they felt to be their heaviest burden."[39] The home also found jobs for widows, furthering their independence and ability to care for their children.

Pittsburgh's Good Samaritans opened homes for aged as well as younger widows. The German Protestant Home for the Aged, the Episcopal Church Home for Orphan Children and Aged Women, the Home for Aged Protestant Women, the Home for Aged Protestants, and the United Presbyterian Home for Aged People sheltered widowed and elderly women in Pittsburgh during the last quarter of the nineteenth century. Pittsburgh also had two separate homes for elderly African American women, both founded in the 1880s by white women, and one Catholic old-age home, the House of the Little Sisters of the Poor, established in the early 1870s.[40]

Few cities matched Pittsburgh's attention to impoverished widows. The nature of the economy fostered concern for widows at both the formal and informal levels. Collections for those widowed by industrial accidents commonly took place at the mill gates. Given the paucity of employment opportunities for older women, the high accident rate produced many bereft and dependent widows.[41] Reacting against the city's minimal assistance, private charities helped widows' families stay together. Unlike Fall River, where municipal authorities used outdoor relief to sustain the city's industrial structure and private philanthropy was limited, official Pittsburgh abandoned widows, the unemployed, and underpaid, while middle-class women reformers and working-class families picked up the pieces.

Charity in Baltimore

Baltimore fell midway between Pittsburgh and Fall River in its awareness of widows' welfare needs. Women from this port city's well-established commercial and mercantile elite created one of the United States' first general societies devoted to widows' and older women's welfare. Perceiving a need to shelter impoverished women, Sarah Mickle, a member of a "fashionable sewing circle," founded the Impartial Female Humane Society in 1802. The society housed and furnished work to poor women, believing that if they sought "work publicly[,] they would have to submit to a remuneration wholly inadequate and perhaps be exposed to insult and temptation." Baltimore also had industry-specific organizations dedicated to assisting widows. The widows of seamen attracted special attention from organizations such as the Society for the Relief of Widows and Orphans of Seamen and the Charitable Marine Society, which paid benefits to members and families of deceased members.[42]

Devotion to widows' needs became part of the rationale for charity in Baltimore, although without the vigilance characteristic of Pittsburgh charities. Asserting that three-quarters of all Baltimoreans lived on the edge of poverty, in 1860 the Baltimore Association for Improving the Condition of the Poor (BAICP) noted that the death of their main breadwinner had driven "another widow and another little band of orphans on the barren harvest of the sewing woman's needle." The BAICP identified the longstanding poverty of working-class families and the constricted job opportunities for widows as responsible for their immiseration. From its founding in 1849 until the depression of the 1890s, about 15 percent of the BAICP's caseload involved widows for whom the association tried to find domestic situations, frequently placing their children in foster homes. It thus adhered to the model of assistance in which family separation and the employment of mothers and older children were the norm. Since the city gave little or no outdoor relief, preferring to run its own institutions (e.g., the city almshouse) or give small sums to privately run homes, the actions of the BAICP and similar private charities determined the type and amount of help given to widows and other needy individuals.[43]

One group of widows received particular attention in post–Civil War Baltimore. The Home for Confederate Widows and Mothers opened in 1885 to provide a pleasant home for the widows and mothers of Confederate soldiers. Set up and managed by the Ladies' Confederate Memorial and Aid Association, this home provided for a small number of widows. Its precarious financial condition underscored the limits of private philanthropy, which was dwarfed by the more sustained efforts embodied in Union veterans' federal pensions and survivors' benefits and state-sponsored homes for ex-Confederate soldiers farther south. Maryland gave the Confederate widows' home a $1,000 annual grant, while the Beneficial Association of the Maryland Line (ex-Confederate) contributed $2,937 to help support 274 former Confederate soldiers or their widows at the turn of the century. About two-fifths of the 204 Union veterans' widows in Baltimore enumerated in the 1890 census drew federal pensions.[44]

Overall, federal widows' and veterans' pensions did little to offset the poverty of urban widows. In the 1880s about half of all northern war widows, mostly resident in small towns and rural areas, received federal pensions. Civil War widows constituted about 10 percent of the nation's total widowed population but only 3 percent in heavily immigrant Fall River, 5 percent in Baltimore, and 8 percent in Pittsburgh. Thus, relatively few urban widows could turn to veterans' organizations in times of trouble.[45]

Veterans or survivors' benefits mostly went to whites, even though a number of African Americans had fought in the Civil War.[46] Baltimore's black community simultaneously struggled to maintain legal rights in an increasingly hostile climate and to establish welfare associations for the less fortunate.[47] In 1865, 11 percent of those assisted by the BAICP were black, with the number increasing to 31 percent by 1892. In the decade following the Civil War, a number of homes opened for African American elderly and orphans. The African Methodist Episcopal Church funded and managed the Aged Men and Women's Home. Opened in 1870, it had, according to the 1901 Charity Organization Society directory, a "board of colored directors" and was "supported by donations from colored persons and societies." It charged a $100 entrance fee and required each new resident to have "an outfit and furniture for a room." Its managers promised to provide the home's residents care for their lives or as long as they maintained "good behavior." It shared the parental ethos of many homes by strictly controlling residents' behavior. Being under church auspices gave additional stability to the Aged Men and Women's Home, which survived for over a century.[48]

African American ex-servants experienced particular difficulties in finding housing when they could no longer work. This led a group of affluent white women to establish the Shelter for Aged and Infirm Colored Persons of Baltimore City in 1883. Run on maternalist lines, it succored aged widows and single women who had served white families until they grew too old for heavy work. The shelter's managers believed there was "no class more helpless when old than faithful colored women who have lived from hand to mouth all their days."[49] They cited self-interest in appealing to the city and the state for support: "We are really offering to lighten the public burden, for if not cared for here, these women would have to go to the almshouse." The city appropriated $500 for the shelter in 1892, although it gave no money to the other charitable homes for the aged at this time. Even with this donation, the shelter eked out a bare existence. Unable to fulfill the demand for its services, it had a long waiting list by the turn of the century. The shelter included a few black subscribers, who, according to the racially segregated donation list, contributed small sums of cash as well as flour, sugar, ham, and bushels of fruit. The largest donations came from white women who retained an interest in their former help.[50]

Baltimore had segregated religious as well as secular institutions. In 1869 the Little Sisters of the Poor established a home for worthy persons over the age of sixty, but it accepted only white Catholics. It opened a twenty-bed "wing for colored women" in 1884 but made no provision for African American men. Exclusion from this very large institution constituted yet another misfortune for older African American men who needed sheltered housing. Apart from the Aged Men and Women's Home, which housed but a handful, the city almshouse was the only care facility serving them. The probable reason for this rests in the origin of many charitable institutions. Where the community they served played a role in founding them, it defined the population to be helped. Where they were paternalistic or maternalistic, however, they sustained only a portion of the needy population, in accordance with the founders' perceptions. Hence the Aged Men and Women's Home established by the African American community housed men as well as women, but the Shelter for Aged and Infirm Colored Persons, founded by white women as a place for superannuated domestic help, contained only women. Baltimore's white charity establishment pondered its neglect of the African American population and accepted the initiative of black ministers and teachers to undertake friendly visiting. By 1895 the BAICP had twelve district boards, eight white and four black, with a roster of 250 women who visited families and conducted sewing classes. However, it gave little sustained financial assistance to its clientele.[51]

Immigrants constituted about one-fourth of those aided by Baltimore's private charities in the last quarter of the nineteenth century, about twice their proportion of the population. Many ethnic groups established facilities in Baltimore to house women and men, with little special institutional emphasis on widows.[52] The old-age homes tended to take both sexes, although women predominated, as they did in the elderly population in general. Thus the General German Aged People's Home, or Greisenheim, as it was familiarly known, established in 1882 by the Allgemeine Arbeiter Kranken Unterstützungs Verein (the general workers' illness benefits society), offered "the aged of their race" a place to "spend the declining days of life in comfort and security." Funded and managed by the Ladies Aid Society, the Greisenheim housed a population that was approximately three-fifths women, a proportion similar to that of the A.M.E.'s Aged Men and Women's Home and the Home for the Aged run by the Little Sisters of the Poor.[53]

Baltimore's Jewish community provided both indoor and outdoor relief to widows and the elderly, principally assisting people in their own homes. Widows headed about one-third of the four hundred families aided by the Hebrew Benevolent Society at the turn of the century, with the elderly and infirm (some also widowed) constituting one-fifth. The Hebrew Ladies' Sewing Society distributed over five thousand garments, five hundred pairs of shoes, and over three hundred pounds each of coffee and sugar; it also gave small sums of money to poor persons. The Hebrew Hospital and Asylum (established in 1890) helped a limited number, housing only forty-one inmates.[54]

The Charity Organization Society (COS) of Baltimore, founded in 1883, was the largest and most influential of the modern charities but tendered only outdoor relief. With its mixed-sex board and female employees (including Mary Richmond), it devoted more of its resources and attention to widows than did the BAICP, whose all-male directorate ran a wood yard where poor men chopped logs in return for lodging. The proportion of widows represented in the COS caseload varied with the state of the economy but averaged about one-third, a lower proportion than that for the Pittsburgh Association for the Improvement of the Poor but greater than that for the Associated Charities of Fall River. The COS staff engaged in friendly visiting and investigated individual cases. The visitors maintained that lonely elderly widows welcomed their attention, although the recipients rarely set their feelings about these cross-class exchanges on paper.[55]

The COS wanted to rationalize philanthropy by coordinating the efforts of the well intentioned and to transfer expenditure on the poor from the public to the private purse. Mary Richmond counseled against "unwise philanthropy," agreeing with Josephine Lowell, of the New York COS, that charity is an act of kindness from one individual to another, while public care is open to political influence. Taxpayers, in this view, should not be forced to give up what they need for their own families to support a "dissolute neighbor's" family. The Baltimore COS published numerous case histories to illustrate the progress of systematic charity, frequently featuring widows, orphans, and the elderly, whose "worthiness" seemed self-evident. Such vignettes emphasized the role of the visitor as facilitating employment rather than providing cash assistance. Typical of this genre, one such account relates how a COS visitor procured a lightweight sewing machine and a better class of sewing jobs for an aged grandmother, which enabled her to support her disabled, widowed daughter and two young grandchildren.[56]

COS activists worried how "women bereft of the natural breadwinner for their children" could maintain "a proper family life in a real home." "Subtle dangers to the character of [the widowed mother's] boys and girls lie in the relief she must receive and in her necessary absences from home to earn in her husband's stead." In such cases, they averred, it might be better to place the children in a local institution and hope that a proper treatment plan would allow the family to live together after "strength and skill" had been gained.[57] Amos G. Warner's report on Baltimore charities, commissioned by the COS in 1887, argued that "normal family life for each individual is undoubtedly better than life in an institution; but a family dependent upon continual doles is not a normal family."[58] Neither was a household headed by widows, according to the Henry Watson Children's Aid Society (HWCAS), an organization dedicated to fostering children from economically or socially unstable backgrounds. These sentiments resulted in the removal of hundreds of children to orphanages and foster homes and undermined widows' efforts to keep their households intact.[59]

Through the end of the nineteenth century, charity workers in Baltimore, like their counterparts in Fall River, regarded widowhood as but one of several problems to be resolved by scientific charity.[60] Reform organizations in both cities emphasized getting the poor to work, with little regard for maternalist gender conventions. Like Fall River's with its textile mills, Baltimore's economy offered plentiful, albeit poorly paid, work for women in its female-intensive garment industry, canneries, and kitchens. The COS in Baltimore favored employment over relief, even if it meant removing children from their homes and boarding them in institutions or with private families. In contrast, the fundraising efforts of Pittsburgh's charitable women provided residential places and income support for widows. Scientific philanthropists condemned this approach as "unregenerate charity," but its proponents recognized that widows and their families suffered because of the lower wages and restricted employment opportunities available to women and children.[61]

The Coming of Widows' Pensions

As long as charity remained a local concern, its coverage varied widely between jurisdictions and reflected individual social, economic, and political systems. In 1900 most extrafamilial support for widows came from private organizations. By 1920 almost all northern and western and a few southern states had passed mothers' or widows' pension legislation providing assistance to impoverished widows with young children. Against the persistent opposition of organized charity, the pension movement grew from nothing to a tidal wave in the 1910s. It garnered support from the trade union movement, newspaper chains, mass-market magazines, the National Congress of Mothers, suffragists, and the Women's Christian Temperance Union.[62] Despite the movement's national scope, however, regional variations persisted in the levels of assistance given to widowed mothers of young children. Moreover, these pensions, which were modeled on poor relief rather than a social-entitlement model, provided poorly for those they purported to assist.[63]

A number of theories have been advanced to explain the rapid spread of widows' pensions. Theda Skocpol located the impetus for pensions within the state and included voluntary organizations as integral contributors to the emerging social-welfare consensus. Mark Leff posited that a decline in the extended family left a vacuum of support that pensions filled. Leff's suggestion seems unlikely, however, for overall levels of family extension remained stable in the late nineteenth and early twentieth centuries for most Americans and actually increased among African Americans, the group least likely to obtain assistance. It is true that fewer younger widows lived with their parents, largely because their own increased economic activity enabled them to maintain independent households, but family extension rates actually increased among older widows (who were not the target of these pensions) as they moved into their daughters' and sons' households.[64]

Many historians have attributed the successful campaign for mothers' pensions to maternalist reformers' affirmation of motherhood. Linda Gordon has described a gendered welfare strategy in which pity rather than entitlement held sway, whereas Susan Sterett examined the constitutional arguments that limited pensions to poor women rather than extending them to all mothers. Marriage, according to Nancy Cott, was seen as a public institution, and by extension so was motherhood, which became a form of service to the state. It was thus both morally acceptable and economically efficient to pay poor women to care for their children when the alternative would be institutionalization. The unanimity among maternalists should not be overstated, however: these women came from diverse social classes, ethnic and racial groups, and religious traditions. They did not necessarily share a perspective based on a particular interpretation of gender roles, and even where groups from different classes or races agreed on the importance of motherhood, they differed in their visions for accomplishing their objectives.[65]

Early analysts of widows' pensions worried about local structures' impacts on welfare provision. As the pioneering social reformer Edith Abbott put it, "local responsibility leads directly to irresponsibility."[66] It certainly resulted in great variation in the availability and distribution of such pensions, depending not just on the vagaries of local politicians but also on different conceptions of women's roles. While altered constructs of women's and children's economic and social roles prompted many reformers to oppose maternal and child employment in fin-de-siècle cities, not all did so, as the Fall River experience shows. Still, a belief in the politics of difference and the difficulties of combining employment and motherhood led many social activists to advocate state-subsidized motherhood. Fears of race suicide through the neglect of (white) children, a desire to keep young people in school so they could be acculturated in American values, and the increased importance of women's voices in social welfare all contributed to the application of maternalist values to aspects of public policy.[67]

Yet differences persisted between cities and states and between urban and rural areas. Despite a general consensus about the need for pensions (some charity workers excepted), the amounts granted to the widowed mothers of young children differed greatly from the North to the South and from city to countryside. Moreover, the stipends were rarely sufficient to let mothers leave the labor force and care for their children. State legislatures passed programs in response to popular pressure, but it was up to local officials to implement them. Payment regimes varied from one place to another. Public sentiment might result in the passage of a law, but local officials often provided little if any funding, as was the case in Maryland through the 1920s.[68]

Widows' pensions were part of the surge of child-centered activism and its many results: compulsory education legislation; laws regulating child labor in factories, shops, and offices; the Children's Bureau; and the Sheppard-Towner Act. The emphasis on childhood as the formative period for economic productivity and political responsibility led many people to support public or private aid to young children channeled through their mothers. The Mothers' Pension League of Allegheny County stated that "children who are poorly prepared for life run a greater chance of becoming dependent when they have become adults." Helping the young, it was argued, would benefit the state in the long run through lower levels of delinquency and higher levels of productivity. State legislatures enacting pensions in the 1910s regarded them as an "integral part of the legislative machinery for child conservation."[69]

Widows' pensions targeted the well-being of children, not mothers, thus merging the welfare of the two groups. Pennsylvania campaigners for mothers' pensions, such as the charity worker Helen Tyson, were not "concerned with the mother of the children as an individual; she could meet her own financial difficulties in most cases, provided she were free for self-support. Only in her relation to her children does she need financial assistance, and her service to them has seemed valuable enough to the State to deserve recognition and aid."[70] This viewpoint simultaneously ignored the persistent wage and employment discrimination that women suffered and foregrounded an ideology that regarded motherhood and breadwinning as mutually exclusive. Pension legislation signified a belief in child rearing as women's primary role and as worthy of social recognition, yet few states provided pensions large enough for mothers to stay at home. Massachusetts strongly encouraged widows' employment, while many western states permitted maternal employment if the juvenile court or other authorities agreed that such work did not harm the mothers' health or lead to neglected children. Most other states declined to pass legislation regarding maternal employment and encouraged it in practice.[71]

Pensions exemplified "the whole trend of modern thought in relation to child conservation," according to Helen Tyson's report written for the Public Charities Association of Pennsylvania. The association claimed that, having previously neglected poor widows with young children, society was paying "a heavy penalty in broken homes, preventable sickness, juvenile delinquency, child labor," and other social ills. Applying conservation metaphors to human resources, the Pennsylvania conservationist Amos Pinchot likened child protection to forestry: "If you strike a sapling with an axe it may live but it will grow up a scarred tree. If you give a child a bad start, you cannot expect it to become a strong man or woman or a first rate citizen."[72] Pennsylvania's board of education described mothers' assistance as an "integral part of the legislative machinery for child conservation," adding that compulsory education and child labor laws can be effective only when the widowed mother of young children has a decent income "independent of their illegal and pitifully precarious wages."[73]

Pensions were charity as well as conservation measures, so states barred property owners from receiving them. Hence, most pension families came from modest backgrounds. One study found that over half (54 percent) of the late fathers had been unskilled workers, while 36 percent held skilled positions. A mere 4 percent had worked in clerical or professional posts. Studies indicated that family wealth in pension families was "pitifully small." States designed and implemented widows' pensions for the poorest widows, referring to them as "indigent" (Pennsylvania), "dependent and neglected" (Illinois), or merely "dependent" (Massachusetts). The legislators who drew up plans for mothers' aid intended it for the poorest children.[74]

Various factors conspired to keep pension numbers low. Financial limitations imposed by parsimonious state legislators meant long waiting lists, while racism and a citizenship criterion barred other needy widows from the pension rolls. As a result, few widows left the labor force, and few adolescent half-orphans completed their educations. The Pennsylvania Mothers' Assistance fund encouraged academically able children to remain in school but recognized the difficulties: "With our limitation of funds the pressure toward work at the age of 14 is almost irresistible in the interest of aiding other families in which there is greater need."[75] Financial constraints undermined the value of pensions as a child-welfare tool, notwithstanding their avowed purpose of protecting the young.

The charity establishment failed to prevent public funds from being expended on widows' pensions, yet they did mold pension legislation and administration. The emphasis on moral motherhood meant that most jurisdictions assisted only widows, even if the wording of the legislation permitted more a general distribution of funds. Widows constituted more than four-fifths of pension recipients; almost all the rest had incapacitated, incarcerated, or institutionalized spouses. Anxiety that public money not encourage socially unacceptable behavior visited the supposed sins of the mother or father on the child. The Massachusetts State Board of Charity believed that to assist mothers with illegitimate children would offend "the moral feeling of respectable mothers, and would thus do violence to a traditional sentiment that is inseparable from a respect for virtue." Such thoughts led many states to refuse aid to children born out of wedlock or whose mothers did not conform to social or sexual conventions. Widows' assistance legislation regulated maternal behavior to establish the sort of home that social workers and legislators regarded as ideal, stipulating who could reside in a pensioned household and what sort of relations widows could enjoy with the opposite sex.[76] Pensions thus legislated a particular view of motherhood. The widow who did not conform jeopardized her own and her children's chances of public assistance.

Despite, or perhaps because of, rising levels of wage labor among younger mothers in the late nineteenth and early twentieth centuries, the widows' pension movement opposed maternal employment as a distraction from child rearing and home management. Rather than leave such matters to chance, Progressives invoked the power of the state to ensure conformity to their social values. The Supreme Court accepted the state's interest in "the proper discharge of [a mother's] maternal functions—having in view not merely her own health, but the well-being of the race."[77] Opposition to mothers' work extended even to those tasks that women performed precisely because they enabled them to attend to their domestic preoccupations. Whether rolling cigars, sewing, shelling nuts, or making artificial flowers, women pursued these tasks at home, thus combining income production with family responsibilities. Industrial homework narrowed the ever-widening gap between home and workplace; the same reformers who favored widows' pensions opposed household manufacturing.[78]

Of course, pension advocates similarly disapproved of employment that took mothers away from home. The New York State Commission on Relief for Widowed Mothers argued that the "work available to such women outside the home inevitably breaks down the physical, mental, and moral strength of the family." The commission added that it disrupts "home life through an inadequate standard of living and parental neglect due to the enforced absence of the mother at a time when the children most need her care."[79] In their eagerness to see that children received adequate care, pension supporters equated working women with neglected children. Motherhood became not one activity among many but rather women's sole legitimate endeavor. Annie Marion MacLean summarized her investigation into women's employment in 1910 by declaring that woman's prime function "must ever be the perpetuating of the race. If these other activities render her physically or morally unfit for the discharge of this larger social duty, then woe to the generations that not only permit but encourage such wanton prostitution of function."[80]

The mothers' pension movement even questioned widows' competence to raise children without partners. The loss of the father, according to Pennsylvania's *Manual of the Mothers' Assistance Fund*, deprived "the family of affection and discipline as well as of their means of support." For this reason Pennsylvania "fathered" its dependent children through the appointment of unpaid county boards of trustees that administered funds and provided paternal "supervision and guardianship of the families."[81] Women without husbands needed not only male earning power but also public supervision in order to fulfill their motherly duties.

Maternalist anxiety for the welfare of widowed mothers and their children reinforced a societal blind spot over widowed fathers and their offspring. Mothers' or widows' pensions were just that. They rarely supported fathers or members of the extended family who looked after dependent children. Men without wives usually had jobs that paid better than those available to women without husbands, but their child-care problems were just as great. Moreover, unless they had coresident older daughters, female relatives, or domestic servants, they often lacked the domestic knowledge needed to manage a household. A trustee of the Allegheny County Mothers' Pension League summarized prevailing misconceptions about widowed fathers: a widowed man, she wrote, will solve the problem of single parenting by "installing a housekeeper, and by the end of six months or a year settles the entire problem to his satisfaction, by providing his children with a step-mother."[82]

Nonetheless, the large number of institutionalized widowers' children attests to the difficulties of combining income production and family care for men as well as women. A tabulation of the reasons for institutional care in Pittsburgh in 1907 revealed that 156 children out of a total of 663 had suffered the death of their mothers; 123 had lost their fathers. An additional 36 had been abandoned by their fathers after their mothers' deaths. With respect to the parents, 29 widowers showed such "defects of character" that their children were taken from them, as did 12 widows.[83] Unsupported fatherhood thus posed a grave problem for families that social-policy makers rarely acknowledged or took seriously.

The pension movement manifested the growing social unease about family separation as a means of providing for widows' children. As early as 1893 the Associated Charities of Boston proclaimed the superiority of the Massachusetts system of outdoor relief because it supported families at home instead of institutionalizing the children.[84] In 1909 Theodore Roosevelt's address to the Conference on the Care of Dependent Children crystallized the principles of home rather than institutional care: "Home life is the highest and finest product of civilization. . . . Children should not be deprived of it except for urgent and compelling reasons." The conference's executive committee recognized the local base of welfare; it wanted each community to determine the form of aid given to poor mothers, "preferably in the form of private charity rather than of public relief."[85] The committee viewed private-sector assistance as preferable, but in fact that sector had already proved insufficient to the task.

Pension advocates and many of their opponents agreed that widowed mothers of young children needed assistance to keep their families together. Few accepted the hard-line stance of the New York Charity Organization Society's general secretary, Edward Devine, who claimed that putting children in institutions is beneficial since it removes them from mothers who are not a "pure, moral influence." Mary Richmond also spoke out against pensions, fearing they would become another form of indiscriminate giving. In her view, careful guidance from charity workers would set the broken family to rights, but largesse from the state would only encourage dependency. Charity Organization Society members preferred privately funded assistance, accompanied by treatment plans adjusted to individual needs, over publicly funded pensions.[86]

Widows' pension advocates asserted the state's new role in child rearing. The New York State Commission on Relief for Widowed Mothers declared, "The normal development of childhood is one of the main functions of government. The best education requires a proper home training and it thereby becomes the duty of the State to conserve the home as its most valuable asset whenever factors, other than the improper guardianship of the parents, threaten its destruction." As a result, the commission called for the "reorganization of all existing relations between the State and its dependent families."[87] In 1910 the pension proponent Hannah Einstein, of New York, argued that a widow has a right to pensions since she has "rendered service to the state by becoming a mother" and has continued to "render a social service by caring" for her children. Einstein, like President Roosevelt, believed it better to board children with their mothers than to place them in foster homes. Aid should be given "as a civil right," not as a charity.[88] As the battles over widows' pensions in Baltimore, Fall River, and Pittsburgh illustrate, however, even the acceptance of pensions in theory did not lessen the stigma of charity in practice, especially since most states vested the administration of pensions in the local poor board.[89]

Mothers' Pensions in Three States

The places examined here exemplified many of the successes enjoyed and dilemmas faced by the mothers' pension movement and the continued importance of local constructions of welfare.[90] Pennsylvania passed its enabling legislation in the initial wave of this activity. The Pennsylvania act derived from the wing of the mothers' assistance movement that viewed pensions as a right, not charity. These proponents declared, "The word 'Charity' does not enter into the category of the movement. The very foundation of the Mothers' Pension idea is to eliminate the thought of public alms giving."[91] They asserted a mother's right to receive support while raising young children, arguing that pensions give the state value for its money, conserve childhood, and preserve mothers from the worst aspects of trying to be both fathers and mothers to their children.

Pennsylvania passed its original pension law in 1913 but did little to implement it in its first year. No boards of trustees had been appointed to distribute money, and the state's auditor general questioned the legislation's constitutionality. Concern over this state of affairs led to the formation of the Mothers' Pension League (MPL) of Allegheny County, which conducted a vigorous campaign for the appropriation of funds and establishment of administrative mechanisms. The league's president, Rabbi J. Leonard Levy, credited "the advocacy of this movement by an excellent group of young women" with advancing the "cause of the impoverished mother and widow." Women did indeed play an important part in the MPL's meetings and policy formation, but they deferred to men in official positions; the league's first officers were all men, primarily rabbis, ministers, and priests. Still, both women and men served on its boards of trustees and as advisers.[92]

The league garnered support through a self-styled propaganda campaign that included public meetings, special sermons preached in the city's churches, and public Mothers' Day celebrations. It sold mothers' pension buttons when the Pittsburgh Pirates played at Forbes Field on the Fourth of July, raising nearly $1,000 toward its legislative campaign. It also set up a straw poll at the 1914 Pittsburgh Exposition. Of 30,000 ballots cast, only 100 opposed pensions. Within two years the strength of popular support in the Steel City, with its high rate of industrial accidents, had led to an amended bill and increased budget, which the state appropriations committee reduced in an effort to keep taxes low.[93]

The enactment of the Pennsylvania Workmen's Compensation Act in 1916 gave some widows another potential source of financial support. Families that received this compensation for fatal industrial accidents could not obtain mothers' assistance, however, so "workmen's comp" was of limited assistance to widows. Furthermore, it excluded workers suffering from occupational diseases such as "miner's asthma," so their families had to endure the long wait for widows' benefits. Such limitations made the distribution of mothers' pensions particularly important in the heavy industrial centers where iron, steel, mining, glass making, and railroading exacted a high price in occupational injuries and deaths. Pittsburgh's employment structure suggested to local pension advocates that the demand for pensions would be proportionately greater in Pittsburgh than in Philadelphia or rural districts.[94]

Fathers' causes of death in pensioned families indicates their vulnerability to accidents and diseases associated with poverty. Nearly half the men whose families subsequently received mothers' assistance died between the ages of thirty-five and forty. Even during the influenza epidemic of 1918, accidents claimed 13 percent of the fathers who died, as did pneumonia, a frequent legacy of these accidents. While 27 percent died from influenza, tuberculosis killed another 12 percent. Of course, the problems of tuberculosis did not disappear with the father's death. Widows struggling to support their children by sewing or doing factory work frequently succumbed to the white plague.[95] Their susceptibility led the supervisor of mothers' aid in Massachusetts to express concern over the presence of tuberculosis among her clients. "Over-work, undernourishment, and crowded and unsanitary housing conditions probably caused the father's illness," wrote Elizabeth F. Moloney, "and if the children are to be saved, these conditions must be remedied as far as possible." Tuberculosis was responsible for the father's death in 28 percent of Massachusetts pensions families. Mothers and children thus needed to be examined for signs of the disease and placed under the supervision of the state board of health. Many states—including Pennsylvania—adopted similar policies, so that by the early to mid-1920s most mothers' aid families received checkups for tuberculosis and other health problems.[96]

Pennsylvania Mothers' Assistance Fund officials petitioned the legisla-ture to transfer funds from rural to urban counties because of city dwellers' high mortality rates. The lawmakers complied in 1920, concurring with the widespread belief that widows' poverty was primarily an urban problem. Yet widows in the countryside also experienced real difficulties. Despite lower living costs, they found it difficult to make ends meet, because employment opportunities in such areas were few and low paying. Even during the labor shortages of World War I, women in rural Pennsylvania earned only fifty to seventy-five cents a day as domestic help. In any event, mothers' pensions were no panacea for those in either setting: with an average grant of less than twenty dollars a month, they supplemented but could not replace maternal employment.[97]

An investigation into the Pennsylvania Mothers' Assistance Fund con-cluded that "in the past, society has been all too proud of the widow who seemed able to carry the double burden [of employment and motherhood] alone."[98] Mothers' assistance made only small inroads into that double bur-den, pension proponents' maternalist rhetoric notwithstanding. In 1920 a mere 16 percent of widowed pensioners described themselves as "not gain-fully employed." According to those administering the state's assistance fund, 38 percent were "engaged with a fair degree of regularity in gainful work." The rest did domestic or farm labor or took lodgers. Limited skills complicated by child-care responsibilities meant that pension mothers took "whatever poorly paid work they [could] do in the home or during the hours when they [could] leave the home."[99]

Welfare authorities in Massachusetts pondered the relationship between widowhood and child labor. Two Bay State investigations recognized the problems widowed mothers had in supporting their minor children but queried whether widowhood per se raised the level of child labor. The Massachusetts Child Labor Committee discovered in 1912 that only 8 percent of the fourteen- and fifteen-year-old workers in New England had widowed mothers, a fact that reveals much about overall poverty levels and the value placed on children's contributions to the family economy. Moving contrary to the era's conventional wisdom, the committee declared that "the 'poor widow' is not the cause of child labor." It recognized that both low parental wages and unsteady employment contributed to the continued presence of young workers in factories and sweatshops. State legislators nonetheless assumed that working fourteen and fifteen year olds supported widowed mothers with earnings that were "absolutely essential to the continuance of the family above ground."[100] They regarded widows' and orphans' poverty in a special light, however, holding them blameless for their impoverishment. Their problems stemmed from economic circumstances rather than moral defects. Nevertheless, the system implemented in Massachusetts provided for moral guidance as well as economic assistance, even though it did little to prevent young adolescents from laboring to support their families.[101]

In 1913 Massachusetts established a mothers' aid system, under the auspices of the state's board of charity, that granted dependent mothers an income while their children were below working age. A settled income would enable them to keep their children at home and in school rather than place them in an institution or put them to work. While the board claimed it made concessions to the sensitive feelings of widows who resented being tarred with the charity brush, mothers' aid closely resembled outdoor relief.[102] The state supervisor of mothers' aid outlined the Massachusetts philosophy: "The Massachusetts Mothers' Aid Law provides weekly cash grants of sufficient amounts to enable a fit and needy mother to bring up her dependent children properly in her own home. The aid rendered is not in the nature of a pension. It is relief which is granted only when the public relief officers are satisfied, after diligent inquiry into all proper sources of support for the family, that there is need of aid from public funds."[103] The Massachusetts approach pauperized widows and made their aid contingent on close supervision of their families to determine whether the mother was indigent and worthy and would spend the relief money in the best interests of the children and household. Unlike poor relief, which tended to be distributed without close supervision, mother's aid in Massachusetts rested on a law that mandated inspection of the widow's household by the overseers of the poor every four months to determine whether she used the subsidy "for the proper maintenance of the home." If not, the overseers terminated her assistance.[104]

The state charity board specified that mothers had to provide "a high standard of home care." It sermonized, saying, "The mother of little children who will not attend conscientiously to their diet, cleanliness, health, and conduct for the sake of an adequate income, steadier possibly than were her husband's wage, is not the sort of woman Massachusetts wants to help under this act." Unless the mother conformed to the accepted norms of maternal behavior, the children were deprived of assistance, a policy that punished the children for circumstances beyond their control. It referred unmarried mothers' aid applications directly to the board of charities and cut off aid to mothers who subsequently conceived children out of wedlock.[105]

Widows with savings of over $200 or more than $500 equity in their homes could not get pensions; neither could those who acquired their homes after their husbands' deaths. This had serious consequences for widows who used their insurance money to pay off the debt on the family home or to take out a mortgage. They were expected to be frugal and provident, but state law barred those with insurance policies on themselves or their children from the mothers' aid rolls.[106]

Some Massachusetts residents felt that having charity authorities administer mothers' aid demeaned the recipients. Even so, the Massachusetts Board of Charity held it logical to distribute mothers' aid through the overseers of the poor, since the criteria for relief meant that it went only to the poorest families. Massachusetts nevertheless accepted that it was wrong to treat the "thrifty worthy mother" like a pauper. Instead, it announced, "the worthy applicant for mothers' aid" should receive "every consideration" at the hands of the overseers. The board of charity urged each city to appoint a "mothers' aid secretary," who would receive applicants in a separate room, sparing them the indignity of passing through the charity door. The board sometimes sent mothers' aid funds by registered letter to save mothers a long journey accompanied by small children.[107] While ameliorating the worst of charity's stigma, it nevertheless kept a close watch over mothers' aid recipients through inspections and an annual review of each case. The social workers and legislators who designed the system aligned it firmly with contemporary charitable practices. It centralized the aid given to widows, required adherence to statewide standards, and reduced the discretion of the local overseers of the poor. Unlike other forms of relief, mothers' pensions required widows to be not just poor but also fit mothers, which in Massachusetts, with its heavily feminized labor force, did not preclude employment outside the home.[108]

According to the Massachusetts Board of Charity, "to insist that the mother shall not work, regardless of home conditions, would tend to discourage that desire for thrift and independence which is an essential element in society." There was some recognition that family size would affect whether mothers could take outside employment. The board held that "any competent woman in good health should be able to support herself and one child." As a result, mothers' assistance went primarily to large families or those where health problems made maternal supervision absolutely essential.[109] In a state with plentiful (if poorly paid) employment for women and a long history of married women's economic activity, mothers' aid supplemented women's own efforts to support their families. The state did not permit middle-class standards of domesticity and motherhood to interfere with essential virtues such as frugality or self-help.

The outdoor relief tradition in Massachusetts eased the way for the passage and implementation of pensions, even though cities differed in their willingness to provide for their widows. In contrast, Maryland (and its major city Baltimore) had a distinctive tradition characterized by private charity and public and private institutions but no outdoor relief. The state did not give pensions to widowed or other lone mothers until the start of the Great Depression. Demonstrating the close links between reformers and activists across the United States, Maryland pension advocates appealed to the Mothers' Pension League of Allegheny County for assistance. The league furnished "many important details" of the first proposed act to appear before the legislature. Even so, the bill "failed through the political antagonism caused by linking it with partisan questions which the majority of the legislature opposed." In 1916 Maryland passed a poorly drafted mothers' assistance act that allowed cities and counties to establish widows' pensions but did not require them to do so. The legislation gave mayors discretion over funding and supervision mechanisms.[110]

In Baltimore this situation led to a ferocious fight over the administration and financing of mothers' pensions, which enabled the mayor to avoid implementing the pension legislation. This development occurred in the context of a reform movement led by wealthy business and professional workers that won a sharp curtailment of city expenditures in the 1910s, after the completion of many capital improvement projects prompted by the great Baltimore fire of 1904. Influenced by Baltimore's vigorous private charity establishment, imbued with a tradition of municipal support only for institutions, and pressured by large taxpayers to restrict charitable expenditures, the mayor and the city's board of estimates opposed open-ended charity, which is how they classed widows' pensions. Events in Baltimore demonstrate maternalist reformers' limited influence. Despite vigorous pressure from within the city and concern expressed by reformers across the nation, there was no way to force the mayor to fund pensions or treat them as an entitlement rather than charity.[111]

Maryland's law provided aid to widows who had children under the age of fourteen and were unable to support their children while maintaining their home. The law was intended to "promote home life for dependent children under the guidance of their mother." At the same time, it permitted Baltimore's mayor and city council to devolve implementation to the supervisors of city charities. This turned it from a pension measure into overt charity. Under the influence of organized charities, Baltimore's supervisors of city charities proposed investigating every case and hearing three witnesses for each applicant. Baltimore's city solicitor believed the law to be invalid, although the city did not test its constitutionality through the courts. Instead, it allocated a minuscule sum for administration and distributed no pensions at all.[112]

Mayor James H. Preston opposed pensions because of the potential cost to Baltimore's taxpayers. He believed they would pauperize the recipients and classed them as charity to "be handled by the Supervisors of City Charities." Mothers' assistance, he said, should be "put into the hands of men who are discriminating, fair-minded, and brave enough to administer it wisely in the interest of the taxpayers, as well as the recipients of the charity." Preston could have appointed a separate board for mothers' relief but chose to treat pensions as dole, outraging the organizations that campaigned for mothers' aid and many individuals who favored pensions as a civic right, not a demeaning handout.[113]

The vociferous national and local opposition to incorporating these pensions into the charity system underscored the conflict between scientific philanthropists and pension advocates over the nature of the pensions themselves. The mayor's opponents believed that "all elements of charity should positively be eliminated from such relief." Many objections to the mayor's adamant refusal to appoint a mothers' relief board came from ordinary citizens rather than political activists. Some sixty artisans and clerks signed a petition urging the mayor to set up a mothers' relief board separate from the charity authorities. A group of neighbors, including clerks, bookkeepers, shopkeepers, building tradesmen, and railroad workers, protested to the mayor, arguing,

"The embarrassment attached to his plan would rob the recipient of any joy or happiness obtained therefrom, and more likely would lead to a desire to do without the help, thus depriving the children of necessities."[114]

Matilda Weekes, the widowed mother of two grown daughters (a nurse and a teacher), claimed that the amendment to the pension act, which gave the mayor the power to administer its provisions through the supervisors of charities, had been inserted at the behest of those "actively opposed to the spirit of the bill." Another of the mayor's correspondents described his actions as unspeakable and "never intended by those who worked so hard" for the bill's passage. The Women's Christian Temperance Union disapproved of his "mean trick" in subverting the law's purpose, while a petition to the mayor asserted that throughout the United States the mothers' pension movement had "been in no way considered a charitable proposition." The signatories to this petition represented the Baltimore Federation of Labor, ministers and religious organizations, the National Congress of Mothers, the Maryland Woman Suffrage Association, civic associations, and fraternal organizations. These documents all show that community groups, trade unions, fraternal lodges, and ordinary citizens, as well as women's organizations, fought for pensions.[115]

Given the wrath of the "most intelligent and persuasive people in Maryland, people whom [the mayor] as a politician should not [have wished] to offend and displease," why did he oppose pensions so vehemently?[116] Part of the explanation centered on money and rested with the nature of municipal politics in the Progressive Era. The recently established board of estimates, which included the mayor, checked local council members' proclivities to spend lavishly in pursuing reelection. The mayor worried about the costs of pensions, concurring with one of his correspondents that "the law [would] be an expensive piece of legislation" and telling the city's newspapers that since the law's passage, he had been overrun with "well-dressed prosperous looking widows who [were] after pensions." He added sternly: "We certainly have no money in Baltimore to give away any such sums as this will eventually lead to." In addition, Mayor Preston sided with the charity establishment in thinking that pensions should be either privately funded or under the control of scientific philanthropists, who were well represented among the supervisors of city charities. Indeed, he viewed the issue as one of charity and saw "no substantial objection to the word": "The relief given will be charity no matter what you call it."[117]

The mayor received letters and telegrams from across the country protesting his stance. He responded sharply to the Manhattan Borough president, Marcus M. Marks, saying that he did not need advice from him. He claimed

Baltimore's situation differed New York's, since his city's supervisors of charities also administered hospitals and general welfare work. Henry Neil, the self-styled father of widows' pensions, protested that wherever organized charity administered pensions, "their control [had] not been for the benefit of the mothers and children but for the benefit of organized charity." Letters from Hannah Einstein, Sophie Loeb, officials from the New York State Commission on Widows, and other pension supporters across the country only served to harden the mayor's opposition.[118]

Many of the defenders of widows' pensions regarded the scientific charities with distaste. Writing as a "citizen and a taxpayer," F. B. Lee asked the mayor to separate pensions from charity: "You must know that the Federated Charities is run almost as a private business and apparently solely in the financial interests of a few." Others complained that the city's charities were "mainly for the benefit and uplifting of the families of drunkards, convicts, and ex-convicts," so that self-respecting widows should not receive aid from the same source.[119]

One of the few people who wrote to the mayor in support of his stance believed there should be no pensions at all. Writing from Prince George's County, Mr. E. Marriott labeled pensions "a swindle upon the taxpayers, demoralizing to citizenship, and corrupting to beneficiaries." He claimed they would lead to a vast scheme of lying and debauchery because women would misrepresent their children's ages to obtain assistance. Widows' pensions, he said, would encourage shiftlessness and family separation. If we read between the lines, however, Marriott's correspondence with the mayor suggests another motivation for resisting pensions: racism. Marriott complained that many African American children would "come under the provisions of this very liberal and free-for-all bill," which would encourage immorality. At a time when southern and border cities and states consciously restricted public expenditure to whites, this writer expressed a common racially charged sentiment. Southern states enacted pension legislation late and funded it poorly as a means of keeping taxes low and preventing blacks from benefiting. Baltimore's wholly inadequate appropriation for African American schools in the Progressive Era suggests that racism played a significant role in the poor public services provided.[120]

African American widows had extremely high rates of labor-force participation; conversely, they had very little chance of obtaining pensions or other publicly funded assistance.[121] Chronic employment discrimination meant that they depended heavily on private charity when self-help efforts proved insufficient. In 1920 they made up 39 percent of Baltimore's Family Welfare Association caseload but only 14 percent of the population. Mothers' pensions would have shifted this burden from private largesse to public entitlement and, in a city where African Americans retained some political rights, public accountability.[122] The city's resistance to pensions and reliance on private charity kept impoverished African American widows at work in other women's kitchens or dependent on handouts. This approach ensured a lower tax rate and some measure of social control through careful selection of beneficiaries. The mayor did not indicate the extent to which he opposed pensions for these reasons, but Children's Bureau officials expressed the belief that racism lay behind southern unwillingness to fund pension schemes.[123]

The vigorous protests against the mayor's intransigence were to no avail. Once assured that state legislation did not prevent Baltimore from shunting the supervision of pensions to the supervisors of city charities, he did precisely that, and no widows received assistance. The unwillingness to implement the mothers' pension legislation kept many widows in the labor force when they might otherwise have been able to reduce their working hours. When Maryland passed effective pension legislation in 1929, the system had all the hallmarks of scientific charity, including a network of friendly visitors to provide individual guidance to widowed women and the Mothers' Relief Auxiliary, which organized outings and little treats for those on the pension rolls. Although funded by the taxpayers at large, it remained firmly rooted in the private-charity model.[124]

Racism and Ethnocentrism in Mothers' Pensions

The purpose of pensions was to conserve childhood, but not all poor children or their mothers had an equal chance of obtaining state support. African American widows accounted for only 1 to 3 percent of the pension families, despite constituting a disproportionate share of urban widows.[125] Initially most states refused to grant pensions to foreign-born women until they obtained their first or final citizenship papers, thus discriminating against their (typically) American-born offspring. Eligibility requirements became less onerous by the mid-1920s, when three-quarters of the states with pensions granted them to aliens. Fourteen states still required a residency period of one to two years, while nine states stipulated three- to five-years' residence. Five states mandated that the father had to have been a resident at the time of his death.[126] Such provisions curtailed assistance for recent migrants and further discriminated against African American widows who joined the Great Migration in search of a better life for themselves and their children.

Even states with relatively liberal provisions discriminated in their implementation of pensions, especially in the first decade. For example, Pennsylvania initially favored native-born whites in the distribution of mothers' assistance. In 1920, 65 percent of the state's pensioned mothers were Pennsylvania-born whites, 4 percent came from other states, 11 percent had been born in northern Europe, 18 percent were from southern and eastern Europe, and 1 percent were described as "Negro." Of the nearly 2,000 families that received pensions from Pennsylvania in 1920, only twenty-six were African American.[127] Given their high levels of poverty, the Pennsylvania figures suggest the true magnitude of the bias against African Americans exhibited throughout the United States in the early years of widows' pensions.

The regional pattern of the pension movement accounted for some of their restricted access. Southern states, concerned to keep labor and governmental costs low and to avoid granting services to black people, gave little public support to widows; they appropriated small sums and reserved pensions for white widows. Since most African Americans lived in the South, where few states granted pensions, they had a smaller chance of obtaining pensions, even if all other things were equal. All other things were not equal, however. The power of the state reinforced the existing racial hierarchies to the extreme disadvantage of African American widows, single mothers, and their children. For example, Tennessee, the first southern state to pass a pension law, granted virtually no pensions to African American widows through the first years of the Depression.[128]

Theda Skocpol attributed the lack of pensions in southern states to low levels of literacy and female reform efforts' devotion to education rather than pensions. As important as educational reform was, race and racism were crucial subtexts running through the southern welfare story. State legislators wished to attract industry through low taxes, low wages, and a docile labor force; denying services to African Americans bolstered that strategy. Although southern states provided some institutional welfare services to blacks, these occurred on a separate and decidedly unequal basis. Conditions in Maryland's segregated almshouses, for example, were truly appalling. The neglect of African American widows and children paralleled discrimination against blacks in education, sanitation, and other public services.[129]

According to Emma Lundberg of the Children's Bureau, the question of aid to African American children caused "some controversy in the District [of Columbia,] as it does in some of the Southern states—no doubt being the main reason why six states now have no mothers' pension law."[130] Five of these states—Mississippi, Alabama, Georgia, South Carolina, and Kentucky—had large African American populations. When pension legislation was finally enacted, the distribution was racially biased. African Americans constituted a mere 9 percent of the pensioned mothers in Maryland in the early years of the Depression, despite their great poverty and significant numbers in the population.[131]

Other discriminatory factors included social workers' value judgments about moral motherhood. African Americans encountered discrimination in the distribution of aid and social services because of both race and marital status of the mothers. Using Linda Gordon and Sara McLanahan's calculations based on the 1900 census, about 3 percent of white children and 11 percent of African American children lived with never-married mothers. While a number of states permitted unmarried mothers to receive pensions in theory, in practice illegitimacy was understood to constitute a prima facie indication of maternal unworthiness.[132] Since single motherhood was more widespread in the African American community, social workers deemed a greater proportion of these families unpensionable.

Pensions provided subsistence for a minority of widows, though rarely enough to enable a mother to stay at home unless she had employed children living with her. The conservation of even white childhood took second place to fiscal parsimony in most states, while—their greater poverty notwithstanding—most African American widows and orphans remained outside the pension safety net entirely. The values represented by pension legislation were later incorporated into the Social Security Act, so that supervision of the mother, an implicit assumption that wage earning (even if necessary) should be discouraged, and racial bias all became features of that landmark legislation.

In the three states and cities examined here, the rhetoric of pensions as rights, relief, or charity made some difference to their funding and distribution. Ironically, the charity model in Massachusetts provided more liberally for widows' pensions even though inequities remained among jurisdictions. Widespread support for the passage of legislation in Pennsylvania did not translate into adequate funding as legislators and local officials sought to keep taxes low. The lack of funding in Maryland carried a racial subtext and a preference for continued institutional expenditure. Whether mother's pensions were viewed as child-conservation measures or aid to overburdened mothers, minimal appropriations and ethnic and geographic biases in distribution undercut their value as a means of ending maternal employment. Young widows' rates of economic activity increased during these years. At best, pensions stemmed but did not turn the tide of family breakup. Children's Bureau officials expressed the expectation that mothers' pensions would curtail the institutionalization of children, but they had not achieved this goal by the end of their first decade. In 1923 widows' children accounted for 26 percent of the children in institutions but only 17 percent of those attended to by child-caring agencies, which suggests that widows still turned to orphanages for help in times of crisis.[133] Widows' pension legislation signaled disapproval of mothers who breached the divide between female domestic and male breadwinning functions. The distribution of these pensions depended on local factors, and despite their designation as pensions, such funds continued to carry overtones of charity, not entitlement.

4 The Implementation of Widows' Pensions

Rightness of character is most likely to be found in homes where
the mother spends much of her time with her children, rather than
leaving them to the indifferent care of the neighbors or to the perils
of the street.

—Baltimore supervisors of city charities to mothers' relief
grant recipients (1929)

As the previous chapter reveals, the values that led to the passage of widows' pension legislation in the early twentieth century translated into varied funding regimes dependent on local economic and social structures. The implementation of these laws confirmed they could improve the material lives of poor mothers' children, but only if legislators appropriated sufficient funds and officials disbursed them fairly. In practice, uneven allocation meant that the laws benefited some single mothers and orphans to the exclusion of many others. These diverse funding and distribution patterns presaged the Social Security Act of 1935, which expanded on existing state welfare provision for dependent children and their mothers but accepted great variations across the United States.[1]

The Social Security Act also assisted the elderly, the disabled, the unemployed, and (through the 1939 amendments) older widows. It incorporated many of the assumptions behind existing widows' pension programs with little debate and continued to divide allocations for children according to their mothers' marital statuses. The Social Security Act and its revisions consolidated gendered and racially charged attitudes toward labor and subsistence, resulting in unequal protection for men and women and for different races, as will be discussed in chapter 5. Its initial neglect of older widows reflected their omission from social programs in the early twentieth century. To understand subsequent national welfare legislation, we need to evaluate these laws and the political attitudes that preceded them within an analysis of the effectiveness of widows' and old-age pensions.[2]

In this chapter I investigate the implementation of widows' pensions in the 1920s and early 1930s, the impact of differing pension/relief philosophies, and the problems of older widows. I examine national distribution patterns and those in Massachusetts, Pennsylvania, and Maryland before considering differences among Fall River, Pittsburgh, and Baltimore. The three states took distinctive approaches to mothers' assistance, ranging from comparatively well-funded relief (Massachusetts) to poorly financed entitlement (Pennsylvania) and outright heel dragging (Maryland). Massachusetts was the most generous state, using a relief model of public welfare to distribute funds widely. It had a relatively inclusive attitude toward eligibility and no waiting lists. Pennsylvania eschewed the relief ethos, regarding mothers' assistance as a right. The ultimate aim of the Allegheny County Trustees of the Mothers' Assistance Fund was "to place every needy and deserving widow under its care and supervision," yet inadequate state funding led to long waiting lists. Maryland's reluctance to contribute state funds to finance widows' pensions produced continued dependence on private charities. Widows and orphans there found little public assistance outside institutional settings. Local variations persisted as Fall River, Pittsburgh, and Baltimore continued their distinctive approaches to social-welfare practice.[3]

The Children's Bureau estimated that fewer than one-third of those eligible for pensions received them. The first nationwide survey of pension distribution, which was undertaken by the bureau in 1921–22, discovered that forty states had mothers' aid laws, altogether helping 45,825 families but with great variations among jurisdictions. The proportion of children aided in the mid-1920s ranged from 1 per 10,000 in Virginia to 38 per 10,000 in Minnesota. In patterns later reflected in the design and implementation of Social Security, northern and western states and urban areas in the 1920s distributed widows' pensions with relative generosity. Few southern states enacted pension laws, and the few bills that made it to the statute books attracted little or no funding. By 1931 five additional states and the District of Columbia granted pensions, doubling the number of assisted families. The Children's Bureau concluded that expanded provision within existing pension states accounted for the increase, since the southern states still disbursed few pensions.[4]

Restricting pensions to preferred racial and ethnic groups kept costs low and preserved existing racial hierarchies. Most jurisdictions overtly discriminated against widows of color. Southern states rarely gave pensions to African Americans, while southwestern states routinely discriminated against Mexican American widows. Three southern states with very large African American populations (Georgia, Alabama, and South Carolina) had no mothers' pensions as late as 1930, and in three others (Mississippi, Kentucky, and Maryland) provision dated only from 1928 or 1929. Many other states that distributed few or no pensions also had large nonwhite populations. As a result, relatively few pensions (about 3 percent in 1930) went to women of color. This paltry figure nonetheless represented an increase from the earliest days of mothers' assistance.[5] Exclusion from pensions wreaked great hardship on African American widows and their families. One Baltimore woman expressed it this way: "If you only knew how strongly I was inclined to allow myself the pleasure of staying at home with my children while they were too young to be alone." Mrs. Datcher got up at 5 A.M. and left for her job cleaning homes in one of Baltimore's affluent white suburbs by 6 A.M. She felt this made it impossible for her to get her children off to school properly. Subsequent access to a mothers' pension in the 1930s enabled her to look after her family without pauperizing them.[6]

Although discrimination existed in the North as well as the South, children of color saw their chances of benefiting from pension legislation increase during the 1920s as African Americans migrated northward and to cities. As late as 1930, however, only one-fifth of all African Americans lived in the North, and two-thirds of those in the South resided in rural areas. As I pointed out in the previous chapter, even discounting racial prejudice (if such a thing were possible), African Americans would still have been less likely than whites to receive pensions because of their concentration in poorly served sections of the nation.[7]

The available data are suggestive but sketchy, since many jurisdictions did not collect racial statistics. Of pension states with sizable black populations, North Carolina, Florida, Virginia, Mississippi, Arkansas, and Tennessee assisted only a handful of African American widows or none at all in the 1920s, while Ohio and Pennsylvania together accounted for about half of all widows' pensions known to be granted to African Americans. Twenty-four large cities with significant black populations reported the race of mothers' aid families to the Children's Bureau in 1931. Most, but not all, of those serving their black residents poorly were in the South or Southwest. Houston, Knoxville, Memphis, Jacksonville, Tampa, and Wilmington denied pensions to African American widows completely. Some northern cities also discriminated consistently against widows from ethnic minorities. Chicago, Milwaukee, Indianapolis, and Detroit made inadequate provision for black women and their families. In a number of other northern cities, the proportion of pensions distributed to African Americans reflected their numbers in the population, although not necessarily their numbers among the widowed or impoverished.[8]

In the 1920s rural households of all races suffered from the perception of child poverty as an urban problem. The majority of mothers' pensions went to big-city families. States that authorized assistance for country dwellers typically did so at a rate lower than that for urban residents. Wisconsin's pension legislation, for example, granted maximum monthly pensions of $40 per family in counties with fewer than 300,000 inhabitants, regardless of the number of children in the family. Mrs. J. S. Hahan, a widow in Kahoka, Missouri, informed the Children's Bureau that her pension was only $15 per month because the Missouri Board of Charities had no more money to give her. Her plight attested to the narrow margin on which many rural widows and children survived. The woman owed $15 for coal, $16 for sorghum, $9.40 on a hog, and $8.33 for rent. Her major source of income seems to have been a cow, which she hated to give up. "I have sold over $50 worth [of milk, presumably] from her this summer," she wrote, going on to express fears about the upcoming winter: "I do not know where the feed will come from." She lacked money to buy shoes, clothes, or books for her children, despite her efforts at self-help.[9] The notion that country living was somehow less expensive than city life belied the reality of the former: marginal existence on small farms at a time of general agricultural decline.

The Children's Bureau concluded that relief was "disproportionately inadequate outside the large centers of population." The overall level of employment was far lower for rural women than for their urban counterparts, and alternative sources of income were less numerous in the countryside (there were few lodgers in rural communities and less call for domestic servants). These facts might have disposed county officials toward generosity in the distribution of pensions, but generally they did not.[10] More typically, rural and small-town women encountered unsympathetic responses from charity administrators. The rural South in particular lacked the charitable infrastructure or political will to sustain these families in their own homes. In 1922 Mary Brewer, who lived in a small North Carolina town, wrote directly to the Children's Bureau seeking help. She believed she could make a living for herself and her three children if she "just had anything to start with." Mrs. Brewer's letter to the Children's Bureau indicates that charity authorities in southern states still regarded orphanages and domestic service as the best mechanism for the care of dependent children and their mothers: the letter reports that the State Board of Charity wished to put her young children in an institution so she could take a live-in position, regardless of the anguish that separation would cause the family. Moreover, southern states gave such small amounts that few mothers could afford to leave the labor force. Arkansas granted an average of $4.33 per month, while Florida, Texas, and Louisiana gave about $10.00 per family in 1931.[11]

Even comparatively generous cities and states restricted the overall numbers of families assisted and disbursed widely disparate amounts, ranging from fourteen dollars a month in Idaho to a maximum of sixty dollars in Massachusetts. Few localities gave pensions to all those who applied for them, limiting their effectiveness as a child-conservation measure. In 1926 the United States contained sixty-two cities or counties with populations greater than 100,000. Over half assisted 20 or fewer children per 10,000 residents. Indianapolis, Richmond, St. Louis, and Kansas City were the least generous (aiding 1–4 children per 10,000 residents), while Cambridge, Oakland, St. Paul, Boston, San Francisco, New York, and Salt Lake were especially charitable with 33–45 children helped per 10,000 residents.[12]

Demand vastly outstripped funding in major industrial cities such as Pittsburgh and Chicago. In 1923, 477 Pittsburgh families received allowances, with nearly as many stuck on the waiting list. Chicago aided over 1,000 families but had between 500 and 600 others that it could not yet assist. In 1926 the Pennsylvania Mothers' Assistance Fund reported that 3,480 families were receiving pensions, but others languished for as long as two years before their pensions came through. Nor did the long waiting lists account for all the unmet needs. In 1920 Chicago turned away nearly 800 mothers without permitting them to register their children's names for pensions because of the "inadequacy of the appropriation." Once the new year's funds had been allocated, the Cook County agent allowed these mothers to put in applications and take their place in the queue for funding. Following investigations into suitability, Chicago assisted only the most urgent cases. Throughout the era of city- and state-funded pensions, inadequate legislative appropriations meant that waiting lists remained long and much need went unmet. Just before the nation's economy plunged into depression, there were 1,500 women on Cook County's pension waiting list, and one estimate put the number of eligible women not receiving assistance as high as 10,000.[13] Throughout the 1920s localities differed widely in their willingness to appropriate resources for these programs, leaving many mothers with no choice but to work, pension rhetoric notwithstanding.

Most states that granted pensions supervised the families closely to ensure conformity with prevailing social norms. This revealed one of the contradictions inherent in the pension system: although designed as a child-welfare measure, these states abandoned the children of sexually nonconformist mothers. In doing so, the "sins" of the mother could be, and were, visited on the children through the curtailment of aid to supposedly immoral mothers. The refusal of pensions to never-married or divorced mothers in many states indicates the moralizing that accompanied mothers' assistance. In 1919 only ten states made provisions for families headed by divorced and deserted women, while three included unmarried mothers in their eligibility lists. Pennsylvania, Illinois, and Minnesota granted pensions to the legitimate siblings of an illegitimate child "if all indications point to [the woman's] being a good mother."[14] States tinkered with the qualifications for pensions through the 1920s but still confined them primarily to widows and maintained a close watch on the recipients' behavior.

When queried about the removal of funding from a mothers' aid family, Baltimore's secretary of charities averred that "it is of utmost importance that mothers of girls and boys should live upright, moral lives." Ironically, the caseworker called the mother in question "one of our most attentive and cooperative mothers." She worked first in a cannery and then in a boardinghouse. A social worker making a home visit discovered her caring for twins whom she claimed belonged to a neighbor. After repeated questioning, "Josephine" admitted they were hers; she said that a man who worked in the pool hall attached to the boardinghouse had raped her. The city stopped her pension because she did not report the rape and lied about the twins. Her five other children lost all support because she was too mortified to admit the sexual assault and subsequently became pregnant.[15]

The assumption that women who had children out of wedlock (for whatever reason) should not be publicly supported meant that at the start of the Depression, about 85 percent of the women receiving mothers' assistance were widows, a figure little changed from the previous decade. Most of the rest had incapacitated or incarcerated husbands. Although some state legislatures sanctioned pensions for never-married mothers, few such women ever obtained them. In 1934 only about 1 percent of mothers' aid in Michigan went to unmarried mothers, despite their legal eligibility.[16] Their children were just as impoverished as those of widows (and possibly more so in the case of women from ethnic or racial minorities), but states refused aid because of the social disapprobation of the mothers' behavior.

The Implementation of Mothers' Pensions in Massachusetts

As these examples attest, state and local jurisdictions differed with respect to their interpretations of mothers' assistance laws and their willingness to appropriate relief funds. Moreover, even states with relatively generous mothers' assistance programs implemented distinctions in aid levels. In 1913 Massachusetts became one of the first states to pass a mothers' aid bill. During its first year of operation, the new system provided pensions for 1,253 widows,

411 women listed as "not widows," and 4,998 children of both groups. The overseers of the poor had previously helped only two-fifths of those families now in the mothers' aid program, so mothers' pensions clearly provided for a real and previously unmet need. The new system was somewhat more generous than the old one, thus improving the standard of living in assisted families. Mothers' aid did not benefit all widows in Massachusetts, however: in about one-fifth of the cases investigated by the state mothers' aid visitors, the families had their financial assistance disallowed. Where this happened, the municipality's overseers of the poor offered assistance at the lower, poor-relief level.[17]

In 1924 the mothers' aid supervisor Elizabeth F. Moloney described pensions as "relief with a plan," a program modeled on what were then considered to be the best charitable practices. To ensure that no unworthy women obtained assistance, local overseers of the poor hired "trained women investigators" to visit families. The Massachusetts State Board of Charity concluded in 1915 that the overseers were "doing much better work under the mothers' aid law" than previously. They considered how each individual family's problems could best be managed by making "a suitable and comprehensive family plan." After a detailed investigation, the local relief visitor determined the amount each family needed in accordance with its "former standards of living, its racial food habits, and the ability of the mother to cook and sew for the children, to keep her house clean, and to manage her income wisely." This approach, elaborated in the 1924 report of the state board of charities, meant that stipends varied by race, ethnicity, and the visitor's evaluation of the mother's performance in discharging her maternal duties. Although subjective, the Massachusetts system aided slightly better-off lone mothers without pauperizing them first. It accorded well with the state's goal of furnishing sufficient aid to let mothers "bring up their children properly in their own homes." At the same time, it legitimized variations in standards based on social workers' perceptions of need.[18]

During the generally prosperous 1920s and parlous 1930s, the Bay State continued to assist widows, married women with incapacitated husbands, and a few divorced mothers of young children. Massachusetts allocated nearly $3,000,000 for relief in 1925. It thus compared favorably with Pennsylvania, which set aside about half that sum for a population twice as large. As a result, Massachusetts mothers did not endure the lengthy waits for assistance typical in Pennsylvania.[19] Several circumstances explain the Bay State's relative generosity. Based on a relief rather than an entitlement model, these payments accorded well with the state's longstanding commitment to supporting poor but worthy members of the community from public funds. Additionally, a shared funding base made widows' pensions more acceptable. The state contributed about 40 percent of the cost of pensions, which eased the burden on local taxpayers and facilitated their generosity.

Massachusetts taxpayers targeted their philanthropy at morally acceptable mothers who were long-time residents of their community. Fearing that former residents might return to the state to claim benefits or that nonresidents might be lured there in search of assistance, Massachusetts protected itself from "welfare tourism" by restricting the pensions to families that had lived in the state at least three years.[20] The local overseers of the poor granted temporary relief at a much lower level to recent migrants, sexual or social nonconformists, and women otherwise ineligible for the state supplement.[21]

Mothers' assistance workers in Massachusetts used the program as a means of Americanization. Like the Sheppard-Towner Act, widows' pensions served as vehicles for transmitting "American" values to immigrant mothers. Local mothers' assistance supervisors stressed that foreign-born, non-English-speaking mothers needed to realize the importance of learning the dominant language. They regarded Americanization as very important, because, they said, "anything that helps a mother to understand and discipline her children helps her to be a more valuable member of society and helps her children to become better American citizens." Some jurisdictions held regular Americanization classes or arranged for home-based English lessons for groups of mothers with young children. The state's board of charity praised the Lowell overseers for cooperating with the Americanization supervisor, furnishing her with a list of foreign-born mothers. By introducing each one to her, the overseers placed "the seal of their authority on her efforts." It is unclear whether these mothers received the impression that attending English classes was mandatory for obtaining mothers' aid, but local overseers certainly saw it as their duty to inform the mothers of the opportunities open to them.[22]

The composition of mothers' aid families in Massachusetts altered in the 1920s, indicating a degree of flexibility among state officials and a willingness to respond to new population trends. At the end of World War I, widows headed 84 percent of the families receiving assistance, and all pensioned families, whether headed by widows or by disabled or absent husbands, supported about the same number of children. Ten years later widows had slightly smaller families than did two-parent pension households, although there is nothing in the state board of charity records to indicate whether this reflected smaller family sizes per se or a greater willingness to assist mothers with only one child.[23] If the latter, this reversed the earlier belief that mothers could provide an adequate standard of living if they had just themselves and a single youngster to consider. The number of pensioned families declined in this decade, moving from 3,793 in 1919 to 2,603 in 1929, only to increase sharply once the Depression took hold and employment opportunities collapsed (see table 16).

Massachusetts represented one extreme of the pension continuum, for it granted a relatively large proportion of its pensions to households headed by separated or divorced women instead of limiting them to widows by statute or custom. Across the 1920s the number of women applying for assistance to bring up young children declined, although more sharply for widows than for nonwidows. Not surprisingly, by the Great Depression increasingly numerous and diverse families had come to depend on mothers' aid, with nonwidows experiencing the sharpest increase. As the economy weakened, the proportion of nonwidow-headed families among those on mothers' assistance rose from less than one-fifth to one-third. A shift in the (former) husband's status attended this rise, and the principal reasons for obtaining support among this group changed from total incapacity of the father or desertion to imprisonment or divorce (see table 17).[24] From the early years of the Depression, divorced women made up a growing share of mothers' aid recipients in Massachusetts, while deserted women's share shrank, indicating that couples formalized their separations and that authorities accepted divorcees' claims more readily.

In Massachusetts mothers' assistance resembled the poor relief it partially

Table 16. Family-Structure Statistics of Massachusetts Pension Families

Year	No. of widows	Children/ widow	No. of nonwidows	Children/ nonwidow	Percentage widow headed
1919	3,199	3.12	594	3.16	84%
1924	2,416	2.94	484	2.95	83
1929	2,085	2.76	518	3.00	80
1934	2,840	2.91	1,072	3.02	73
1937	3,474	2.73	1,608	2.86	68

Source: Data from Massachusetts State Board of Charity, *Annual Report,* for years 1913–37.

Table 17. Status of Husbands in Massachusetts Nonwidow Pension Families

Status	1919 ($n = 594$)	1924 ($n = 484$)	1929 ($n = 518$)	1934 ($n = 1,072$)	1936 ($n = 1,608$)
Ill	51.3%	54.8%	46.5%	45.4%	45.1%
Absented	40.1	38.0	38.2	32.3	27.8
Imprisoned	2.9	3.5	8.1	5.9	6.4
Divorced	5.7	3.7	7.1	16.4	20.8

Source: Data from Massachusetts State Board of Charity, *Annual Report,* for years 1913–36.

supplanted, with some of charity's stigma removed and some expansion in numbers and income across the state. The state board of charity stoutly maintained that mothers' aid was "not a pension." It was "*relief,* given out of the public treasury to a fit and needy mother of dependent children after the fact [had] been established that there [was] *need of aid* and that the mother [was] fit." Massachusetts continued to support the families of ill and insane men during the Depression and made greater provision for divorced women and the wives of prisoners during the economic crisis. It did so despite recognizing its system to be expensive, because the enabling legislation mandated that assistance levels "be sufficient to enable the mother to bring up her children properly in their own home."[25]

The Bay State thus accepted responsibility for providing an adequate standard of living for widows and other lone mothers. Like most other states, however, it restricted its beneficence in certain areas. The local and state charity authorities removed about one-fifth of their pensioners from the rolls during the 1920s, either because older children earned enough to support the family or because the youngest child had reached the age of fourteen (later sixteen).[26] If mothers remarried, the state assumed that the new partner would care for the offspring of the late husband. Local authorities transferred some mothers to other forms of relief because they had not lived in the state for three years prior to applying for their pension. (Widows who moved to another town or city within the state lost their pension, but the state usually paid the cost of reinstating it in the new locality.) Finally, local authorities removed women from the relief list if they concealed assets or kept male lodgers, which Massachusetts, like many states, prohibited. Then, too, some mothers removed themselves by placing their children in orphanages or with relatives so that they could work full time.[27]

The Bay State rejected children born out of wedlock altogether, since their illegitimacy meant that their mothers did not conform to public definitions of fit motherhood. In every report the supervisor of mothers' aid noted that a number of widows lost their assistance because they either had given birth to an illegitimate child or had been arrested for habitual immorality, intoxication, or the illegal sale of liquor. The practice of removing women from the mothers' aid rolls for "nonconformity with policies" or "unfitness of mother" continued through the Depression, despite the desperate poverty of such families and the professed aim of providing for the "citizens of tomorrow."[28] As in the case of fathers who deserted, public officials expressed their reluctance to support such families for fear of encouraging misbehavior among its citizens. The Massachusetts Department of Public Welfare regulations mandated that a year elapse between desertion and aid, arguing that an immediate transfer of the father's responsibility to the state "would be encouraging desertion on the part of certain irresponsible fathers."[29] In such instances, that state's ideological commitment to conventional gender roles merely punished the children of absconding fathers and sexually nonconformist mothers.[30]

Shifting part of the financial burden of supporting widows and orphans from local jurisdictions to state treasuries increased the number of widows aided, yet the continued emphasis on local management resulted in wide variations across the state. About half the communities in Massachusetts had established mothers' aid programs by 1915. All large cities and towns disbursed relief, although many smaller ones did not, with the cities differing significantly in the amount of mothers' aid they distributed. The more munificent jurisdictions, such as Boston, granted generous allowances to mothers' aid families. In fact, Boston and its near neighbors accounted for almost half the mothers' aid cases, indicating the pension system's big-city orientation even in such a highly urbanized state as Massachusetts. Fall River stood out as anomalous in aid provision under the new system. The fourth-largest city in the state in 1920, it ranked eighth in the total number of women assisted, placing approximately the same number of widows on mothers' aid as had been helped under the old relief system.[31]

Boston, Cambridge, and Lowell had the highest proportion of aid cases (about 10–15 per 10,000 residents throughout the 1920s), while Fall River and Springfield had the lowest (2–5 cases per 10,000). This standardized calculation of pension distribution does not take into account local variation in the number of needy widows. Using the 1920 census to determine the number of widows in each city shows that Boston, Cambridge, and Lowell assisted about 12 to 16 percent of widows aged fifteen to forty-four; New Bedford and Worcester helped 10 to 11 percent; but Springfield and Fall River aided only a parsimonious 4 to 7 percent (see table 18). Thus (using maternal age as a proxy for age of children), it appears that only a small minority of mothers with young children benefited from mothers' pensions even in this relatively generous state, and of course older widows received no assistance from these funds at all.[32]

Many factors accounted for these discrepancies in aid levels. Larger cities typically had more highly developed charitable systems than smaller ones did, even within the same state. Boston, at one extreme, had hundreds of charities, homes for the aged, widows' assistance societies, and orphanages. Possibly the charitable mindedness of its inhabitants led to generous pension provision. Yet size alone cannot account for altruism toward unfortunate widows and children, since some smaller cities distributed more pensions

Table 18. Massachusetts Widows Receiving Mothers' Assistance, 1920

City	Total no. of widows	Widows aged 15–44	No. of widows aided	Percentage of eligible widows aided
Boston	35,055	6,845	1,091	15.9%
Cambridge	5,308	974	121	12.4
Fall River	4,579	795	59	7.4
Lowell	4,779	880	123	14.1
New Bedford	4,903	1,032	109	10.6
Springfield	5,681	971	42	4.3
Worcester	6,761	1,146	111	9.7

Source: Data from Massachusetts Department of Public Welfare, *Annual Report, 1920* (Boston, 1921), 81; U.S. Bureau of the Census, *Fourteenth Census,* vol. 2 *Population 1920: General Report and Analytical Tables* (Washington, D.C.: GPO, 1922), 468, 471, 482, 493, 498, 527, 533.

per capita than larger ones did. No clear correlation between population size and pensions obtains except for the largest and smallest cities. Fall River gave about one-third to one-fourth as many pensions as Boston did, but a number of small cities and towns responded to widows' needs with Bostonian generosity rather than Fall River stinginess. Proximity to Boston had some influence on the availability of pensions, but the correlation is weak. Cambridge gave generously, but Newton and Somerville did not. Region within the state seems also to have made little difference to the proportion of pensions issued. Some cities and towns north of Boston, such as Lowell, granted pensions freely; others, such as Lynn, did not.[33]

Local values, industrial structure, racial and ethnic mix, and expectations regarding women's employment all played a part in determining the proportion of pensions granted. Three cities with approximately the same number of widows exhibited quite distinctive approaches to their support, with Lowell and New Bedford being far more generous than Fall River was. Lowell, with its more diversified economy, had a much lower employment rate for married women and a smaller proportion of foreign-born whites than did Fall River.[34] Fall River, a one-industry town with an economically and ethnically divided population, had a long history of poor municipal services and low taxes. In contrast, New Bedford's and Lowell's higher taxes financed more municipal services and widows' pensions. The differences among the three cities illustrate their distinctive interpretations of welfare policy, which were influenced not only by the usually dominant forces of economy, employment, race, ethnicity, and gender but also, apparently, by less tangible factors such as civic pride.[35]

Under the old poor laws Fall River had restricted relief to those who had no children to work in the mills or who were too weak or burdened to seek work there themselves. Extreme residential segregation by ethnicity and religion, the smallness of the middle class, and the prevalence of religious antagonisms and ethnic suspicions fostered an atmosphere of segregated aid and ethnocultural and familial self-help but little private or public charity. The control that Fall River's elite exercised over philanthropy combined with the city's ethnically and geographically fragmented working class to yield a hostility toward city aid that even subsidies from the state purse could not overcome. The constant pressure from the Fall River charitable establishment clearly helped to keep mothers' assistance rates low, as it had done with poor relief previously, and served as a brake on aid in bad times as well as good.[36] Further limits on relief emerged from the sentiment, common in the city, that women and children should work and from the law's parallel stipulation that mothers should continue employment even if alterations had to be made in the hours worked or in child-care arrangements. Indeed, the notion that children should work in the mills as soon as, or sometimes before, they were legally eligible for employment had widespread acceptance in Fall River.[37]

The relationship between employment and mothers' assistance was not straightforward, although state charitable authorities recognized that job scarcity for young people could destabilize widow-headed families. It became increasingly difficult for fourteen to sixteen year olds to find employment in the early 1920s, so more stayed in school. The Massachusetts Department of Public Welfare concluded that this was "a blessing in disguise to the children, who [were] thus given a chance to get more schooling than they would otherwise [have been] allowed." In 1925 Fall River's economy experienced a sharp downturn, with fewer than one-half its textile workers regularly employed at the beginning of the year. This meant that older children who contributed a significant proportion of their wages to support their mothers' aid families either worked half-time or were unemployed for months at a time. The state and local contribution to these families increased, but the number of families on mothers' aid remained static, indicative of the local overseers' reluctance to expand the roll, regardless of the state of the economy.[38]

As mothers' assistance unfolded in Massachusetts, Fall River became more parsimonious, while Lowell took the opposite tack. In 1915 Lowell granted 8.7 pensions per 10,000 residents; the figures for Fall River and Boston were 4.4. and 13.7, respectively. Although the number of pensions fluctuated in all cities, by 1929 Lowell was granting mothers' assistance to more households, as were 25 percent of Massachusetts towns and cities. Fall River, however, restricted access despite the distress caused by the closure of the textile mills. In 1929 it assisted only 3.3 families per 10,000 residents. Mothers in Massachusetts thus found pensions only a partial solution to the problems of bringing up children on their own. Nearly half those who left the welfare rolls became self-supporting through the earnings of children old enough to work, using the pensions as a stopgap until their children reached the legal age for employment.[39]

The Implementation of Widows' Pensions in Pennsylvania

Widows' pension practices in Pennsylvania differed in crucial aspects from those of mothers' assistance in Massachusetts. Employing an entitlement model in a state that had long abandoned outdoor relief, Pennsylvania helped widows but few other single mothers through most of the decade. It gave small grants and had long waiting lists. Like Massachusetts, the Keystone State adopted a residency requirement of three years (later shortened) to keep women from traveling there in search of benefits. An underlying assumption of both Massachusetts's and Pennsylvania's pension legislation was that mothers with only one child could support themselves. While one-child families were technically eligible for relief, the inadequacy of the appropriation meant they rarely received any support. Neither did property owners. Both states permitted a small amount of equity via home ownership but limited this to $1,500; further, they countenanced only limited savings—up to $400 in Pennsylvania and up to $200 in Massachusetts. As in Massachusetts, the state government paid for a significant proportion (50 percent) of the mothers' assistance costs in Pennsylvania.[40]

Unlike Massachusetts, however, Pennsylvania allocated money on a county-by-county basis. Whereas widows in rural counties with few applicants might get help quickly, those in large cities endured a long hiatus between applying and obtaining funds because demand was so great. Although the state doled out appropriations in proportion to county size, with big cities getting the lion's share, the sums were pitifully small, amounting to $35,100 each for Philadelphia and Allegheny counties in 1915–16. The next four largest counties, with populations ranging from 200,000 to 1,000,000, each received $8,775, while the ten smallest counties had $585 to distribute. Not surprisingly, the large cities found their grants insufficient. Pittsburgh received 1,843 applications in 1916, of which it investigated between 800 and 900, even though it could fund only 100.[41]

These funding limitations were tragic for applicants with meager resources, and more than three-fifths of those who applied had no savings, property, or insurance.[42] In addition, inadequate information about the new system caused some of the delay between widowhood and application for aid. In the first few years of the Mothers' Assistance Fund, only 30 percent applied for a pension during the first year of widowhood. By 1920 better information about the existence of pensions had increased the proportion to over 50 percent. In fact, Philadelphia welfare officials administered the fund in a small upstairs room, choosing a somewhat out-of-the-way location because they worried they would be overrun with requests. Once they stenciled "Mothers' Assistance Fund" on the windows, applications poured in, although it took some families two years to secure assistance. Waiting lists skyrocketed during the influenza epidemic of 1919, and funding delays continued to be a problem until the New Deal. In her 1924 annual report, the state supervisor of the Mothers' Assistance Fund charged that the length of the waiting lists was "a perpetual reproach to the State and travesty of the purpose of the Law."[43]

Despite its lengthy waiting lists, Pennsylvania was one of the very few states to distribute pensions without apparent racial prejudice. The trustees of the Mothers' Pension League of Allegheny County proudly proclaimed, "Absolute fairness has been the rule; no amount of pressure or influence has ever made us deviate from that rule. The first and last mothers recommended were colored women."[44] Pennsylvania's even-handed policy ensured that African American women had access to pensions while other states denied them. In 1920, 1 percent of widows' benefits in the state went to black families; a decade later African American widows secured 8 percent of Pittsburgh's pensions and 16 percent of Philadelphia's, somewhat exceeding their share of the population (6 and 11 percent, respectively).[45]

Again, the value of pensions granted varied from city to city and between urban and rural areas, although it did not correlate directly with city size or cost of living. In 1925 Pennsylvania issued an average $11.53 monthly payment to each child covered; the specific amount ranged from $15.65 in tiny Union County, where eight widow-headed households enjoyed support, to a paltry $8.23 per month in Crawford County. Philadelphia and Pittsburgh, with 3,400 and 2,084 children on the pension roles, respectively, approximated the statewide funding average. Grants fluctuated from year to year according to state appropriations, so that in 1926 the per capita monthly sums shrank by $1 to $6 per child, with the smallest counties exhibiting the greatest funding volatility.[46]

Such small grants did not permit widows to leave the labor force. Moreover, the low wages paid to women meant that even employed widows found it difficult to support their families. Although mothers had jobs in over one-third of all pension families, their earnings were too low to maintain the household because they could find only "unskilled, poorly paid, and very laborious" occupations. With the employment levels of widows rising across the decade, social service personnel described their "double efforts to be mother and father, caretaker and wage earner," as "nothing short of heroic." Widowed mothers throughout the state contributed about one-fifth of the total family income in pension households, while the grant from the state accounted for about two-fifths. Mothers' pension administrators believed the state grant too small to maintain even a bare subsistence standard of living.[47]

This inadequate provision propelled many widows' children into premature employment, negating the original purpose of pensions as a child-conservation measure. While the mothers' assistance administrator concluded that such young children made relatively insignificant contributions to family budgets, even small sums made a big difference to poor widows (see table 19). A 1925 study conducted in Philadelphia discovered that one-third of the fourteen- to sixteen-year-old children in mothers' assistance families had jobs, three times more than the figure for all the city's children in this age range. Virtually all the working children of widows left school early because their families desperately needed the extra income. Over half these families already received the maximum grant available, but a number endured cuts in their grants due to inadequate appropriations. These young children earned modest amounts (no more than six to eight dollars per week), but their families' poverty made even small contributions to the family coffers very welcome.[48]

Mothers and young adults coresiding with the family each contributed about one-fifth of widows' aid families' income in Pennsylvania, while children aged fourteen to sixteen supplied 4 percent. Older children in Pittsburgh accounted for nearly one-quarter of the family income, while children

Table 19. Income from Specified Sources in Widows' Aid Families, Pennsylvania, 1926

Income source	Allegheny[a] (n = 501)	Philadelphia (n = 738)	State average (n = 2,404)
Mothers	24.2%	20.4%	20.8%
Older children (>16)	24.7	22.0	23.4
Children (14–16)	2.4	4.8	3.9
Relatives	2.3	1.9	1.8
Boarders	5.8	8.3	6.6
Mothers' Assistance			
Grants	38.8	37.4	39.4
Charity	0.9	4.6	3.2
Unions, lodges	0.9	0.6	0.9

Source: Pennsylvania Department of Public Welfare, *Report of the Mothers' Assistance Fund, 1926* (Harrisburg, 1926), 36.
[a]Pittsburgh comprised the vast majority of the population of Allegheny County.

under the age of sixteen contributed about 2 percent. Fewer young children worked in Pittsburgh than did in Philadelphia (5 percent), largely because of the dominant industries in these cities. Other relatives donated modest sums to pension families, but they also aided widows through baby sitting and other in-kind contributions. A 1926 Mother's Assistance Fund report stated that relatives were "the most natural source of aid," but it warned of their shortcomings: "They usually come from the same economic group, and by the time the family can be accepted for assistance their help may be either exhausted or withdrawn." Charities at the eastern end of the state assisted more widows' families than did those in Pittsburgh. Unions and fraternal organizations gave little sustained cash assistance to widow-headed households in either city during the 1920s. Fraternal organizations did aid distressed members through illness and burial benefits, and a number maintained orphanages or old-age homes.[49]

Notwithstanding Pittsburgh's relatively low incidence of female employment, widows in the Steel City contributed slightly more of the family budget than did their sisters in the City of Brotherly Love. Philadelphia widows had lower levels of employment outside the home but were somewhat more likely to take in boarders. Although it may at first seem surprising that a smaller proportion of Pittsburgh widows monetized their domestic labors, the reason lies in the nature of the city and rules governing pension entitlements. Pennsylvania allowed female lodgers but limited male residents in pension households to fathers, brothers, or other male relatives. This prevented Pittsburgh widows from the time-honored practice of using home and domestic skills to supplement their income, for most of those seeking room and board in Pittsburgh would have been men separated from their families. Philadelphia, with its larger female employment base, would have had more women searching for the board and lodging widows provided.[50]

The administrators of pensions claimed, "The proper care of children does not leave the average mother much time to do the extra work necessary for boarders or lodgers. Besides, unless home conditions are carefully watched[,] the presence of strangers in the home is as a rule not desirable."[51] Two distinct models of motherhood and the home operated here. Early twentieth-century maternalist reformers believed the home to be a sacred place, solely dedicated to raising the family. As a result, the proportion of boarders in white middle-class households dropped away to almost nothing by 1920.[52] Working-class women, however, still used their homes to produce an income through industrial homework and taking in boarders. This enabled them to fulfill their vision of good motherhood, but it conflicted powerfully with middle-class assumptions about the ideal home and family life.[53]

Male lodgers necessarily competed with home and family for the widow's attention; beyond that, they might jeopardize her moral standing. The handbook of the Pennsylvania Mothers' Assistance Fund claimed that men with money to spend might lure widows into improper behavior. To protect pension families from temptation, these jurisdictions forbade widowed mothers from undertaking the one money-making activity they could have combined with child care and household management. Widows who persisted in suspect behavior suffered the consequences. After close investigation, Pennsylvania disqualified one-sixth of the families on its pension rolls, mostly for immorality, taking in unrelated boarders, or concealing assets.[54]

Although the state used an entitlement rather than a relief model, Pennsylvania mothers' assistance authorities were anxious to demonstrate that the pensions supplemented but did not replace widows' and children's efforts to be self-sustaining. After taking pension funds into account, slightly over half the covered families (54 percent) had incomes equal to those earned by the widows' late husbands, but the rest had considerably less. Pension administrators acknowledged the deficit: "Assisted families are not raised by the grant above the economic group in which they have always lived."[55] One-third of the Pennsylvania pension families managed to keep themselves out of debt without resorting to "undesirable" sources of income, such as premature child labor, maternal employment without adequate supervision for the children, industrial homework, or night work. The other two-thirds faced one or more of three circumstances: debt, young people who worked full time, or inappropriately employed mothers. Pensions thus had a modest impact on child labor in the Keystone State, although their origins reflected sentiments about childhood similar to those manifested in the campaigns against child labor and in favor of compulsory education elsewhere.[56] Widows with pensions were clearly better off than those who were unable to obtain them, but they were not "gilt-edged widows," as some claimed.[57] Instead, most widows and other mothers bringing up children on their own scraped by through dint of hard labor and help from their children and their families, with some subsidy from the state. Even that subvention came at a price—the systematic supervision of and intervention into working-class family life, a process that pensions in Baltimore made explicit.

The Implementation of Widows' Pensions in Maryland

Characteristic of southern and border states, which were unenthusiastic providers of widows' pensions, Maryland passed effective enabling legislation only on the eve of the Great Depression, and even then it allowed local authorities to decide whether to implement the law's provisions. As with the previous campaign to assist widows, in 1916, Baltimore responded reluctantly following a concerted effort on the part of local women's organizations. The battle for widows' pensions fought in Baltimore between 1929 and 1933 refutes the idea that women lost interest in these matters after they got the vote. At the grass roots they certainly did not, even if at the national level passage of maternal and child health-care legislation absorbed their attention.[58]

The list of Baltimore and Maryland organizations that lobbied for mothers' pensions closely resembled that of the Coalition of 100 a decade earlier, ranging across classes, religions, and fraternal and civic groups in its efforts to ensure pensions in 1916. The women's auxiliaries of the machinists' union, the Baltimore and Ohio Railroad, the Veterans of Foreign Wars, and the American Federation of Labor joined the Council of Jewish Women, the Woman's City Club, the Women's Club of affluent Roland Park, the United Jewish Charities, Maryland Children's Aid Society, the Parent-Teachers' Association, and the Women's Auxiliary for Mothers' Relief (WARM) in lobbying the state and city for the passage of an enforceable act to aid widows and the families of permanently disabled men. The city's big organized charities stood aloof from the campaign, however, and social workers opposed it altogether. Contemporary welfare analysts credited WARM with responsibility for the new pension law's passage. This organization consisted of "worthwhile women who through a fine sense of public spirited citizenship ... rendered noble service to the Department [of Public Charities] and the city at large."[59]

Despite their efforts, it took several years before Baltimore distributed more than a pittance to widowed mothers. WARM and the Women's Progressive League lobbied the mayor to appropriate more funds for urgent cases as the Depression worsened. They launched newspaper and radio campaigns to bring the issue to public attention and put pressure on the city. The Women's Progressive League sponsored fund-raisers for needy families, while WARM adopted a two-pronged approach redolent of traditional charity organizations. Members visited needy mothers and children and gave them little gifts. At Christmas WARM and other organizations provided treats specifically chosen for poor children of different ethnic and racial groups. Other groups, too, stepped up at Christmastime. The "Colored Division" of the Athletic League entertained seventy-nine African American children from the pension rolls, and Catholic charities looked after the Catholic children. The Empty Stocking Club (a charity dedicated to making Christmas a real holiday for poor children) held a party, and the Advertising Club gave shoes and stockings to the needy. The Women's Progressive League, the Housewives' Alliance, the Federation of Republican Women, the Twentieth Century Club, and individual kind souls gave food baskets. Local chapters of the Catholic Daughters of America, the Moose, the Elks, and the Masons also contributed Christmas treats for pension families.[60]

The Women's Auxiliary for Mothers' Relief also used its political connections to lobby the city and state for improved levels of assistance. Once the state made mothers' relief mandatory in 1933, WARM led a successful suit against Baltimore's intransigent mayor, forcing him to use the full amount appropriated for mothers' pensions. Baltimore officials had contended that the state requirement for mothers' relief violated home rule. Although the courts rejected this interpretation, the city kept some applications pending for four years. Through the mid-1930s the city still institutionalized and fostered many children from very poor families rather than pay to keep them at home. Members of the Women's Progressive League and WARM coalition hoped that adequate relief would finally end the removal of children from their mothers' homes because of poverty, but that did not happen during the Great Depression. And here as elsewhere, race played a role. Public authorities placed a disproportionate number of African American children in foster homes, where their host families principally sought their labor, not their welfare.[61]

Both the city's large charity establishment and its child-care institutions had vested interests in retaining the status quo. The city had contracts with various local institutions to accommodate ostensibly neglected children, but it also lodged destitute children in orphanages and children's homes. Baltimore gave various agencies grants to house children such as those of the late William Isaac Jones. Mr. Jones, described as a man of little education, worked as a laborer until his death from heart disease in 1922. His widow was unable to care for their five children, so the city placed the three youngest in private institutions; the older two looked after themselves the best they could while she worked as a servant.[62] Another woman, a mother of six widowed for five years, tried hard to keep her family together but failed. Having exhausted her small savings and insurance policy, she placed three of her four minor children in different homes while keeping the youngest with her. The casework records describe her two married children as "young and with income only sufficient for their own families."[63]

Thus, although Baltimore accepted responsibility for pension assistance to widows, it did so reluctantly and kept the program at a low level. In the first full year of operation, the city dropped fourteen women with large families from the fifty-two on the pension rolls because it lacked funds.[64] In a maneuver that presaged the approach taken by the Aid to Dependent Children program, the city allocated funds only for the maintenance of the children;

the mother had to "forage for herself." Relief workers in Baltimore believed that "every woman knows that she can work some time," so even mothers described as "incapacitated" obtained no appropriation under this program. Despite pressure from the organized women of the city, at the depths of the Depression Baltimore lagged behind all other major U.S. urban areas when it came to the number of distressed families to which it gave mothers' aid. In 1933 it funded sixty-five cases of mothers' aid, far fewer than the 143 old-age pensions it granted.[65]

In 1933 Maryland made 235 mothers' aid grants statewide. The fiscally conservative state assisted only one family per 10,000 people that year, a rate exceeded by other southern states with mothers' aid programs (averaging 2–5 families per 10,000 people), Massachusetts and Pennsylvania (6–7 per 10,000), and New York and Wisconsin (the most generous at 16 and 24 families per 10,000, respectively). Those lucky enough to obtain benefits did receive reasonably high monthly grants, with the exact amount left to the discretion of the granting agency rather than specified by law. Like those in other states, Maryland's legislators ensured that only those widows with a long-term association with the state could obtain help; they, too, limited aid to citizens resident in the jurisdiction for at least three years.[66]

A combination of population volatility and overt racial discrimination meant that African American families had less chance of receiving mothers' assistance than did other Baltimoreans, despite their need. As was true in other cities, the black female population in Baltimore was concentrated at the lower end of the economic spectrum: 87 percent were domestic service workers or laborers, and another 10 percent were semiskilled and skilled workers (primarily dressmakers or food-processing workers), so they were unlikely to have had savings to sustain them in widowhood.[67] Poverty notwithstanding, residency requirements disqualified some of the African American widows who joined the expansion of the city's black population in the interwar years.[68] In 1930 African American widows received only 9 percent of the pensions, although 18 percent of all Baltimoreans were black. They contributed 22 percent of the names on the waiting list and made up 40 percent of Family Welfare Association cases. That they obtained any aid at all reflects the African American community's comparative political strength in Baltimore.[69] Nevertheless, racial prejudice, inadequate funding, and the economic collapse that disproportionately affected Baltimore's black population collectively militated against adequate support for African American widows. As a result, the story of Mrs. Dora Datcher was all too typical. Mrs. Datcher waited for two years before getting a widow's pension, and even then she had to continue working to supplement the $11.77-a-week stipend.[70]

Mothers' assistance recipients, regardless of color and ethnicity, endured scrutiny of their behavior. In keeping with the tenets of scientific philanthropy, the professionalization of social work, and the maternalist ethos behind mothers' assistance legislation, casework and counseling became essential parts of the pension process. Unlike recipients of soldiers' or retirement pensions, women receiving mothers' pensions had to exhibit a demeanor acceptable to those giving the money. The widow needed to be a "fit person, morally and physically, to bring up her children."[71] Casework notes frequently described maternal conduct in language similar to that of charity visitors: on the one side were descriptions such as "very superior type," "one of our highest type women," "splendid spirit," or "most cooperative"; on the other were those such as "has not cooperated to the fullest extent," "very antagonistic," or "very nervous and easily discouraged."[72] Caseworkers' assessments could result in the revocation of the pension, which suggests that these programs had more in common with private largesse than with public entitlement.

Social workers monitored Baltimore widows' maternal behavior to ensure their children learned "lessons of thrift and industry, the principles of good citizenship and a spirit of loyalty" to city, state, and country. The city sent a letter with a stern warning to all widows: "The moral tone of your home must be at all times such as will make for the development of good character in your children and . . . you shall require of them proper regard of . . . [relevant] religious observances." The supervisors of city charities expected widows to conform to traditional notions of motherhood and domesticity: "Rightness of character is most likely to be found in homes where the mother spends much of her time with her children, rather than leaving them to the indifferent care of the neighbors or to the perils of the street." They added, "Spend as much of your time in your home and with your children as may be practicable." In return for granting the widow a pension, Baltimore required that the home be kept clean and orderly at all times and that the children be properly clothed and "in a neat condition." In addition, they were to receive regular and sufficient nourishing food "properly prepared" and be constant in their attendance at school. Such expectations were seemingly straightforward and no more than most mothers, given sufficient income, would provide for their children.[73] Yet the city assumed that poor mothers needed supervision and instruction to fulfill their maternal functions, while the elderly persons to whom it granted old-age pensions at this time did not endure equivalent supervision or scrutiny of their morals.

Baltimore gave its widows no opportunity to forget these injunctions on their behavior. It directed widows not to "mislay, mutilate, or destroy" the letter of instruction that accompanied notification of the pension. It further announced that a visitor from the supervisor of city charities would periodically read over the instructions with each recipient to ensure "the maintenance of the best family life."[74] Baltimore mandated bimonthly inspections of pensioned families to ensure that beneficiaries conformed to its requirements. As in most pension schemes, the city threatened to withdraw assistance if the caseworker believed that the widow behaved inappropriately. The penalties for noncooperation were dire: a widow with six minor children had her pension "withdrawn for lack of cooperation," as did a mother of seven. Another with five children lost her pension because there was "a man involved." Deviant conversation from a "non-cooperative and unworthy" widow cost her city support, too.[75]

Thus, pensions in the three cities and states had some similarities but also important differences. All welfare authorities wished to limit pensions to worthy mothers and required long-term residence in the relevant locale. Massachusetts had an explicit public-relief model built on its history of small sums given to paupers in their own homes, with the ironic consequence that there was a much shorter wait for aid there than in the other states. Pennsylvania considered its mothers to be worthy pensioners but made such paltry appropriations that many widows never obtained help. Maryland, the last to institute pensions, used a relief model, had a blend of public and private assistance, and—unusual for a southern or border state—provided aid to blacks as well as whites, albeit on a lesser basis. Custom and usage in the three cities meant that Fall River provided less adequately for its widows and orphans than did other cities in Massachusetts, seemingly with little local opposition. Strong women's groups in Pittsburgh and Baltimore urged local authorities to be generous in their funding but lacked the political influence to win sufficient appropriations. Baltimore's tradition of charitable noblesse oblige gave rise to a voluntary organization dedicated to augmenting mothers' assistance grants with treats, trips to the country, and baskets of food and clothing. Yet even these well-intentioned women could not compensate for the inadequate aid granted by the parsimonious local government.

The Impact of Widows' Pensions

Although they helped individual families, pensions failed to produce as great an impact on children's and widows' welfare as reformers had intended. Again, funding levels remained low, and they varied from city to city and state to state, with many jurisdictions never distributing any pensions at all. Both local and national data pointed to the desperate financial difficulties encountered by many families, even those on the mothers' assistance rolls. A

1923–24 Children's Bureau study found that the amount of the grants given out (rather than the maxima specified in legislation) varied from twenty to fifty-two dollars per month in northern and western jurisdictions. Southern states provided even smaller sums. The ten states with the highest per capita expenditure on widows' pensions all sat north of the Mason-Dixon line, while seven of the ten with the lowest expenditure were below it. The South accounted for ten of the fourteen states assisting fewer than six families per 10,000 inhabitants. Only two of the fourteen states pensioning thirteen or more families per 10,000 were in that region.[76]

At the start of the Great Depression, state widows' or mothers' pensions helped some 220,000 children across the nation to reside in their own homes. Nonetheless, the putative desire to substitute home care for institutional provision notwithstanding, widows' children continued to be overrepresented in public facilities. Indeed, the number of children in orphanages and foster homes rose in the 1920s and 1930s, so that by 1933 there were approximately 102,000 children in foster homes and 140,000 in orphanages. In other words, dependent children in institutions and foster homes outnumbered those who were sustained in their own homes by pensions. The number of children in orphanages fell only after the New Deal and the enactment of the Aid to Dependent Children program.[77]

Given the rhetoric of the movement, another indicator of pension success would have been a decline in the proportion of employed widowed mothers, since keeping mothers at home was widely reckoned to be the best way to bring up children safely and soundly.[78] Yet economic activity among widows rose throughout the pension era as part of the general response to consumerist pressures, the curtailment of child labor, and the expansion of women's employment opportunities. Over half the pension recipients worked in order to make ends meet. As a result, according to an investigator into pensions in Pennsylvania in 1928, mothers spent "too much of their time and strength" working, "sometimes to the hurt of the children," and in many cases the families fell below the minimum standard of living "necessary for health and efficiency."[79] Widows' participation in the labor force receded only between 1930 and 1940, supporting the hypothesis that the Social Security Act's Aid to Dependent Children program, whose funds were more liberally available than were state- and locally funded widows' pensions, led some widows (as well as divorced, deserted, or never-married mothers) to leave the labor force. Pensions might have improved individual family financial situations but had little overall impact on widows' employment rates. Despite maternalist rhetoric, pensions were inadequately funded and typically made no provision for mothers to stay at home. Age-specific employment rates for widows demonstrated the extent to which widows' economic activity increasingly substituted for child workers in this era. In 1890 about half the widows under the age of forty-five were in the labor force. By 1930 over two-thirds of all widows in this age bracket worked for wages.[80]

Employment rates for African American widows were even higher. More than four-fifths of African American widows in this age group had jobs. Such high rates of economic activity testify to pensions' near irrelevance to the well-being of most African American widows, unmarried mothers, and their children. The racial biases incorporated into the administration of mothers' aid, the limited distribution of pensions in the South, and the concentration of African American women in that region all help to explain why African American widows' employment continued unabated in this era. African American widows and never-married mothers scrubbed floors, picked cotton, and washed clothes at a time when some white widows received state aid or, in the case of older widows, relied on their children for support.[81]

Pensions did have some success keeping ten to fifteen year olds out of the labor force. Yet it would be an oversimplification to say that the decline was due entirely to mothers' pensions, as the decrease in economic activity by young African Americans indicates. In 1910 nearly half of all African American youths worked (mostly as agricultural laborers and servants). By 1920, 22 percent did so, and by 1930, 16 percent of all ten- to fifteen-year-old African Americans were economically active. The decrease cannot be related to widows' pensions, since these children's mothers were the least likely to obtain pensions, or to labor laws, since few states banned children from farm or service jobs. Instead, mandatory education requirements, the growing use of agricultural machinery, urbanization, and the substitution of maternal for child labor all contributed to this transition.[82]

Through the 1920s mothers' assistance administrators interpreted state enabling legislation in widely divergent fashions. Local customs and wage-earning opportunities influenced the extent to which pensions curtailed the employment of young children. As (northern) state labor laws increasingly restricted legitimate employment opportunities, the number of working fourteen and fifteen year olds decreased, although some parents lied to census takers and other officials about their children's ages or economic activities. There were great variations in school attendance and employment across different localities, even within a state. Some jurisdictions interpreted the law to mean that mothers' aid children should go to work as soon as they could get employment certificates, while others kept them out of the labor force, even past the minimum age for leaving school. Thus, in Fall River's neighbor, New Bedford, Massachusetts, 54 percent of the fourteen- and fifteen-year-old children of mothers' aid families attended school, and the rest worked in the local factories. In Berks County, Pennsylvania, only 29 percent of mothers' aid children went to school at fourteen or fifteen (the rest were in the textile mills), but in Pittsburgh this figure reached 81 percent. Demand as well as supply factors limited the number of young workers: employers increasingly preferred adult workers and grew less resistant to the regulation of child labor.[83]

Mothers' assistance came into existence for philosophical, compassionate, and economic reasons: there was widespread sentiment that mothers were the best people to look after their children at home. It was both more humane and cheaper to have them do so. Inadequate funding levels and conflicting intentions meant that pensions did not succeed entirely in removing widows and children from the labor force. Even in Massachusetts, where a relief model prevailed and funding came closest to being adequate, there was never enough money for women to stay at home. Neither, in jurisdictions such as Fall River, was there agreement that mothers should withdraw from the labor force. In Pittsburgh, where such beliefs were more strongly held, inadequate provision made this an impossibility, as it did in Baltimore, where belated funding limited mothers' assistance to a small number of widow-headed families.

Old-Age Assistance at the State and Local Levels

Irrespective of their uneven distribution, widows' pensions made an important social and political statement about the appropriate use of mothers' and children's time. They had little relevance, however, to the vast majority of widows who dropped off the social-policy radar once they were no longer young mothers raising children on their own. The proportion of widows over the age of sixty-five grew during the Progressive Era, from 32 percent in 1890 to 40 percent in 1930. By comparison, 24 percent were under the age of forty-five in 1890, declining to 18 percent at the start of the Depression. While a growing fraction of younger widows entered the labor force, older widows encountered great difficulty in finding work, even if they were physically capable of doing the sort of domestic service or factory work they had done before marriage. A study of older workers in Maryland between 1920 and 1930 indicates that only 2 percent of Baltimore's female workers were sixty-five or older, although 7 percent of white women and 2.3 percent of African Americans were in that age group.[84]

Older widows managed through a combination of savings, employment, assistance from their children, and charity. Childless widows found it especially difficult to survive and constituted a significant proportion of the institutional population. A number of homes, including the Baltimore Humane and Impartial Society and Aged Woman's Home, refused admission to those who had living children in the belief that they should care for their elderly parents. Those without children lived in dread of ending their days in the poorhouse. Mrs. Lizzie Chris, seventy-one, who had no surviving children, wrote to the director of Pittsburgh's Department of Charities to explain that she needed help making ends meet. She lived in one room on the South Side and did plain sewing when she could get it. She wished to avoid joining her sister at Mayview (the city home) and hoped the city would assist her through a small cash stipend.[85]

As the economy deteriorated, Mrs. Chris's strategy of self-support combined with aid from the city or private charity became more difficult. Fewer households hired independent seamstresses or domestics, and there were almost no other places for them in the economy. While a few had recourse to private or employer pensions, veterans' benefits, savings, or their families as a means of sustaining themselves in later life, many others turned to local charities or ended their days in the almshouse. A number moved in with their children or more distant kin and "contributed generously to the support of the family until the depression deprived them of their livelihood," according to the Massachusetts supervisor of mothers' aid in 1934. Coresidence was not a panacea, however, because the Depression stretched children's resources, and many had no room to house elderly relatives.[86]

Widows composed a significant portion of the aged poor, although older men dominated the poorhouse population. Policy makers believed that families were more likely to help an aged mother than to aid her male counterpart.[87] Some men benefited from occupational pensions in the early twentieth century, while city and state old-age pensions went to the indigent poor of both sexes. The United States, according to some commentators, lagged behind other industrial nations in its general old-age provision, although certain constituencies benefited. Veterans' pensions after the Civil War provided for many elderly native-born white men in the North, some foreign-born men, and a few African Americans and their widows. By 1894 these pensions took up nearly two-fifths of the national budget.[88] As Theda Skocpol's research has indicated, however, antipathy to party politics and potential corruption curtailed the spread of such noncontributory pension systems. At the same time, the number of private employer plans increased in the 1910s and 1920s, but these provided for very few women. Locally based systems grew slowly because of fears that they would reduce a state's competitive advantage, especially as industries began to move to low-labor-cost, low-tax states in the early twentieth century.[89]

While younger widows attracted attention as the mothers of young children, social-policy developments for older widows arose from a general concern for the elderly. Efforts to provide specific assistance to older people accelerated during the 1920s and 1930s, motivated by a perception that they had fared badly during the industrial era. Old-age unemployment rose in the early twentieth century, especially during the 1930s, when employers let go older managers as well as production-line workers.[90] Vigorous campaigns by organizations such as the American Association for Labor Legislation and the American Association for Social Security led to old-age assistance plans in a number of states in the 1920s. Such programs attempted to avoid the stigma of poor relief by providing poor older citizens with an income that would not be seen as charity. Pensions, one advocate concluded, constitute "rewards for a long life of faithful and honorable service to society" and should carry no social stigma.[91] Not all sectors of society agreed. While accepting public provision of institutional relief, the courts could be unsympathetic to government efforts to provide systematic assistance to the elderly in their own homes. Fraternal organizations and industrial unions in Pennsylvania lobbied hard for state old-age pensions in the 1920s, yet the state's Supreme Court declared the Old Age Assistance Act unconstitutional because it provided for the elderly in general rather than just the poor.[92]

The small number of employment-based programs in this era favored male industrial workers; almost all were in heavy industry. The few in banking and the insurance industry required long service for the same employer, hence few women qualified. In addition, some municipal and state employees, including teachers, received occupational pensions in the early twentieth century. States that did manage to pass old-age pension acts usually did so on a county-option basis, enabling communities to grant them if they so wished, but few did. A number of cities, including Baltimore, furnished retirement pensions to specific groups of municipal workers, typically police and firemen who either had been injured in the course of duty or had completed long periods of service. In 1916 Baltimore established pensions for city employees earning less than $1,000 per year, and in 1922 it permitted firemen to retire on half-pay once they completed twenty consecutive years of service. This act also provided relief to widows and children of firemen killed on duty. Several years later Baltimore extended its retirement system to include teachers once they reached the age of seventy.[93]

Elderly women of modest means, women who had not been in the labor force during their married lives, service workers, and African Americans of both sexes had little access to private or employer-based retirement plans. State-supported old-age pensions offered them help. Public noncontributory old-age assistance programs expanded on existing charitable and relief provisions, broadened their coverage, and served as outdoor relief without the stigma of charity. They circumvented the constraints of employment-based programs for older widows who had not worked for wages for many years and did not have "jobs" from which to retire. Potentially, they expanded access to include domestic workers and racial minorities of both sexes, who rarely came under the scope of employment-based programs.[94]

For groups outside the private and employer pension systems, particularly the infirm, widows, and the former working poor, city and state old-age assistance programs meant the difference between relative autonomy and the poorhouse, dependence on children, and destitution. Noncontributory old-age assistance plans relieved families from the responsibility of caring for their elders. This accorded with the contemporary belief that poor families would disintegrate if they had to care for younger and older generations simultaneously. These pensions also reflected the growing revulsion against institutionalizing the elderly in almshouses. Although the proportion of elderly (over sixty-five) in almshouses had not increased in the early twentieth century, that of the over fifties did, so that by 1923 they made up four-fifths of the total poorhouse population. Designed as outdoor relief, pensions provided a cost-effective and humane means of caring for those who did not need specialized facilities but who could no longer compete in the labor market. Enabling legislation typically forbade granting pensions to the residents of homes for the elderly, whether maintained by city, state, or private organizations.[95]

Such facilities housed a small proportion of the aged. Allegheny County had about a dozen residential facilities catering for the elderly, including the (Negro) Aged Ministers and Laymen's Home, the Allegheny Widows' Home, and sectarian institutions run by the Jewish, Catholic, Baptist, and evangelical communities of the Pittsburgh area. These had a capacity approaching 1,000 residents, while the Mayview city home housed about 500 older residents. Baltimore institutions represented a similar range of racial and religious organizations and contained approximately 1,500 residents in 1930, of which 16 percent were African American and the rest were white. Fall River's Catholic charities provided aid to their coreligionists, but the city had only one general old-age home in addition to the city poor farm. As the Depression deepened, such institutions could not meet the demand for aid, increasing the pressure for outdoor relief or pensions for the elderly.[96]

Government and charities responded to the Depression by vastly increasing the amount of money spent on sustaining the unemployed. In 1929 over two-fifths of all urban relief funds were spent on special entitlement programs, but as unemployment rose, so did direct-aid and work-relief expenditures. By 1931 the proportion of relief funds devoted to entitlement programs shrank to 20 percent, falling to a mere 9 percent by 1933, although the amount more than trebled. In 1929 mothers' assistance programs received the lion's share of these funds (92 percent). A small amount went to blind people (nearly 8 percent), and less than 0.5 percent went to the elderly. In 1929 only a few, scattered cities granted old-age pensions; by 1935 three-fifths did so. As with mothers' pensions, pronounced regional biases existed: few cities in the south Atlantic and south-central sections of the United States spent any money on old-age assistance through 1935. Nevertheless, in that year the elderly accounted for 52 percent of special entitlement spending; mothers' pensions took up only 41 percent, and the blind received 7 percent.[97]

In the early 1930s most jurisdictions granting aid to widows and the elderly gave preference to the latter in both number and amount of pensions given. In 1931, when state and municipal funding for these constituencies peaked, widows and their dependent children in eighty-five urban areas received nearly $46 per month for an average family of four (about $11.50 per person). Old-age pensioners typically received $30 per person per month. By 1935 payments to both groups had declined: the average monthly allowance for widows' families had dropped to $40 ($10 per person), while that of the elderly was $21 per person.[98]

Baltimore trailed behind other states and cities in provision of old-age assistance. In 1933 the nation's most generous jurisdiction, New York City, had 8.64 pensioners per 100 people over the age of sixty-five. Massachusetts had 3.64; California, 2.66; and Montana, 5.65, with the average pension-granting state assisting about 5 percent of the elderly. Massachusetts limited such pensions to people over seventy, yet by 1936 it had 28,300 persons on its old-age assistance rolls, receiving an average of $23.59 per month. The state paid one-third of the benefit, which went only to citizens who had been resident for at least five of the preceding nine years. Baltimore had 143 pensioners, although it received 1,318 applications and had many senior residents. Social investigators reckoned that if the city matched the nationwide average, there should have been about 2,000 pensioners in it.[99]

Maryland's old-age pension provided for assistance at the discretion of the county, with no state subsidy. This thrust the burden for supporting the impoverished elderly directly on cash-strapped cities. Each recipient in Baltimore got a maximum of $30 per month, but there could be only one pension per family, so a married couple received no more than a single person's entitlement. The average pension was about $21, with a range from $7.50 to $30. The vast majority of pensioners were native-born whites, despite

Baltimore's ethnically diverse population. African Americans constituted about 10 percent of the old-age pensioners, which seemed fair to the city's Family Welfare Association. In fact, blacks constituted a larger proportion of the aged poor, since the laboring and domestic-service jobs they had typically held left many unable to save for their old age.[100]

The distribution of old-age pensions in Baltimore during the early 1930s demonstrates their significance for elderly widows, who made up the largest category of recipients: 39 percent were widows, 14 percent were widowers, 22 percent each were married or single, and 3 percent were described as "remarried." The majority apparently had no living children and so faced old age on their own, while the rest seem to have had children who were unwilling or unable to support their parents. Maryland's old-age pension act prohibited aiding elderly persons who had a "child or other person responsible under the law of Maryland for his/her support and able to support him/her." Those with children may have obtained aid from them in the past, but unemployment meant there were no funds to share. The social background information also indicates that these first pensioners came from the poorest strata of the population; Baltimore charities had assisted three-fifths of them previously.[101]

While the proportion of older women in the labor force increased slightly during the 1930s, older widows fared badly in hard times. Cases detailed by Baltimore's Family Welfare Association show that age, widowhood, and gendered earning patterns impoverished many. Social workers described Mrs. Terrett as "a dear little old lady," but her employer of eleven years fired her because of her age. At the time of her dismissal, she earned eleven dollars per week, enough to live on but not enough to save for a comfortable old age. Her daughter wanted to house her but, with seven children and an out-of-work husband, simply could not. Instead, various Catholic charities assisted Mrs. Terrett. The Society of St. Vincent de Paul paid her rent but could not find employment suitable for an older woman who was not strong enough to do domestic work. The St. Mary's Ladies of Charity sent her a weekly sum for food, and her friends left small sums for her insurance and gas bill.[102]

Other families combined forces, with older widows moving in with their sons or daughters.[103] Indeed, coresidence was a common response to the worsening economic condition. In some cities as many as one-quarter of the households contained widowed parents, siblings, or two-family groups.[104] While the Depression no doubt drew some families closer together, doubled-up families were not necessarily happy families. As the economic decline worsened, families' abilities and willingness to help support widowed mothers decreased. At least some in these households bitterly resented the privations forced on them by having to provide for a widowed mother or a grown daughter and her offspring.[105]

Nor were philanthropic groups able to support the growing number of elderly who applied to them. Charities that had for many years assisted the elderly found their donations waning and their caseloads increasing three- or fourfold.[106] Local communities foundered under the burden of unemployment and widespread poverty among children and the elderly. The New Deal shifted the onus of supporting the unfortunate to the national government, and through the Social Security Act of 1935 it began making systematic provision for the fatherless and the elderly.

Tracing the development of mothers' assistance during the 1910s and 1920s has highlighted the social response to the changing family economy and the outcry against child labor, family separation, and the employment of women with young children. The experiences of widows and orphans in the three cities demonstrates the diversity of pension regimes and the inadequacy of funding in most jurisdictions. Limited sums meant that few widows were able to emulate the middle-class model of maternal focus on home and family, should they have wished to do so. The political response to the Great Depression legislated the family wage through New Deal welfare systems.[107] The Depression exacerbated doubts about women's place in the labor force and led to the division of the poor into those eligible for employment (men and single women) and those for whom relief seemed the appropriate response (mothers). The solutions to poverty adopted under the New Deal followed the paths pioneered by mothers' pensions during the 1910s and 1920s, incorporating their basic philosophy and establishing a federal-state partnership in which the federal government provided much of the funding while states controlled the administrative mechanisms and distribution.

At the start of the Great Depression, mothers' pensions provided a subsidy to a minority of widows with young children and, more rarely, to the wives of permanently incapacitated men, some divorced or deserted women, and a few never-married mothers. They restricted the form of work these women could do but rarely provided sufficient income to support the dependent family completely. Based on one vision of good mothering, they reinforced the belief that a "mother, under our ordinary competitive system, cannot be the breadwinner and home maker at one and the same time particularly if the children are of tender age."[108] This statement recognized the double burden and disadvantages endured by mothers in the labor market.[109] In the 1920s and 1930s most states accepted maternal employment on the part of those women receiving pensions, however reluctantly, if only because legislatures were unwilling to appropriate funds sufficient to let mothers remain outside the labor force. The employment crisis of the Great Depression increased resentment against female economic activity, especially for mothers and married women. Government policies incorporated highly gendered employment and welfare models. These placed single mothers at an economic disadvantage and discounted the employment of older women and widows in pension entitlements. The original Social Security legislation made no provision either for mothers to look after their young children or for older widows to obtain a pension.[110]

While some have argued that the Social Security Act and other federal relief and welfare legislation "enforced traditional work and family roles," I contend that the roles reinforced were not traditional but rather associated with one sector of society (the middle class) and possibly sought by the working class.[111] Women's employment outside the home had been rising throughout the twentieth century, and the labor-force participation of mothers with young children (especially widows) rose sharply.[112] As unemployment increased, so did the outcry against maternal employment. It is against that background that one must view the relief, employment, and welfare policies of the Great Depression and the New Deal.

5 Widows and Orphans First?
The New Deal and Its Legacy

While we watched for the aged and the blind watched for themselves,
nobody watched for the poor widows and orphans and they got stuck.
—Dr. Abraham Epstein (1939)

The New Deal incorporated existing patterns of racial and gender stratifi-
cation into employment and welfare legislation. It distinguished between
locally administered welfare programs for women and a national expansion
of men's rights as workers and family breadwinners.[1] Through the Social
Security Act, the New Deal differentiated between federal programs that
principally benefited white male workers and those that provided charitable
assistance—at the discretion of state and county welfare officials—to people
of color and white women. White men obtained rights to public jobs, to unemployment compensation, to old-age pensions, and to higher pay; African
Americans and other racial minorities and white women got poor-law-type
aid contingent on their locality, marital status, and conformity to sexual
norms. While widows continued to fare better than other single mothers
did, all women suffered from the exclusion of their principal occupations
from the entitlements granted under the Social Security Act, such as old-age
and unemployment insurance.[2] As well intentioned as many New Dealers
were, they nevertheless built contemporary hierarchies of race and gender
into legislation designed to save one version of the American way of life and
consequently gave economic security to white men as workers while relegating all others to the status of dependents.[3]

In this chapter I marshal national, state and local data to explore the
treatment of widows during the Depression and the New Deal. I examine
the various schemata that had a significant impact on widows, single mothers, and their offspring; the ramifications of the Social Security Act (SSA)
for widows and dependent children; and the shift from widows' pensions to
Aid to Dependent Children (ADC). Where appropriate, I continue to focus

on Pittsburgh, Baltimore, and Fall River, since the New Deal legislation that codified the welfare state did not end regional discrepancies in provision.[4]

The New Deal's emphasis on getting men back to work displaced or marginalized women generally and widows specifically. The ideology of the family wage earner received federal sanction even though, or perhaps because, more women became economically active in the 1920s. The concentration of widows and married women in a limited number of occupations and the assumption that they should look after their families rather than compete in the labor force had widespread support. Most of the women active in social-policy formation in this period—for example, in the overlapping networks of the Children's Bureau, the settlement-house movement, and Chicago School of Social Work—believed that, as Grace Abbott put it, a "mother's services are worth more in the home than they are in the outside labor market."[5] Social activists worked hard to protect mothers, but this frequently came at the expense of their full economic citizenship.

Combining a national and a local focus enables us to probe how hierarchies of race and gender affected responses to the economic crisis. The implementation of widows' pensions and the Social Security Act's provisions for dependent children (but not survivors' benefits) differed greatly among geographical areas. Rather than view the SSA in isolation, in this chapter I examine the New Deal's ramifications for older and younger widows and for mothers bringing up children on their own. In some cases, such as the SSA's provision for old-age assistance and support for dependent children, the links to race and gender were direct and obvious. In others, ranging from the Agricultural Adjustment Act to the National Industrial Recovery Act, the Federal Emergency Relief Act, and the Works Progress Administration, the connections are perhaps less apparent but real and important nevertheless. These acts asserted a racialized and gendered economic hierarchy that denied full citizenship for women and people of color and weakened their relative standing and legitimacy in the workplace.[6] As the federal government expanded its direct intervention into economic matters, it extended employment rights for a portion of the population in the industrial sector while largely ignoring or relegating to relief programs the agricultural and domestic-service sectors of the economy, mostly staffed by women and racial minorities.[7]

The events of the 1930s, including New Deal legislation, reduced labor-force participation rates among widows from 34 to 30 percent. This ran counter to the generally rising levels of female economic activity during the early twentieth century and the Depression itself. In 1930, 24.8 percent of women over the age of fifteen had jobs; in 1940, 25.8 percent of those aged fourteen and over were in the labor force. Even though the 1940 census tabulations of economic activity included fourteen year olds, who were more likely to be in school than at work, female employment levels still rose slightly. Moreover, widows' and wives' tendencies to hold jobs outside the home moved in opposite directions at this time. The proportion of employed wives rose from 12 to 16 percent,[8] despite federal and state legislators' efforts to curtail their presence in the labor force, especially in government jobs.

Families could no more manage on a single income at this time than they could previously, so more wives entered the labor force, effectively replacing their children as ancillary wage earners. Given the economic pressures experienced by families in the 1930s, it at first appears counterintuitive that widows' employment rates declined. The restriction of scarce jobs to one preferred group of a certain race and gender, both in public and private employment, partially explained the downward trend. Local and federal authorities chose to place widows on relief rather than find suitable employment for them, edging younger widows (previously the most likely to be economically active) out of the labor force.[9] White men got jobs on the construction projects that dominated New Deal work-creation programs. They had better protection under the National Recovery Administration, and they benefited from discrimination against their potential competitors (racial minorities and women).[10] There is some evidence that widows did not depart from the labor force voluntarily. Even after the passage of the Social Security Act, they constituted a disproportionate share of women seeking work. In 1940 about 15 percent of economically active women were widows, but they accounted for 18 percent of all job applicants.[11] Unable to locate either private or public employment, they began leaving the labor force and turning to New Deal relief schemes.[12]

Anxiety about men's status as breadwinners during the Great Depression reinforced the tendency to regard women's economic activities and needs in terms of their family status, regardless of actual circumstances. Key New Dealers, including members of the Committee on Economic Security, conceptualized work as that performed by white men in industrial settings. The legislation they drafted, including the unemployment and retirement provisions of the Social Security Act, privileged and protected those workers, not necessarily because they consciously intended to discriminate against women or ethnic minorities, but because they sought to strengthen the position of industrial workers through social insurance programs supported by the federal government in partnership with the states.[13] As a result, the New Deal "aged" and "gendered" economic participation, condemning the labor of children and older people and devaluing that of women. Various employment programs reserved scarce jobs for men but shifted women onto relief.[14]

New Deal reformers subscribed to a vision of motherhood that constrained even as it enabled, largely ignoring women except as the mothers of dependent children. Progressives and New Dealers alike believed that a good mother stays at home to look after her children and remains outside the labor force. New Deal responses to the Great Depression simultaneously improved widows' likelihood of receiving assistance and restricted their economic strategy to dependency. Described by the historian Linda Gordon as a "dead weight crushing the imagination of welfare reformers," the family wage ideology relegated women to the economic sidelines and decreased levels of economic activity for widows, at least in the short term.[15]

The New Deal addressed widows' needs—which had earlier been met by combining wage earning, charity, and child labor—by giving them the status of wards of the state. The widespread use of emergency assistance (rather than work relief) and Aid to Dependent Children (rather than employment) defined widows and other single mothers as peripheral to the economy. Maternalist policies supported such mothers at subsistence levels while discouraging maternal employment, especially for white women.[16]

Political compromises meant that localism remained a key determining principle in the distribution of aid to single mothers. States retained control, within certain broad parameters, over eligibility criteria for welfare programs such as ADC but not for programs in the Social Security Act's entitlement sections, notably those for old-age insurance or aid for the blind, which the federal government controlled.[17] Frances Perkins, President Franklin D. Roosevelt's secretary of labor, believed that allowing the states to put their stamp on any program "that intimately affects the daily lives of people" would damp down southern objections to the act.[18] Unemployment insurance fell somewhere between the two categories, as Suzanne Mettler has observed, because it simultaneously gave states more authority but retained a measure of national control. It also privileged white male workers, who were more likely to be the full-time, long-term workers that unemployment insurance covered. By excluding part-time workers and the occupational sectors most closely associated with widows (domestic service and agriculture), it reinforced the divisions in American society between male economic security and female welfare dependence.[19]

Widows' (Un)Employment during the Great Depression

Widows and other lone mothers suffered high levels of unemployment and occupational displacement during the Great Depression, with little protection from measures designed to ensure economic stability. Their concentration in domestic service and agriculture left them exposed to the ill winds of unemployment. Early New Deal programs put them in a position of relative disadvantage by concentrating on the male sectors of the economy for their public expenditure. This made it difficult for widows to earn a living for themselves and their families. A Women's Bureau study of the Depression's effects on wage-earners' families in South Bend, Indiana, based on interviews with 1,468 women in 1932, concluded that "married women and those who had been married fared worse than single women during this time of unemployment." It found that one-fourth of the widowed, separated, or divorced female workers employed in 1930 and one-third of married women employed then had been out of work for the entire year, whereas fewer than 10 percent of this group's single women were caught in similar straits. The Agricultural Adjustment, Civil Works, and Works Progress Administrations all preferred to hire men, especially white men, leaving women comparatively disadvantaged.[20]

The distribution of widows within occupational spheres helps explain why some left the labor force during the Depression and others were especially vulnerable to unemployment and occupational displacement. The sectors in which the poorest widows worked—agriculture and domestic service—suffered severely in the 1930s, for the economic downturn undermined agricultural markets, and many urban families fired their household help. As a result, the number of widowed farmers (a few owners but mostly tenants and sharecroppers) and domestic servants decreased. While more affluent and educated widows held on to their managerial and professional jobs or found suitable federal employment schemes, rural and unskilled women had more difficulty locating work.[21]

Widows in agriculture suffered because Agricultural Adjustment Administration (AAA) payments enabled landowners to mechanize production and evict tenant farmers and sharecroppers. The AAA favored farm owners in its set-aside programs, payments for acreage reductions, and parity programs. Women made up a tiny minority of farm owners but a substantial portion of agricultural laborers. African American widows were especially vulnerable, since they had smaller holdings and no representation on the local farm committees that oversaw the cotton-crop reduction programs. Overall, black farmers fared badly at the hands of the New Deal. The Swedish sociologist Gunnar Myrdal concluded that agricultural policies, especially the those of the AAA, were directly responsible for the drastic curtailment in the number of sharecroppers and tenant farmers.[22] With farm owners using crop subsidies to shed workers, the overall proportion of African American women working farm jobs decreased from 27 percent in 1930 to 16 percent in 1940.

The census reckoned that nearly one-third of unemployed women of color had been farm laborers, indicative of the displacement and unemployment this group endured. In contrast only 3 percent of unemployed white women reported farm labor as their previous occupation.[23]

According to the Federal Emergency Relief Administration (FERA), the greatest concentration of impoverished female-headed households were found among the blacks in both cotton belts and the whites of the eastern cotton belt and in the Appalachia-Ozark area. About 13 percent of rural families on relief consisted of mothers with an average of three children under the age of sixteen. Nearly 20 percent of these families contained people over the age of sixty-five, and in 5 percent the widow sustained an aged parent or parents as well as her own young children. Fewer than one in five of these rural widows had jobs. Those lucky enough to work earned modest sums, averaging thirteen dollars a week to support four people. In the same period two-fifths of the male householders located employment, earning twice as much as their female counterparts did.[24]

Limited employment opportunities and the scarcity of relief in rural counties meant that country widows and their children endured great hardships during the Depression. A white mother of four, widowed at the age of twenty-four, told the sociologist Margaret Hagood that her children had so little to eat, she did not know how she kept them alive. Widows who retained their farm or sharecropping tenancy relied heavily on child labor at crucial times in the agricultural calendar. Sons and daughters helped plow, plant, weed, and harvest, frequently staying home from school for days or weeks at a time when their mothers needed them. Many widows returned to their parents' farms, compounding the poverty of old and young alike.[25]

Other displaced rural women moved to the city, seeking employment in already overcrowded labor markets that offered few jobs. Studies of the urban-relief population show consistent overrepresentation of female servants, especially among women of color. During the Depression, over half of all unemployed nonwhite women had been domestic servants or service workers. In contrast, fewer than 25 percent of unemployed white women had previously worked in this sector. The Federal Emergency Relief Administration (FERA) claimed there was "evidence of a serious depression in domestic service, complicated by the racial factor, low wages, and the relative ease with which such service [could] be dispensed with by the household which has met economic adversity."[26] Overall, former domestic and service workers formed 51 percent of those seeking jobs in 1936, although they had constituted 30 percent of the female labor force at the start of the Great Depression. By contrast, in 1930 about 36 percent of all employed women worked in clerical and professional occupations, but only 26 percent of the unemployed women registering with the U.S. Employment Service sought work in those fields.[27]

An investigation conducted by the University of Pittsburgh's Bureau of Business Research in the winter of 1930–31 discovered that three-fifths of the female relief applicants in the Steel City were African Americans, as were one-third of the men, although blacks constituted only 6 percent of the adult population. Most of these women had been domestic servants, and the men had held common laboring positions. Even in 1939, as the Depression receded, African Americans constituted nearly one-fifth of unemployed women, largely because servants still suffered higher levels of unemployment than did other women.[28] Thus, the decision to exclude domestic help from the unemployment-compensation provisions of the Social Security Act put women of color at a significant disadvantage, whatever the rationalizations behind the decision.[29]

Surveys in Baltimore, Washington, and New York confirmed the deterioration of conditions in domestic service in the 1930s and the serious problems this posed for widows from racial minorities clustered in this occupation. Employers preferred to hire white women; the Depression gave them the opportunity to do so. As unemployment increased throughout the economy, unemployed white women "traded down" to less socially desirable employments, including private household service. This in turn displaced thousands of African American women servants. Black women in Baltimore, for example, had held about two-thirds of the nursemaid positions in 1928 but only one in ten by 1934. New York witnessed flourishing "slave markets" where African American women, desperate for work to support themselves and their families, stood on street corners hoping for offers of a day's work.[30]

Bosses across the nation took advantage of surplus labor to lower wages, so that by 1940 about half of all domestic servants earned less than $200 a year. Since on average widows working as domestics each supported two dependents, these cost-cutting measures left their families in extremely precarious positions.[31] Women in nondomestic occupations, too, suffered lower wages and higher levels of unemployment as the Depression combined with industrial relocations to reduce wage levels and transfer jobs from the North to the South. When the textile industry moved from Massachusetts to lower-wage southern states, women's and children's employment opportunities declined in the former area. The mills transferred some of their male overseers and superintendents but none of the female operatives. Widows who had previously combined wage earning with mothers' pensions became more dependent on the state, since neither they nor their children could find work. The southward flight of capital did not even benefit widows in that region, for employers used the relocation to decrease remuneration.[32] Low wages in textiles undermined wage levels in other industries such as tobacco, which also employed large numbers of women. Moreover, New Deal agencies did little to improve women's economic standing. National Recovery Administration wage codes incorporated differentials by region, race, and sex, permitting continued discrimination against women from all racial and ethnic groups.[33]

Moreover, female factory operatives endured high levels of unemployment throughout the Depression (with clothing workers being hit especially hard), depressing wages further. Although they were 23 percent of all gainfully employed women, their ranks accounted for 35 percent of unemployed women in 1937. Even when the Depression began to lift, widows still constituted a disproportionate number of those seeking work in manufacturing. They made up 11 percent of the operatives and kindred workers in 1940 but about 17 percent of those searching for work in factories and as seamstresses.[34]

The Depression further curtailed widows' use of their children as wage earners. Sending children into the labor force had become more difficult by this time. New Deal efforts to restrict child labor succeeded despite objections from child-employing textile manufacturers, newspaper publishers, and a strict constructionist Supreme Court. The number of working fourteen and fifteen year olds fell by two-fifths between 1930 and 1940.[35] Nationwide, the proportion of employed sixteen to nineteen year olds decreased slightly in these years, from 40 percent to 35 percent for boys and from 23 to 20 percent for girls. National legislation led to a convergence in employment rates between cities. The proportion of employed older teenagers in Fall River tumbled during the interwar years, moving from 70 percent in 1920 to about 25 percent by 1940. The level of working adolescents in Baltimore had not been as high (53 percent for boys and 43 percent for girls), and had dropped 19 and 12 percent, respectively, by the eve of World War II. Pittsburgh, never welcoming to young workers, witnessed a near-disappearance of employed adolescents; by 1940 only 7 percent had jobs.[36]

A significant improvement in young people's educational levels accompanied these changes, yet they also meant that families in general, and those headed by widows in particular, either turned to adult women as wage earners or depended on relief. While many children worked, even those in two-parent families, the nature of their contribution to the family economy altered. They now had part-time jobs after school and provided the basic necessities only in "severely deprived families."[37] Thus at the same time that widows were finding it more difficult to locate work, their traditional strategy of relying on their children as ancillary breadwinners was becoming less feasible. These constraints forced them to rely heavily on charity and relief to survive.[38]

Widows and Relief during the Great Depression

Depression-era assistance schemes reinforced the dignity of men of all ages as breadwinners, while policy makers overlooked women or distributed small sums to keep them out of the labor market. The Civilian Conservation Corps, designed, in Franklin Roosevelt's words, to get young people "off the city street corners," aided young men but ignored young women, who also suffered from unemployment.[39] Programs aimed at women, whether mothers' aid or cash rather than relief work, intensified dependency and forced widows and other single mothers to subsist on less money than men obtained. Almost all the early work relief went to men employed on construction schemes of one sort or another. The Allegheny County Emergency Association gave jobs to men in 1932 and 1933 but none to women. It also gave to these men's families food orders that were 20 percent larger than those furnished to households on direct relief, so as "to meet the increased needs of the worker." Families headed by a man on work relief thus had more to eat than did those headed by women on mothers' assistance.[40]

Mothers' assistance programs expanded and modified during the early 1930s to meet the exigencies of the Depression. Massachusetts, for example, supervised mothers' aid families less stringently than it had previously. It mailed out checks fortnightly instead of insisting that widows collect them weekly from local boards of public welfare. The state supervisor of mothers' aid felt that this was acceptable for "worthy cases" but inadequate for those mothers who were poor managers, so social workers verified the expenditures and incomes of a growing number of recipients. Baltimore's pension system provided for supervision through the supervisors of public charities and a corps of volunteer visitors. Only 267 of the city's families obtained mothers' aid in the early years of the Depression. The state of Maryland made no contribution to mothers' assistance, which helps explain Baltimore's continued reluctance to help widows with young children. In Pittsburgh, however, the number of mothers' aid families increased from around 800 a month in 1928 to between 1,300 and 1,400 per month in the early 1930s. As in Massachusetts, Pennsylvania city and state governments divided the cost of these pensions, enabling local authorities to be more generous than they otherwise would have been.[41]

The total amount expended on mothers' aid and the number of women and children receiving pensions rose during the early years of the Depression.

Nevertheless, the amount granted per family decreased slightly, while regional disparities in pension provision and expenditure continued.[42] Ten northern and western states (California, Illinois, Massachusetts, Michigan, Minnesota, New Jersey, New York, Ohio, Pennsylvania, and Wisconsin) accounted for 85 percent of the expenditure on mothers' pensions in 1934. In contrast, only 4 percent of families receiving mothers' aid resided in the former Confederate states and District of Columbia. Southern states persistently refused to spend tax money on African Americans during the Depression or, at best, grudgingly dispensed insignificant amounts. They disbursed almost no aid to African American mothers and placed few of their children in public institutions. In 1932 New Orleans simply stopped accepting aid applications from African Americans. Local charities such as the New Orleans Family Service Society could not help because of their own deteriorating financial situation, leading the New Orleans organization to report to the Children's Bureau that "Negro families are said to be suffering greatly."[43]

Southern welfare workers concluded that blacks were "bearing the brunt of the Depression in the South." The caseworker who wrote this believed that public authorities intentionally ignored applications for relief submitted by African American widows. These poor women survived by taking in a little washing, begging, and picking over trash cans and dumps for discarded vegetables and fruit.[44] Neighbors' generosity sustained those in particularly straitened circumstances. Maya Angelou describes this phenomenon in an autobiographical account of her childhood in Stamps, Arkansas, during the Depression: "Although there was always generosity in the Negro neighborhood, it was indulged in on pain of sacrifice. Whatever was given by Black people to other Blacks was most probably needed as desperately by the donor as by the receiver."[45] The dreadful economic conditions and an inability to get assistance to tide them over the hard times accelerated the migration from rural areas and the South generally, leading an African American social worker to comment, "Our one big problem is a number of families who have come to Chicago recently from Southern communities. Many of them have been widowed there or left their husbands in prisons and asylums." He hoped that their home communities might have juvenile courts, mothers' pensions, or social legislation that would enable them to get aid. This would be "a much more satisfactory arrangement for them," he added, and would keep Chicago free of responsibility for their welfare.[46]

In 1932 rumors circulated that a shortfall in tax revenues would curtail pensions and increase the institutionalization of children. A number of states and cities did take "pension holidays" pending the receipt of tax revenues. Pennsylvania passed the Talbot Relief Act, which cut mothers' assistance appropriations, but later rescinded it. Some counties in Idaho, Arkansas, and Nebraska also discontinued aid. Most cities maintained their payments, but with lengthy delays in disbursements and unequal treatment for women and men. Pittsburgh's private philanthropic agencies formed a partnership with the city to raise funds for public improvements and employment, but only for men. The city provided skilled labor and materials, while voluntary contributions paid the men's wages for unskilled work. This private aid peaked in 1931; by mid-1932 charitable donations had dried up, leading the city to issue bonds to fund public welfare.[47]

Fund-raising efforts in the private sector collapsed as the Depression lengthened. The Fall River Family Welfare Association's income plummeted in 1931 as the Depression bit harder into middle- and upper-class lifestyles. The association curtailed aid to the poor, halving its caseload between 1931 and 1933. From then on it distributed clothing, food, and other stores on behalf of the federal government. Even before the institution of the Social Security Act, widows and other impoverished mothers relied more heavily on governmental agencies, particularly the federal government, for assistance, increasingly relief rather than employment. The 1934 "Highlights" of the Fall River Family Welfare Association mentions "men employed on the ERA [Federal Emergency Relief Administration]" and "young men sent to the CCC camps." Aid for women, in contrast, consisted of handouts of government clothing, cloth, blankets, flour, and other food.[48] Yet again, men got work and women received charity—if they were lucky.

Women of all ages and marital statuses suffered from the perception of unemployment as primarily a man's problem. Harry Hopkins, in charge of the Federal Emergency Relief Administration, believed that relief demoralized recipients and undermined the independence of their families. "Give a man a dole, and you save his body and destroy his spirit. Give him a job and pay him an assured wage and you save both the body and the spirit." Nor did Hopkins mean *man* in a universal sense. He admitted, "We haven't been particularly successful in work for women."[49] Key New Deal staffers, including Molly Dewson, worked hard to get more positions for women but with limited success. While work-relief programs provided jobs for millions of men, they employed only thousands of women in a limited range of occupations.[50]

A number of scholars have documented the extent to which the New Deal ignored women or treated them as men's dependents, contributing to what Barbara Melosh refers to as "the pervasive erasure of women's paid work."[51] In her study of women, work, and fiction in the 1930s, Laura Hapke argues that women were the literary and cultural scapegoats of the Great Depression.[52] Widows and other single mothers found it difficult to get emergency or work relief precisely because they were eligible for mothers' assistance. Like many men, many women preferred jobs to handouts because work relief paid better and enabled recipients (regardless of their sex) to maintain their self-respect.[53] Few Pittsburgh widows got jobs: if they were "of proved character," welfare officials referred them to the Mothers' Assistance Fund of Allegheny County. Relief administrators in other jurisdictions took a similar approach. An internal memorandum of the Children's Bureau stated that the Temporary Emergency Relief Administration in New York "adopted the policy of allowing no grants from the emergency funds for cases eligible for mothers' aid."[54]

Federal relief sustained many more widows' families than had received mothers' pensions. The proportion of single mothers obtaining government assistance increased sharply during the New Deal as states shifted the support of mothers and children onto federal funds and thus provided for those who might otherwise have languished on city or state waiting lists or been ruled ineligible under mothers' pension laws.[55] Widows perceived themselves as being unfairly treated, and they complained to Secretary of Labor Frances Perkins, Franklin Roosevelt, Eleanor Roosevelt, and the Children's Bureau that they were denied relief because they had a working child as well as younger ones. Pennsylvania relief administrators refused assistance to a widow with a six-year-old son because her older boy earned fifteen dollars per week. She said she had no fuel or clothes and at times no food. Another widow had her pension revoked because two daughters found work, even though she still had three younger children at home.[56]

In 1937 (before Aid to Dependent Children took effect) Allegheny County Mothers' Assistance Fund families continued to work for their own support, but self-help efforts provided less income than they had previously. In 1926 such families earned 60 percent of their income, with mothers' pensions and charity providing the rest. During the Depression this ratio reversed: family efforts accounted for 39 percent of pension family income, and relief payments, for 56 percent. In 20 percent of the families the mother held a job, and in over 40 percent the children entered the labor force. Most of the public funds still came from mothers' assistance appropriations, with a small proportion coming from FERA, Works Progress Administration, National Youth Administration, and Civilian Conservation Corps. The proportion contributed by relatives declined during the Depression, indicative of the strain on extended families and their inabilities to assist widowed relatives. The median income of families reliant solely on mothers' assistance in Pittsburgh was about half that of families with at least one working member, underscoring the financial penalty endured by the former. Divorced, separated, and abandoned women, who were ineligible for widows' pensions, obtained federal relief funds and thus broadened the group helped by the public authorities.[57]

Widows continued to work primarily in the private sector; few got public-work jobs.[58] For all the (male) employment programs created, female counterparts, if they existed, came in dribs and drabs or were quickly abandoned. The Civilian Conservation Corps employed 2.5 million young men, paying them enough to send money home to their families. The short-lived female counterpart employed 8,000 women, did not pay a salary, and was eliminated in a 1937 budget cut. The Civil Works Administration (CWA) emphasized construction projects and provided limited employment for women, principally in painting murals and teaching adult literacy. In Pennsylvania just 3 percent of CWA workers in 1934 were women. Its successor, the Works Progress Administration (WPA), employed millions of men building bridges, libraries, post offices, and roads, but women constituted only 12 to 18 percent of its labor force.[59]

Although mandating that women should be employed, the WPA did not hire widowed and older women in proportion to their numbers in the relief population. For example, women (overwhelmingly widows) headed about 25 percent of the households on Baltimore's relief rolls but obtained only 10 percent of the WPA jobs there. Rural areas had a lower proportion of female-headed households, but these women were overwhelmingly placed on direct relief rather than given employment. Fewer than one in ten female household heads received work relief, "since most work projects in rural areas were designed for male workers."[60] Moreover, even if they were certified as household heads and obtained work, rural widows endured discriminatory wage rates. Their relief jobs paid about half what men earned. By 1937 only 14 percent of the household heads employed on WPA programs were women. Federal relief administrators, seeking to mute criticism, ordered states that employed women in large numbers to cut them from the rolls. When Harry Hopkins discovered that Colorado's WPA register was 27 percent female in 1936, he ordered the numbers slashed to the national average of 16 percent.[61]

There was a startling lack of imagination when it came to finding jobs for women. Most government officials undervalued women's skills, especially if the woman in question had been employed as a servant or had not worked at all. Widows had less trouble being certified as household heads than married women did, but relief workers frequently dismissed their applications because few appropriate work programs existed for them.[62] Each of the three cities in this study had its distinctive approach to women's work relief influenced by its attitudes toward women's work and it willingness to incur fiscal liability for public-works programs. Parsimonious Baltimore's politicians and social workers made relatively few places available to women. In 1933 and 1934 widowed and other female household heads constituted about 20 percent of Baltimore's relief cases, but they obtained fewer than 1 percent of the city's CWA jobs. As the Depression drew to a close, the proportion of women on public-works projects increased but still remained well below their share of the labor force. Women formed 30 percent of the economically active population in 1940, yet they held only 15 percent of public-works jobs. Pittsburgh's women had greater representation among WPA workers and moved into white-collar jobs as the WPA expanded its educational and clerical projects. Fall River, perhaps recognizing women's centrality to family economies and the prevailing acceptance of female economic activity, had by 1940 accorded more women public-works jobs than had most other cities. The large number of widowed household heads on work relief also compensated for their children's decreased abilities to contribute financially following the curtailment of child labor.[63]

Sewing shops employed more than half the women on WPA jobs in 1936. One-fifth undertook clerical, technical, or educational employment, and one-tenth worked in the various WPA home economics programs. In some states the proportion doing sewing climbed higher. In Massachusetts 87 percent of the women on WPA projects machined clothes. Unemployed women in Baltimore worked either in the sewing rooms or as domestic servants. The sewing schemes there ran on a commercial basis and dismissed employees who did not meet production quotas. Gender stereotyping existed even within the limited range of opportunities offered to women. The WPA reinforced the garment industry's sexist division of labor. Men cut out the clothes (traditionally a male monopoly in clothing manufacturing), while women sewed them. This prevented women from upgrading their skills and reinforced their segregation into lower-waged occupations. Toward its end, the WPA increased the number of educational, professional, and clerical projects, enabling already educated women to work at jobs more commensurate with their backgrounds, but it still provided few advancement opportunities for less educated women.[64]

Even when widows managed to get work through the WPA and other public-works programs, they received lower wages than their male counterparts did, in part because the sewing projects paid poorly. Over two-fifths of women on public emergency work earned less than $200 per year, while fewer than one-fourth of the men did so. A small number of women obtained white-collar jobs with the WPA. They accounted for the tiny fraction (1 percent) of women who earned more than $1,400 per year from relief jobs.[65]

Because of the racial and gender politics prevalent in the South, its regional WPA programs provided much less adequately for African American women than it did for whites, although black men were somewhat less disadvantaged. In 1938 African Americans constituted about 10 percent of the U.S. population. African American men made up 12 percent of the WPA workforce, although African American women accounted for a mere 2 percent. White men constituted over 74 percent of the WPA's workers, and white women, 11 percent. Several factors explain this imbalance. As already discussed, the emphasis on construction projects routinely excluded women. While there was a limited acceptance of black and white men working together, especially on outdoor projects, where they might labor in separate gangs, southern mores prohibited black and white women from working together. Few white southerners thought to establish separate projects for black women, who consequently had few opportunities for public employment.[66]

Baltimore thus stood out from other southern and border cities because it gave African American women some access to WPA jobs (see table 20). Baltimore provided three sewing projects for women, two for whites and one for blacks, employing about 900 women. Women who did not manage to get a place in the sewing rooms had only one real alternative: domestic service. Many WPA schemes aimed principally at African American women sought to "improve" their domestic skills by training them as housekeepers. If they did not accept jobs as low-paid domestics, the WPA threw them off the relief rolls, although white women could turn down such work with no penalty. The situation was especially difficult for the disproportionate number of single mothers in the African American community.[67]

In many cases Baltimore housewives demanded that their servants live in. This placed a real hardship on African American widows and other single

Table 20. Whites and African Americans on Public Emergency Work and in Labor Force, 1940

	White men		White women		Black men		Black women		
	PEW[a]	LF[a]	PEW[a]	LF[a]	PEW[a]	LF[a]	PEW[a]	LF[a]	Total
Baltimore	40.2%	57.4%	10.2%	22.0%	44.3%	12.7%	5.3%	7.9%	100.0%
Pittsburgh	58.8	66.1	18.1	24.7	16.4	6.7	6.7	2.5	100.0
Fall River	66.2	79.0	37.8	21.0	—	—	—	—	100.0

Source: Data from U.S. Bureau of the Census, *Sixteenth Census: Population,* vol. 3, *The Labor Force* (Washington, D.C.: Government Printing Office, 1943), pt. 3, pp. 358, 451, pt. 5, p. 12.
[a]PEW = public emergency work; LF = labor force.

mothers trying to balance their own domestic responsibilities with wage earning. They received little sympathy from Baltimore's director of employment for the WPA. He insisted they needed to make sacrifices to find employment. Given these attitudes, it is perhaps not surprising that African American women formed only 5 percent of the workers on public emergency projects, although they were 8 percent of the labor force in Baltimore and a considerably higher proportion of the unemployed. In Pittsburgh, where African Americans got a fairer deal—although not necessarily more diversified employment—7 percent of the WPA workers were black women, even though they were only 3 percent of the workforce.[68]

Variations among local approaches to the distribution of relief and public employment left widows facing different economic prospects during the Great Depression. The New Deal helped more women in Pittsburgh and Fall River get work relief, while Baltimore lagged well behind. The relative munificence of relief authorities in Massachusetts stemmed from the state's well-established acceptance of responsibility for the poorer members of society and its tradition of public outdoor relief. In contrast, Baltimore's mayor throughout the Great Depression, Howard Jackson, was hostile to the New Deal ethos and, in keeping with long-standing Baltimorean tradition, authorized expenditure on public welfare reluctantly and conservatively. Baltimore adhered to its privatist tradition in matters of social welfare; it both eschewed outside help and acted to keep taxes as low as possible. Throughout the Depression the poorest women of the city, widowed African American domestic servants, had little access to public aid and were segregated into poorly paid domestic service jobs—if they managed to get into public-works schemes at all. Pittsburgh blended public and private aid to the unemployed. Its mothers' assistance rolls rose sharply, and there was less discrimination against African American widows in obtaining public employment, but women generally found it easier to get relief than to obtain WPA jobs.[69]

Social Security

The Social Security Act, passed in 1935, comprised national welfare legislation that improved the circumstances of some widows, single mothers, and the elderly but nevertheless excluded many of the poorest Americans. Its key provisions included old-age retirement insurance, old-age assistance (for those not covered by the retirement provisions), unemployment insurance, aid to the blind, and aid to dependent children. It built on the existing local systems of widows' pensions and old-age assistance (both means tested) but also expanded coverage by developing a contributory federal old-age pension system. It was a compromise program that divided authority, making local governments responsible for welfare functions and the federal government responsible for entitlement programs. The Old Age Insurance (OAI) section of the Social Security Act mandated payroll deductions and in turn granted a non-means-tested pension to long-serving full-time workers, mostly in industrial occupations. Designed to ensure the dignity of labor, OAI gave pensions automatically, without interference from social workers or local bureaucrats. There were no restrictions on wealth or property ownership, marking the pensions as an entitlement, not demeaning charity. Based on lifetime employment history, they were not tied to a single employer, as private pensions had been. Among OAI's major shortcomings was its exclusion of large occupational groups, arising in part from regional and racial prejudices and, arguably, from the complexity of collecting pension contributions from individuals and small businesses.[70]

Historians have described the Social Security Act as a "landmark" in American history that transferred welfare provision from voluntary to public institutions and from the local level to the federal government, helping the United States catch up with other advanced industrial nations.[71] Although this is true of the act's social-insurance sections, states retained significant control over the programs for women and children. In fact, the act's implementation had unintended consequences, including the "political marginalization of female administrators, social workers, and surviving maternalist programs," according to Skocpol.[72] Gareth Davies, writing principally about OAI, emphasized its nature as radical in that it severed the connection between benefits and local interpretations of appropriate criteria for granting them. While true of retirement pensions, this did not characterize the welfare portions of the act. The SSA had a decidedly conservative cast in its limited coverage, low benefits, and five-year delay between its enactment and the collection of benefits. Nevertheless, OAI represented a significant break with the past, not least because it committed federal government funding without the states' forming an intervening layer of control.[73]

Many of the most sweeping criticisms of the Social Security Act have come from feminist historians, including Alice Kessler-Harris, who has discussed the way the 1939 amendments embedded "generalizations about male/female behavior in public policies."[74] According to Mimi Abramovitz, the Social Security Act shored up the patriarchal family unit despite women's increased economic activity and men's inability to support their families during the Depression. She claims that it "marked the institutionalization of social or public patriarchy in the contemporary welfare state."[75] Women figured principally as the mothers of dependent children, and the act initially omitted elderly widows except insofar as they might qualify for old-age assistance. It reinforced a particular version of family life contrary to widows' and single mothers' own strategies of combining wage earning and child care.[76]

The insurance sections of the Social Security Act marginalized women by excluding their predominant occupations and making no provision for those who worked intermittently. This was the work of Congress, however, not the Committee on Economic Security (CES), which drafted the bill. Congress restricted the act's coverage, ignoring arguments from the National Association for the Advancement of Colored People, among other organizations, that domestic servants and farm laborers be included.[77] Prevailing class, race, and gender hegemonies, coupled with a desire to keep costs low, resulted in retirement and unemployment programs that provided for industrial workers but not domestic servants, farm laborers, part-time workers, or those who moved in and out of the labor force. There was an underlying assumption that older men would support their wives on their pension income and that men never depend on women financially.[78] The 1935 act made no allowance for widowed survivors of either sex. It also excluded workers in nonprofit organizations, public employment, and educational institutions, many of whom were women. As originally framed, the retirement pension system covered about half the working population, forgoing protection for nearly three-fifths of all women workers and more than nine-tenths of African Americans.[79]

To get such ambitious legislation through a Congress dominated by conservative southern Democrats and others who feared the expansion of federal government, the act's backers had to settle for restricted coverage. Martha Derthick and Gareth Davies have argued that the complexity of collecting worker or employer contributions from myriad small businesses, farms, or households made the exclusion of agricultural and domestic workers from these programs an administrative necessity.[80] It certainly was politically expedient to exclude them. Robert Lieberman has made the case that the Social Security Act was "as national and inclusive as political circumstances and historical legacies allowed," although Jill Quadagno observed that "southern congressmen had no intention of letting federal funds go directly to black workers."[81] These programs were based on white men's occupations and standardized provision keyed to male working patterns.

Legislators, the CES, and the Children's Bureau (which drafted the sections on children's security) omitted older or childless widows, even though administrators such as Barbara Armstrong fought to include them. Armstrong, the director of planning for the CES, recollected that every time she attempted to write survivors' benefits into the proposed legislation, Edwin

Witte, the committee's director, removed them.[82] Concerned about getting the legislation through Congress, the CES assumed that adult children would support widowed mothers. Both Congress and the CES believed that older men deserved a pension based on their former employment, not dependence on their children's largesse. The CES underrated the significance of women as wage earners, despite their sizable presence in the labor force, and excluded agricultural and household workers in a racially based subtext that meant almost no women of color obtained federal old-age pensions in this era.[83]

The Social Security Act assumed a model of family roles in which women stay home to look after children or are supported by their retired husbands or grown children. It entitled (white) men to ensured dignity while relegating women and people of color to a precarious combination of local programs and federal programs with lesser benefits, including Aid to Dependent Children and Old Age Assistance. The legislation's drafters gave little thought to the way mothers bringing up children on their own might sustain themselves. Rather than balance the needs or rights of different family members, the act's authors viewed wage earning as an unnatural activity for mothers and ignored the welfare of older widows. While providing for children, the act disregarded their mothers. In President Roosevelt's view, the Economic Security Act (the act's original name) was a measure for children.

> The very phrases "mothers' aid" and "mothers' pensions" place an emphasis equivalent to misconstruction of the attention of these laws. These are not primarily aids to mothers but defense measures for children. They are designed to release from the wage-earning role the person whose natural function is to give her children the physical and affectionate guardianship necessary, not alone to keep them from falling into social misfortune, but more affirmatively to rear them into citizens capable of contributing to society.[84]

Many shared Roosevelt's vision of family life, which incorporated separate spheres into federal welfare legislation. Edwin E. Witte testified before Congress that these were not mothers' pensions but "aid toward the care of these unfortunate children who have been deprived of a father's support."[85] Conceived as a child-welfare measure, ADC provided no direct support for the mothers who looked after the children. It thus differed from federal stipends paid to veterans' widows and children, in which mothers received a separate allowance. ADC presupposed that the guardians of dependent children would live off the payments channeled through them for their children or, as with widows' pensions, would work as well. The federal government made provision for caretakers only in 1950.[86]

Bureaucratic infighting played a significant part in shaping Social Security, with various interests competing to manage it. The Children's Bureau focused on innovative children's health programs instead of supporting old-fashioned relief systems, but it had considerable expertise in both areas. In an effort to keep costs down, the CES rejected the Children's Bureau casework model and its maternalist notions of supervised motherhood in favor of a more restricted program. The Federal Emergency Relief Administration criticized the Children's Bureau's elitism and emphasis on casework and sought to incorporate assistance to widows and orphans into a general relief program. Congress, dismissing the Children's Bureau's claims to ADC and distrusting FERA's empire building and its boss, Harry Hopkins, gave the newly created Social Security Board (SSB) control over all programs. The SSB subordinated the needs of the very poor to those of the individuals it perceived as worthy of social insurance, the unemployed and retired men, making ADC an "orphan program" in an agency primarily concerned about the elderly and unemployed.[87]

The act provided less well for single-parent families than for the other groups it incorporated. The relatively generous provisions originally envisaged by the Children's Bureau got lost in the wrangle with FERA.[88] Moreover, the House Ways and Means Committee deleted the sections of the bill that would have required states to grant reasonable levels of support to ADC beneficiaries. As a result, widows and dependent children obtained significantly lower levels of federal funding than did other groups.[89] Congress gave states, which paid two-thirds of ADC costs, the rights to impose additional eligibility requirements, control recipients' behavior, and supervise their moral character, as they had done under widows' pension programs. Abraham Epstein, the executive secretary of the American Association for Social Security and a longtime campaigner for old-age pensions, believed that the differences in the federal government's contributions (one-third of ADC costs but half of those for pensions for the blind and aged) made no sense. He attributed this unfair situation to inattention: "While we watched for the aged and the blind watched for themselves, nobody watched for the poor widows and orphans and they got stuck."[90]

A variety of groups fought for increased or improved support for older Americans at the grassroots and national levels. The Townsend movement, the American Association for Old Age Security, and fraternal and veterans' organizations enjoyed a coherent voting strength that widows, other single mothers, and their dependent children lacked. The radical nature of Dr. Townsend's proposals (giving $200 a month to all Americans over the age of sixty and requiring that they spend it by the end of the month) and their immense popularity pushed Congress to assist the aged. The Committee on

Economic Security also sought to distinguish its proposals from "welfarism" by making retirement pensions contributory and graduated according to contributions. This differentiated it from old-fashioned poor relief, which ADC closely resembled, in both its inadequate provision and local control.[91]

The federal government established a maximum disbursement of eighteen dollars per month for the first child and twelve dollars for each subsequent one. Since it did not establish minimums, some states paid wholly inadequate amounts. These rates perpetuated the discrimination between young and old, which appeared with state- or city-funded old-age pensions, and permanently skewed welfare provision in favor of the elderly, who received higher payments.[92] Benefit amounts geared to subsistence standards of living kept down costs and reassured southerners that they would not lose their underpaid labor force.[93]

Blanche Coll described the Social Security Act as a "departure from localism," but many of the law's programs overtly reinforced local control.[94] The federal government exercised some oversight of state regulations for ADC and Old Age Assistance, building, in Children's Bureau chief Katherine Lenroot's words, on a "foundation of federal, state, and local cooperation" that would not lead "into any difficult administrative realms or into any unpredictable costs."[95] Individual state plans had to provide statewide coverage under the administrative oversight of a single statewide agency and contain a mechanism for appeals against the denial of assistance. Since the federal government refused to match in-kind payments, the emphasis shifted to cash provision instead of the demeaning deliveries of charity coal, food vouchers, and secondhand clothing.[96] Yet Congress freed states from federal control by allowing them to impose additional eligibility requirements and to supervise the morals and manners of recipients as a means of ensuring conformity to local norms. The NAACP, among other groups, feared that this would result in discrimination against African Americans in child welfare, but the Ways and Means Committee refused to write nondiscriminatory provisions into the bill.[97]

Local control over ADC appeased southern Congressmen who had spoken against the Social Security bill because it threatened to upset the existing racial balance in their section of the country. The balance of power in Congress gave southern representatives and senators an effective veto over New Deal legislation, so new laws had to conform to southern mores or at least not impinge on them. White southerners did not want federal funds going directly to African Americans or undermining their control over agricultural and domestic workers. Their fears reflected their general concern over the transfer of power from the states to the central government and the potential costs of these measures. Ultimately, the administration of the act gave local authorities significant control, which boded poorly for African Americans and other groups that lacked political power in particular localities.[98]

Representatives of the NAACP and the Federal Council of Churches of Christ in America protested the potential for racial bias in the administration of the Social Security Act at the congressional hearings. They sought, unsuccessfully, to have an antidiscrimination clause included. These speakers pointed out that the "widespread and continued discrimination on account of race or color" meant that "Negro men, women, and children did not share equitably and fairly in the distribution of benefits accruing from the expenditure" of federal funds under the New Deal. The council's George Haynes lamented the "prevailing idea that Negro persons can have such a reasonable subsistence on less income than a white person." The exclusion of farm and service occupations provoked anger from the NAACP's representative, who claimed that the bill deliberately omitted such jobs precisely because many or even most of them were held by African Americans.[99] Subsequent administration of the act indicated an inverse correlation between the proportion of black people in a state and its spending on welfare (especially AFDC).[100]

The laggardly way that states implemented the Social Security Act showed that they cared far more about adult workers and the elderly than about children. A year after its passage only twenty-six states had approved plans for Aid to Dependent Children, although forty-two states had acceptable Old Age Assistance programs. Given their previous record on widows' pensions, it is not surprising that southern states enacted enabling legislation slowly. In other jurisdictions welfare authorities used the new act to shift women off work relief and onto ADC. In 1939 Congress codified this practice in the Woodrum Act, which prevented anyone eligible for ADC from obtaining a WPA job. While widows and other lone mothers might have preferred the higher work-relief payments, strong sentiment that mothers belong at home led to their removal from work-relief projects and placement on welfare. This explicit gendering of work and welfare helps explain the decline in widows' and other single mothers' labor-force participation between 1930 and 1940.[101] Even so, ADC had lower rates of accepted applications than did other programs. In the first few years of operation, the number of elderly receiving assistance was triple that for young people, even though the needy in the latter group were at least as numerous as those in the former.[102]

When southern states finally submitted plans for ADC, they established much lower payments. In 1938 aid per family averaged about $32 per month nationally (or about $13 per dependent child), with Massachusetts giving $65.03 per month but Arkansas proffering a mere $8.14.[103] Southern states also kept African American women off ADC rolls by adopting rules that disqualified them. The "employable mother" regulation, widespread in the South, prevented mothers with school-age children from receiving assistance. Southern welfare administrators believed black mothers could "get along" on a combination of seasonal labor and low-paid domestic jobs.[104] People of color constituted 14 to 17 percent of all ADC recipients between 1937 and 1940, slightly higher than their share of the national population (12 percent). African American children in the South accounted for a smaller proportion of the ADC rolls than their relative numbers warranted, despite blacks' elevated levels of poverty and female-headed households. The higher rates of unmarried motherhood in the black community led southern social workers to deem these households "unsuitable" and refuse them benefits.[105]

Nationally widows and their half-orphaned children made up between 40 and 50 percent of the recipients of ADC in its first years of operation, whereas they constituted about four-fifths of all mothers' aid recipients in the early 1930s. By 1940 divorce had replaced widowhood as the principal cause of marital dissolution among younger women (those younger than thirty-five).[106] Even so, divorcees headed just over one-quarter of ADC families. States assisted few illegitimate children, and some states denied them aid altogether. Initially, at least, city and state welfare officers placed a narrow construction on eligibility, to the detriment of many children raised by single mothers.[107]

Officials in Fall River permitted the number of recipients to rise once the federal government shared the cost. The number climbed from between fifty and sixty mothers a year under the state mothers' aid program during the 1920s to nearly two hundred in the first year of ADC. This occurred despite a "puritanical" local aid administrator who established her own stringent criteria for dispensing aid. She banned illegitimate children from ADC, required a high standard of housekeeping, and insisted that children go to church if they were to be eligible.[108] The first group of recipients had modest means. Most were recent widows (within five years). Few had been in the labor force while their husbands were still alive (fewer than 10 percent), and many were of either French Canadian or Portuguese origin. They received an average of forty-six dollars per month, about the same as they would have gotten on mothers' assistance, but less than the Massachusetts statewide average.[109]

Pennsylvania's Department of Public Assistance altered its regulations following the passage of the Social Security Act to liberalize access. It explicitly extended eligibility to children deprived of their father's support through death or continued absence because of desertion, separation, divorce, or incarceration in a penal or mental institution, which expanded coverage considerably. The number of assisted families nearly trebled between 1935 and 1939, demonstrating the tremendous demand for financial help that local resources had been unable or unwilling to meet.[110]

Baltimore remained reluctant to assist mothers bringing up children on their own. Although the Social Security Board approved Maryland's plans in 1936, the city and state dragged their collective heels. The city's fiscal conservatism and antipathy to public aid meant that many potential recipients of ADC did not obtain assistance. Having described Social Security as "asinine," Mayor Howard Jackson made little effort to implement its provisions for the benefit of Baltimore's lone mothers and children. The state of Maryland played its part in ensuring few families obtained ADC by making wholly inadequate appropriations. While the city authorized aid for 750 mothers in 1936, the state provided funding for only 150. The magnitude of the shortfall is startling, especially in comparison to Pittsburgh's generosity; indeed, in 1937 and 1938 Maryland had to grant general relief to over one-third of the families eligible for ADC because the amounts appropriated were so paltry.[111]

In 1937 the Social Security Board devised amendments to the SSA to mute criticisms of it. Payroll deductions were introduced in that year, although pension benefits had not yet begun, thus reducing consumer spending and inducing the "Roosevelt Recession." Board members were also concerned that widows and orphans lacked sufficient protection and that some states, including Maryland, had been extremely parsimonious in granting ADC. In recognition of this and other inadequacies in the act and its implementation, Congress amended the Social Security Act in 1939. It placed ADC on the same footing as the other shared contribution programs, so that the federal government contributed one-half rather than one-third of the costs. It also raised the age limit to eighteen as long as the children remained in school.[112]

Coverage expanded to include widows by establishing survivors' benefits. The amendments gave women retirement benefits as economic dependents of a man rather than in their own right. The chairman of the Social Security Board described the new benefits as "a family concept," adding, "You just cannot think of these people as individuals. You have to think of them in their family relationships."[113] This mirrored social expectations that men should be families' sole breadwinners, with women and children reliant on them for their support. Married women who worked in pensionable occupations gained little from the revised act because of the maximum limits set on a couple's pension income. Business leaders such as Marion B. Folsom, the treasurer of the Eastman Kodak Company, objected that giving pensions to aged wives and aged widows would "cut down on the benefits which must be paid to the single man in the distant future."[114] In this view, payments to women took money away from men, even though many had worked before or during their marriage.

The architects of the survivors' benefits program took great pains to assure skeptics that it would not harm single men. Dr. J. Douglas Brown, chairman of the Advisory Council on Social Security, explained to Congress that "in order to control the cost of the system," the pension money earned by a woman in her own right would be "telescoped into the amount of old age pension she got through her husband." In other words, she received nothing extra based on her own earnings. Brown explained that as more women entered industrial or other occupations in their early or middle years, they would in effect finance wives' allowances so that they would not be a net addition to the cost of the plan.[115] They would not receive any pension based on their own earnings. Married women who worked subsidized those who did not hold jobs.

Gender biases pervaded these benefits. A male retiree received 100 percent of the pension to which he was entitled. He was credited with 50 percent more for his wife once she reached the age of sixty-five. When he died, she received a widow's pension of half the combined amount. Put slightly differently, a man on his own got 100 percent of a man's benefit, but a woman received only 75 percent. This meant that the widow's standard of living dropped following the death of her husband. If the wife predeceased the husband, however, he lost only her 50 percent. Nevertheless, survivors' benefits meant that nonemployed wives received a pension for life if their husbands had been in covered occupations, which considerably improved their prospects in old age.

In another flagrant example of gender bias, a man could not obtain a pension based on his wife's earning record unless he had been completely dependent on her support. The Social Security Board's pension model simply ignored the rising number of economically active women. Nor did it recognize the growing number of dual-income couples, in which both parties made financial contributions. The debates in Congress assumed that women married men for venal reasons and would entrap foolish old men in wedlock just to get their Social Security benefits. The amended act stipulated that the supplementary wife's pension would be paid only if the marriage had occurred before the husband reached the age of sixty. Divorced women were excluded altogether from survivors' benefits, as were those who were separated. This contributed to the displaced homemaker problem, where women divorced in middle or old age received no pension because their marriages had broken down and their former husbands "owned" their Social Security contributions.[116]

The dependent children of men in covered occupations received benefits, as did widowed mothers, unless they remarried. The widow received three-quarters of the monthly benefits due on her husband's wage credits, and each child received half the father's benefits. Widowed mothers who received survivors' benefits could earn money, although a cap was placed on their earnings. The Social Security Board still regarded widows primarily in their maternal role. They considered and rejected benefits to middle-aged widows, assuming that they would have "more savings than younger widows" and that their children would be able and willing to help them out financially. The board also contemplated and rejected the notion of granting pensions to childless widows under the age of sixty-five because it would present "certain serious anomalies." It claimed that any age criterion would be arbitrary and that lowering women's retirement age would both discriminate against men and substantially increase the cost of the program.[117]

The amended Social Security Act differentiated two groups of mothers and children with drastic consequences. The first group consisted of impoverished lone mothers and dependent children, while the second contained the widows of men covered under the provisions of Social Security retirement clauses. The Social Security Board believed that "to limit pensions to low income widows and orphans would destroy the contributory principle or deny benefits to the higher-income groups which have already made contributions to the system."[118] It privileged those widows and orphans whose husbands and fathers were within the Social Security system while further disadvantaging those outside it. Widows entitled to survivors' benefits received assistance automatically; those on ADC continued to suffer the biases of local welfare workers, means testing, and humiliating investigations into their personal circumstances. Survivors also received a pension for themselves, which was intended to enable them "to remain at home and care for the children," although not until the 1950s did lone mothers on ADC obtain benefits that would permit them to stay home and look after their children.[119]

Paul T. Beisser, president of the Child Welfare League of America, indicated the dangers of leaving ADC in the hands of closefisted state legislatures and relief authorities. He posited that an urban widow with three children needed sixty-eight dollars a month to keep body and soul together. Yet in 1937 thirty-seven states gave less than half that amount, and five gave only one-quarter. The 1939 amendments did not confront this problem directly. They raised the federal government contribution, but this allowed states to reduce their relief expenses.[120] Further, the amendments stigmatized the ADC when it removed widows from the program's roster, for it deleted those traditionally regarded as the worthy poor and morally acceptable. The proportion of ADC children who were orphans declined from about half in 1937 to 21 percent by 1950 and had fallen to only 6 percent by 1969. The amended act discriminated against many nonwhite women whose late husbands or partners did not work in covered occupations. They received the lower ADC payments and remained firmly under the control of local authorities, who could and did cut grants to force recipients into poorly paid jobs or away from "objectionable" sexual activities.[121]

The 1939 amendments did little to alter the racial configuration of old-age pensions in the short run. Domestic service and farm labor remained outside OAI, despite a vigorous campaign by the NAACP and other African American pressure groups.[122] As a result, African Americans and other people of color constituted a tiny proportion of the early recipients of OAI but a larger fraction of those on Old Age Assistance. Between 1937 and 1940 the African American elderly made up 12 percent of Old Age Assistance recipients across the nation, even though they were only 7 percent of the population over the age of sixty-five. Crucially, this program, like ADC, remained under local control, a feature designed to attract the support of white southern Congressmen. States had the right to establish eligibility criteria, and southern ones disadvantaged older African Americans. Old Age Assistance rates were much lower in the South, with few blacks obtaining OAA in that region despite their great poverty. Local control equated with racial preferencing; in Mississippi white pensioners got eleven dollars per month; blacks received only seven dollars.[123]

The first years of the Social Security Act bore out the fears that African Americans would fare poorly under the law unless it contained specific antidiscrimination provisions.[124] While the federal-state partnership benefited many widows and single mothers, those of African, Mexican, or Native American ancestry experienced biased and inadequate provision.[125] This was a direct consequence of pandering to local prejudices in the creation of the welfare state. The states' rights arguments advanced in Congress, principally by southern congressmen, limited federal oversight and deprived women of color of equal protection under the law. The United States established a two-tier welfare state. It provided poorly for many mothers and children because of either race, maternal marital status, or residence.

Conclusion

The New Deal increased public provision for widows and orphans but also continued local variations in welfare. Furthermore, it incorporated gender differentiation in federal government policies. There were significant discrepancies between entitlement programs (aimed at white men, their wives, and orphaned children) and welfare programs that served unmarried mothers and people of color poorly. The amended Social Security Act provided assistance for widows with young children and retirees, yet it stranded many women between motherhood and old age as displaced homemakers, with no pension, no job, and nowhere to turn. The Social Security system demanded the same payments from women and men but for decades provided lower returns to working women on their retirement contributions, effectively privileging families with a single male wage earner. The lack of coverage for occupations in which people of color predominated left this group particularly vulnerable. Black (and other) domestic servants received no Social Security pensions, and neither did those who were, or were married to, farmworkers. Congress subsequently rectified these occupational exclusions when people of color became more powerful politically, but in the short term, they greatly disadvantaged this group.[126]

In a time of economic crisis, the New Deal returned to Progressive Era understandings about the family economy, gender, and race instead of forging a new path or acknowledging emerging family forms (e.g., households headed by divorced or never-married women). Viewed from that perspective it was an old deal, now sanctioned by federal law. Serious and detrimental regional differences continued to discriminate among widowed women—indeed, all women—on racial and occupational grounds. Localism remained the dominant paradigm in social-welfare provision, although entitlement programs were national in scope, benefits, and intent. The Social Security Act undermined women's economic citizenship by discriminating against them, their occupations, and their employment patterns. This seriously disadvantaged elderly women, divorced and never-married mothers, and their children, especially in the South. It built race and gender prejudices into law.[127] A few widows received favored treatment as the wives of men in preferred occupations and as the mothers of their children. The majority of younger single mothers obtained meager handouts, subject to prevailing local customs. Most female heads of households received a less favorable deal simply because they were women and especially if they belonged to racial minorities.

The Social Security system consolidated and reinforced existing racial and gender hierarchies. It kept down the costs of social-welfare policy by providing for women only as mothers and relicts while ignoring their claims to economic equity in their own right. For all the legislative gains made by some groups, notably organized labor, and despite the fact that some women had achieved positions of power, public policy toward widows, lone mothers, and women in general continued to treat them in terms of their roles in the family rather than as individuals. In an age of individualism, gender and marital status defined women as much, if not more, at the end of the Depression as they had at the beginning.

The inability to perceive women except in their family context meant that women's economic situations remained hidden and subsumed under misleading assumptions about family roles and relationships. Southern states in particular tried to limit the number of ADC recipients among African American women bringing up children on their own. In particular, deviation from strict moral codes (e.g., having a second child out of wedlock) would cost them their benefits. Social Security, like other forms of widows' pensions, ignored fathers who looked after their children following their wives' deaths. They could not get a widowers' pension, nor did their wives' earnings accumulate credits for their children's upbringing. This situation was not rectified until the mid-1970s, when Stephen Wiesenfeld sued the Social Security Board to obtain benefits against his late wife's contribution record.[128]

Social Security legislation barely acknowledged the changes that had occurred in demographic trends, women's economic roles, and the family economy during the early twentieth century. It did not address the lengthening empty-nest interval caused by a declining birth rate. It ignored increased female longevity that meant women were widows for far longer and had fewer children to support or house them. It also failed to recognize the demographic changes that took place in the 1920s and 1930s, when divorce rather than widowhood became the most important cause of lone-parent families. The family economy that emerged from the New Deal was substantially different from that of Progressive Era. In 1940 divorcées outnumbered widows among young mothers for the first time in the nation's history. Women refused to stay in unhappy or unsatisfactory marriages or to conform to narrow visions of the way to conduct their social relationships. Thus, divorce, desertion, or illegitimacy, not widowhood, became the predominant causes of poverty among nonmarried mothers and their children. Yet the 1939 amendments disadvantaged these groups.

Whereas young widows had formed the primary category of assisted mothers under state mothers' assistance programs, the Social Security Act, as reformed in 1939, constructed a two-tier system that penalized the majority of potential recipients. Aid to Dependent Children and survivors' benefits differentiated categories of mothers and dependent children. Built on a patriarchal version of family life in which women and children depend financially on men and need the state's close supervision in the absence of a male breadwinner, these programs provided widely differing levels of service and subsistence. Survivors' benefits shared the entitlement approach of OAI, with the federal government automatically funding these widows and orphans. Nonetheless, a means-tested and locally controlled system of welfare benefits under ADC permitted states to provide lower levels of service to divorced, deserted, or never-married mothers and their children.

Localism in welfare permitted discrimination against people of color since states could and did write rules reflecting local economies and racial mores. Each state had its own rules, subject only to the federal ukase that they be the same across a state. Discrepancies among jurisdictions endured, with Baltimore and the South generally providing poorly for women and children on ADC. In practice, distinctions between the supposedly worthy and unworthy poor received federal sanction and established a welfare state that seriously disadvantaged many poor women and children. Southern states in particular used "suitable home" and "employable mother" rules to keep down welfare rolls in postwar America and force certain groups of women off welfare.[129]

Despite these serious limitations, the Social Security Act did transfer resources to many older widows through survivors' benefits. Their inadequacies and gender biases notwithstanding, the 1935 and 1939 legislation gave widows (at least those whose husbands had been in covered occupations) a guaranteed subsistence in old age. As a result, and especially as more women earned credits in their own right, numerous women eschewed turning to their extended families, the recourse (however inadequate and stressful) for their counterparts before 1939.[130] Entitlement programs for the elderly, the disabled, and decedents' survivors gave greater parity of treatment across the United States for those included under their provisions. This was not the case in other aspects of Social Security, such as Aid to Dependent Children and Old Age Assistance.

Between 1880 and 1939 maternalist reformers put children's needs (as they perceived them) first, while some reformers tried to balance women's economic needs with models of good parenting and family welfare.[131] Progressive reformers generally opposed what they regarded as the sacrifice of the individual child on the altar of family need. They believed the good of the state to be inextricably linked to the education and training of the young. These sentiments engendered the fight for mass education and against child labor. They resulted in a new vision of childhood and a new form of family economy in the twentieth century. As children left the labor force, their mothers replaced them, since many families found themselves unable to manage on a single income or state benefits. Nevertheless, widows' employment decreased, unlike that of other women, as benefits supplemented scarce jobs as a means of sustaining their households in the 1930s.

By sanctioning continued local control, by not recognizing the demographic and economic changes occurring in the United States, and by differentiating between entitlement programs and welfare, the Social Security Act perpetrated a two-track assistance system. This systematically disadvantaged most women bringing up children on their own. While older widows eventually benefited from improved gender equity, lone mothers and children remained stigmatized by a locally based welfare system. "Welfare" came to have negative connotations. It abandoned their needs to appease taxpayers who resented aiding the poor, especially those from racial minorities. The increase in middle-class mothers who took jobs outside the home reduced any social willingness to support poor women so they could stay home to care for their children and eliminated any push to ensure a level playing field where the children of poor single mothers might enjoy the advantages given to those from affluent two-parent homes. The United States was and remains all the poorer for this.

Notes

Introduction

1. St. Vincent's Home, Fall River, Boy's Register (1886–1921), 2–3 (manuscript in possession of the St. Vincent's Home; used by kind permission of Sister M. Ludivine and Mr. Jack Weldon, MSW). All names are fictitious to protect privacy.

2. Associated Charities of Fall River, District Conference 3, casework notes (1889), 16–18 (manuscript in possession of the Family Welfare Association of Fall River).

3. Qtd. in Charity Organization Society of Baltimore, *Twentieth Annual Report* (Baltimore, 1901), 33.

4. Mary Richmond, "The Work of a District Agent," in Charity Organization Society of Baltimore, *Annual Report, 1899* (Baltimore, 1899), 21.

5. W. Andrew Achenbaum, *Old Age in the New Land: The American Experience since 1790* (Baltimore, Md.: Johns Hopkins University Press, 1978), 89–90.

6. Margaret Mead and Ken Heyman, *Family* (New York: Macmillan, 1965), 78; Sarah M. Nelson, "Widowhood and Autonomy in the Native-American Southwest," in *On Their Own: Widows and Widowhood in the American Southwest, 1848–1939,* ed. Arlene Scadron, 22–41 (Urbana: University of Illinois Press, 1988); Theda Perdue, *Cherokee Women: Gender and Culture Change, 1700–1835* (Lincoln: University of Nebraska Press, 1998), 139–41. Although illegal, widow-burning still occurs; see Joan Smith, "Murdered by Tradition," *London Independent,* 11 August 2002, p. 21.

7. Helena Znaniecki Lopata, *Widowhood in an American City* (Cambridge, Mass.: Schenkman, 1973); Alexander Keyssar, "Widowhood in Eighteenth-Century Massachusetts: A Problem in the History of the Family," *Perspectives in American History* 8 (1974): 83–119; Linda Gordon, "Putting Children First: Women, Maternalism, and Welfare in the Early Twentieth Century," in *U.S. History as Women's History: New Feminist Essays,* ed. Linda K. Kerber, Alice Kessler-Harris, and Kathryn Kish Sklar, 63–86 (Chapel Hill: University of North Carolina Press, 1995); Theda Skocpol, *Protecting Soldiers and Mothers: The Political Origins of Social Policy in the United States* (Cambridge, Mass.: Belknap, 1992); Robyn Muncy, *Creating a Female Dominion in American Reform, 1890–1935* (New York: Oxford

University Press, 1991); Kay Walters Ofman, "A Rural View of Mothers' Pensions: The Allegan County, Michigan, Mothers' Pension Program, 1913–1928," *Social Service Review* 70 (1996): 98–119.

8. Lisa Wilson Waciega, "A 'Man of Business': The Widow of Means in Southeastern Pennsylvania, 1750–1850," *William and Mary Quarterly,* 3d ser., 44 (1987): 40–64; Claudia Goldin, "The Economic Status of Women in the Early Republic: Quantitative Evidence," *Journal of Interdisciplinary History* 16 (1986): 375–404; Anne M. Boylan, "Timid Girls, Venerable Widows, and Dignified Matrons: Life Cycle Patterns among Organized Women in New York and Boston, 1797–1840," *American Quarterly* 38 (1986): 779–97.

9. Arlene Scadron, ed., *On Their Own: Widows and Widowhood in the American Southwest, 1848–1939* (Urbana: University of Illinois Press, 1988).

10. Julie A. Matthaei reflects on husbandless women in the colonial economy and husbandless homemakers in the nineteenth century in *An Economic History of Women in America: Women's Work, the Sexual Division of Labor, and the Development of Capitalism* (New York: Schocken Books, 1982), 51–73, 136–39. Hasia Diner examines the high mortality rates among Irish men and the consequences for widows' employment in *Erin's Daughters in America: Irish Immigrant Women in the Nineteenth Century* (Baltimore, Md.: Johns Hopkins University Press, 1983). Beyond that, many monographs make scattered references to widows, but few consider them sytematically.

11. Linda Gordon, *Pitied but Not Entitled: Single Mothers and the History of Welfare* (New York: Free Press, 1994), 15–35; Joanne L. Goodwin, *Gender and the Politics of Welfare Reform* (Chicago: University of Chicago Press, 1997), 21–55.

12. For information on inheritance patterns, see Carole Shammas, Marylynn Salmon, and Michel Dahlin, *Inheritance in America from Colonial Times to the Present* (New Brunswick, N.J.: Rutgers University Press, 1987); Norma Basch, *In the Eyes of the Law: Women, Marriage, and Property in the Nineteenth Century* (Ithaca, N.Y.: Cornell University Press, 1982); Marylynn Salmon, *Women and the Law of Property in Early America* (Chapel Hill: University of North Carolina Press, 1986); Lisa Wilson, *Life after Death: Widows in Pennsylvania, 1750–1850* (Philadelphia: Temple University Press, 1992), 39–42. For patterns of support for widows, see Terri L. Premo, *Winter Friends: Women Growing Old in the New Republic, 1785–1835* (Urbana: University of Illinois Press, 1990).

13. U.S. Bureau of the Census, *Special Reports: Benevolent Institutions, 1904* (Washington, D.C.: GPO, 1905), 11. Half the 4,207 benevolent institutions in the United States were founded between 1890 and 1903.

14. Sophonisba Preston Breckinridge, "Neglected Widowhood in the Juvenile Court," *American Journal of Sociology* 16 (1910): 54.

15. Vivien Hart, in *Bound by Our Constitution: Women, Workers, and the Minimum Wage* (Princeton, N.J.: Princeton University Press, 1994), touches on these themes when she contrasts social policy in Great Britain to that in the United States.

16. Ann Shola Orloff, "Gender in Early U.S. Social Policy," *Journal of Policy History* 3 (1991): 249–81.

17. Roy Lubove, *The Struggle for Social Security, 1900–1935* (Cambridge, Mass.: Harvard University Press, 1968). These comments are based on a heated interchange between Lubove and myself at a conference to mark the retirement of Samuel P. Hays at the University of Pittsburgh, May 1991.

18. Mark H. Leff, "The Consensus for Reform: The Mothers'-Pension Movement in the Progressive Era," *Social Service Review* 47 (1973): 397, 408.

19. Andrew Billingsley and Jeanne M. Giovannoni, *Children of the Storm: Black Children and American Child Welfare* (New York: Harcourt Brace Jovanovich, 1972), 72.

20. Jill Quadagno, "Theories of the Welfare State," *Annual Review of Sociology* 13 (1987): 109.

21. Ann Shola Orloff and Theda Skocpol, "Why Not Equal Protection? Explaining the Politics of Public Social Spending in Britain, 1900–1911, and the United States, 1880s–1920," *American Sociological Review* 49 (1984): 728; Theda Skocpol and John Ikenberry, "The Political Formation of the American Welfare State in Historical and Comparative Perspective," *Comparative Social Research* 6 (1983): 87–148.

22. Some states and localities provided retirement pensions for individuals in certain occupations (typically firefighters, police officers, teachers, and other government employees). A few also gave outdoor relief to the impoverished elderly on a systematic basis (William Graebner, *A History of Retirement: The Meaning of an American Institution, 1885–1978* [New Haven, Conn.: Yale University Press, 1980], 15, 163).

23. See Lubove, *Struggle,* chap. 6.

24. W. Andrew Achenbaum, *Social Security: Visions and Revisions* (Cambridge: Cambridge University Press, 1986); Brian Gratton, *Urban Elders: Family Work and Welfare among Boston's Aged, 1890–1950* (Philadelphia: Temple University Press, 1986); Carole Haber, *Beyond Sixty-Five: The Dilemma of Old Age in America's Past* (Cambridge: Cambridge University Press, 1983).

25. Jill Quadagno, *The Transformation of Old Age Security: Class and Politics in the American Welfare State* (Chicago: University of Chicago Press, 1988); Michel Dahlin, "From Poorhouse to Pension: The Changing View of Old Age in America, 1890–1929" (Ph.D. diss., Stanford University, 1983); Daniel Scott Smith, "Accounting for Change in the Families of the Elderly in the United States, 1900–Present," in *Old Age in a Bureaucratic Society,* ed. David van Tassell, 87–109 (Westport, Conn.: Greenwood, 1986); Howard P. Chudacoff and Tamara K. Hareven, "Family Transitions into Old Age," in *Transitions: The Family and the Life Course in Historical Perspective,* ed. Tamara K. Hareven, 217–43 (New York: Academic, 1978); Carole Haber and Brian Gratton, *Old Age and the Search for Security: An American Social History* (Bloomington: Indiana University Press, 1994).

26. Skocpol, *Protecting,* 41. See also Ann Shola Orloff, "The Political Origins of America's Belated Welfare State," in *The Politics of Social Policy in the United States,* ed. Margaret Weir, Ann Shola Orloff, and Theda Skocpol, 37–80 (Princeton, N.J.: Princeton University Press, 1988); Theda Skocpol, "Gendered Identities in Early U.S. Social Policy," *Contention* 2 (1993): 167.

27. Skocpol, *Protecting,* 2.

28. Linda Gordon, "Gender, State, and Society: A Debate with Theda Skocpol," *Contention* 2 (1993): 139–56.

29. Skocpol, *Protecting,* 459; James D. Anderson, *The Education of Blacks in the South, 1860–1935* (Chapel Hill: University of North Carolina Press, 1988).

30. Charles Noble, *Welfare as We Knew It: A Political History of the American Welfare State* (Oxford: Oxford University Press, 1997), 3.

31. Mimi Abramovitz, *Regulating the Lives of Women* (Boston: South End, 1989); Linda

Gordon, "Black and White Visions of Welfare: Women's Welfare Activism, 1890–1945," *Journal of American History* 78 (1991): 559–90; Sonya Michel, "The Limits of Maternalism: Policies toward American Wage Earning Mothers during the Progressive Era," in *Mothers of a New World: Maternalist Politics and the Origins of Welfare States,* ed. Seth Koven and Sonya Michel, 277–320 (London: Routledge, 1993); Kathryn Kish Sklar, "The Historical Foundations of Women's Power in the Creation of the American Welfare State, 1830–1930," in *Mothers,* ed. Koven and Michel, 43–93; Linda Gordon, ed., *Women, the State, and Welfare* (Madison: University of Wisconsin Press, 1990).

32. Peggy Pascoe, *Relations of Rescue: The Search for Female Moral Authority in the American West, 1874–1939* (Oxford: Oxford University Press, 1990).

33. Molly Ladd-Taylor, *Mother-Work: Women, Child Welfare, and the State, 1890–1930* (Urbana: University of Illinois Press, 1994), 138; Muncy, *Creating a Female Dominion;* Linda Gordon, *Pitied,* 19–22.

34. Eileen Boris, "When Work Is Slavery: Disdained Mothers and Despised Others: The Politics and Impact of Welfare Reform," *Social Justice* 25 (Spring 1998): 28–46; Robert C. Lieberman, *Shifting the Color Line: Race and the American Welfare State* (Cambridge, Mass.: Harvard University Press, 1998); Rickie Solinger, *Wake Up Little Susie: Single Pregnancy and Race before Roe v. Wade* (London: Routledge, 2000); Lisa Levenstein, "From Innocent Children to Unwanted Migrants and Unwed Moms: Two Chapters in the Public Discourse on Welfare in the United States, 1960–1961," *Journal of Women's History* 11 (2000): 10–33; Jennifer Mittelstadt, "The Dilemmas of the Liberal Welfare State, 1945–1964: Gender, Race and Aid to Dependent Children" (Ph.D. diss., University of Michigan, 2000).

35. Lieberman, *Shifting,* 6.

36. On the importance of marriage, see Nancy Cott, *Public Vows: A History of Marriage and the Nation* (Cambridge, Mass.: Harvard University Press, 2000). John Fabian Witt describes the relationship between workmen's compensation and the family wage ideology in *The Accidental Republic: Crippled Workingmen, Destitute Widows, and the Remaking of American Law* (Cambridge, Mass.: Harvard University Press, 2004), 126–51.

37. Linda Gordon, "Social Insurance and Public Assistance: The Influence of Gender in Welfare Thought in the United States, 1890–1935," *American Historical Review* 97 (1992): 19–54.

38. Homer Folks, qtd. in Winifred Bell, *Aid to Dependent Children* (New York: Columbia University Press, 1965), 7.

39. Miriam Cohen and Michael Hanagan, "The Politics of Gender and the Making of the Welfare State, 1900–1940: A Comparative Perspective," *Journal of Social History* 24 (1991): 470.

40. Goodwin, *Gender,* 11.

41. Barbara J. Nelson, "The Gender, Race, and Class Origins of Early Welfare Policy and the Welfare State: A Comparison of Workmen's Compensation and Mothers' Aid," in *Women, Politics, and Change,* ed. Louise A. Tilly and Patricia Gurin, 413–35 (New York: Russell Sage Foundation, 1992).

42. Noble, *Welfare,* 60–62 (in chapter 6 Noble explores the backlash against universal benefits, paying rather more attention to race than gender). Social Security retirement benefits, while linked to job category and sex, did not vary by location (see Barbara J. Nelson, "The Origins of the Two-Channel Welfare State: Workmen's Compensation and Mothers' Aid," in *Women,* ed. Gordon, 123–51).

43. Sharon Perlman Krefetz, *Welfare Policy Making and City Politics* (New York: Praeger, 1976), 8. Christopher Howard offers an overview on this topic in "The American Welfare State, or States?" *Political Research Quarterly* 52 (1999): 421–42.

44. Walter Trattner, *Crusade for the Children: A History of the National Child Labor Committee and Child Labor Reform in America* (Chicago: Quadrangle Books, 1970), 150; Frances Fox Piven and Richard Cloward, *Regulating the Poor: The Functions of Public Welfare* (New York: Vintage, 1971), 113–17.

45. Suzanne Mettler, *Dividing Citizens: Gender and Federalism in New Deal Public Policy* (Ithaca, N.Y.: Cornell University Press, 1998), 6; see also Gail Bederman, *Manliness and Civilization: A Cultural History of Gender and Race in the United States, 1880–1917* (Chicago: University of Chicago Press, 1995).

46. Gordon, "Social Insurance," 19–54; Robert V. Wells, *Revolutions in Americans' Lives: A Demographic Perspective on the History of Americans, Their Families, and Their Society* (Westport, Conn.: Greenwood, 1982), 151; Tamara K. Hareven, *Family Time and Industrial Time: The Relationship between the Family and Work in a New England Industrial Town* (Cambridge: Cambridge University Press, 1982), 190. See also Elizabeth Fox-Genovese, *Feminism without Illusions: A Critique of Individualism* (Chapel Hill: University of North Carolina Press, 1991).

47. U.S. Bureau of the Census, *Fourteenth Census,* vol. 4, *Population 1920: Occupations* (Washington, D.C.: GPO, 1923), 478.

48. Henry W. Thurston, *The Dependent Child: A Story of Changing Aims and Methods in the Care of Dependent Children* (New York: Columbia University Press, 1930), 121; Marilyn Irvin Holt, *The Orphan Trains: Placing Out in America* (Lincoln: University of Nebraska Press, 1992), 5; Linda Gordon, *The Great Arizona Orphan Abduction* (Cambridge, Mass.: Harvard University Press, 1999), 11. Child placing peaked after the Civil War but continued through the 1920s.

49. Patrick M. Horan and Peggy G. Hargis, "Children's Work and Schooling in the Late Nineteenth-Century Family Economy," *American Sociological Review* 56 (1991): 583–96; Harold Woolston, "Social Education in the Public Schools," *Charities and the Commons* 16 (1 Sept. 1906): 571 (quotation).

50. See Judith Sealander, *The Failed Century of the Child: Governing America's Young in the Twentieth Century* (Cambridge: Cambridge University Press, 2003), 101–7. The moniker is taken from Ellen Key's book *The Century of the Child* (London, 1900).

51. Pamela Barnhouse Walters and Philip J. O'Connell, "The Family Economy, Work, and Educational Participation in the United States, 1890–1940," *American Journal of Sociology* 93 (1988): 1116–52; S. J. Kleinberg, *The Shadow of the Mills: Working-Class Families in Pittsburgh, 1870–1907* (Pittsburgh, Pa.: University of Pittsburgh Press, 1989), 125; Daniel Scott Smith, "A Higher Quality of Life for Whom? Mouths to Feed and Clothes to Wear in the Families of Late Nineteenth-Century American Workers," *Journal of Family History* 19 (1994): 1–33; Andrea G. Hunter, "The Other Breadwinners: The Mobilization of Secondary Wage Earners in Early Twentieth-Century Black Families," *History of the Family* 6 (2001): 69–94.

52. Diane Kirkby, *Alice Henry: The Power of Pen and Voice* (Cambridge: Cambridge University Press, 1991), 23; Tera W. Hunter, *To 'Joy My Freedom: Southern Black Women's Lives and Labors after the Civil War* (Cambridge: Mass.: Harvard University Press, 1997), 50–51; Horan and Hargis, "Children's Work," 583–96.

53. Alice Kessler-Harris, *In Pursuit of Equity: Women, Men, and the Quest for Economic Citizenship in Twentieth-Century America* (New York: Oxford University Press, 2001), 5–6.

54. Mary E. Richmond and Fred S. Hall, *A Study of Nine Hundred and Eighty-Five Widows Known to Certain Charity Organization Societies in 1910* (New York: Russell Sage Foundation, 1913), 21.

55. See ibid.

56. Sonya Michel explores the tensions between these two groups' best interests in *Children's Interests, Mothers' Rights* (New Haven, Conn.: Yale University Press, 1999).

57. See especially the Supreme Court decision in *Muller v. Oregon*, 1908. See also Eileen Boris, *Home to Work: Motherhood and the Politics of Industrial Homework in the United States* (Cambridge: Cambridge University Press, 1994), 84–85; Helen Glenn Tyson, *The Mothers' Assistance Fund in Pennsylvania: A Brief Review of the Work of the Mothers' Assistance Fund with a Discussion of the Immediate Needs in This Field of Child Care* (Philadelphia: Public Charities Association of Pennsylvania, 1926), 4.

58. New York State Commission on Relief for Widowed Mothers, *Report* (Albany: J.B. Lyon, 1914), 7.

59. All statistical statements, unless otherwise noted, derive from an approximately 500-household sample for each city manually coded from the 1880, 1900, and 1920 U.S. censuses.

60. Children's Bureau, *Mothers' Aid, 1931*, pub. no. 220 (Washington, D.C.: GPO, 1933), 19. Discussions of the gendered political climate and pensions include Paula Baker, "The Domestication of Politics: Women and American Political Society, 1780–1920," *American Historical Review* 89 (1984): 620–49; Alisa Klaus, *Every Child a Lion: The Origins of Maternal and Infant Health Policy in the United States and France, 1890–1920* (Ithaca, N.Y.: Cornell University Press, 1993); Joanne L. Goodwin, "An American Experiment in Paid Motherhood: The Implementation of Mothers' Pensions in Early Twentieth Century Chicago," *Gender and History* 4 (1992): 323–41; Ann Vandepol, "Dependent Children, Child Custody, and the Mothers' Pensions," *Social Problems* 23 (1982): 221–35; Mark Leff, "Consensus for Reform"; Bell, *Aid to Dependent Children.*

61. Viviana Zelizer, *Pricing the Priceless Child: The Changing Social Value of Children* (New York: Basic Books, 1985); LeRoy Ashby, *Saving the Waifs: Reformers and Dependent Children, 1890–1917* (Philadelphia: Temple University Press, 1984); Susan Tiffin, *In Whose Best Interest? Child Welfare Reform in the Progressive Era* (Westport, Conn.: Greenwood, 1982). All these works focus on emerging attitudes toward children.

62. Skocpol, *Protecting*, 30–33; Sophonisba P. Breckinridge, *Family Welfare Work in a Metropolitan Community: Selected Case Work Records* (Chicago: University of Chicago Press, 1924), sect. 4; Grace Abbott, *From Relief to Social Security: The Development of the New Public Welfare Services and Their Administration* (New York: Russell and Russell, 1966); Goodwin, *Gender*, 4.

63. Patricia Huckle, *Tish Sommers, Activist, and the Founding of the Older Women's League* (Knoxville: University of Tennessee Press, 1991), 171–98.

64. *The Eagle Magazine* (Aug. 1925, p. 16) depicted an elderly woman leaning on a walking stick and carrying the small bundle of her worldly goods as she trudged uphill to a dilapidated building labeled "Poor House."

65. Goodwin, *Gender,* 10. See also Leslie Margolin, *Under the Cover of Kindness: The Invention of Social Work* (Charlottesville: University of Virginia Press, 1997), 101.

66. John Hope Franklin, "Public Welfare in the South during the Reconstruction Era," *Social Service Review* 44 (1970): 379–92.

67. Gwendolyn Mink, "The Lady and the Tramp: Gender, Race, and the Origins of the American Welfare State," in *Women,* ed. Gordon, 92–122; Theda Skocpol, Marjorie Abend-Wein, Christopher Howard, and Susan Goodrich Lehmann, "Women's Associations and the Enactment of Mothers' Pensions in the United States," *American Political Science Review* 87 (1993): 686–97. See also Eileen Boris and Angelique Janssens, "Complicating Categories: An Introduction," in *Complicating Categories: Gender, Class, Race and Ethnicity,* ed. Boris and Janssens, 1–51 (Cambridge: Cambridge University Press, 1999). Few eastern U.S. cities had more than a handful of Native American, Chinese, or Japanese residents at this time.

68. Steven Ruggles, "The Transformation of American Family Structure," *American Historical Review* 99 (1994): 107.

69. Linda Gordon and Sarah McLanahan, "Single Parenthood in 1900," *Journal of Family History* 16 (1991): 97–116. For information on the informal exchange network within the black community, see Carol B. Stack, *All Our Kin* (New York: Harper and Row 1979).

70. Gareth Davies and Martha Derthick argue that the difficulty in collecting contributions explains the exclusion of these groups ("Race and Social Welfare Policy: The Social Security Act of 1935," *Political Science Quarterly* 112 [1997]: 217–35).

71. Mary Elizabeth Poole, "Securing Race and Ensuring Dependence: The Social Security Act of 1935" (Ph.D. diss., Rutgers University, 2000); Alice Kessler-Harris, "Designing Women and Old Fools: The Construction of the Social Security Amendments of 1939," in *U.S. History,* ed. Kerber, Kessler-Harris, and Sklar, 87–106.

72. Blanche Coll, *Safety Net: Welfare and Social Security, 1929–1979* (New Brunswick, N.J.: Rutgers University Press, 1995), 104, 117.

73. This is especially the case for the African American community.

74. Dana Frank, "White Working-Class Women and the Race Question," *International Labor and Working Class History* 54 (1998): 80–102; Eileen Boris, "'You Wouldn't Want One of 'Em Dancing with Your Wife': Racialized Bodies on the Job in WWII," *American Quarterly* 50 (Mar. 1998): 77–108.

75. U.S. Census Office, *Twelfth Census,* vol. 2, *Population, Part 2* (Washington, D.C.: GPO, 1902), lxxxv-vi, 311, 320, 338 (data are for persons twenty years of age and over); ibid., vol. 3, *Manufactures* (Washington, D.C.: GPO, 1902), pt. 2, pp. 1040–94; *The Charities Record* 4, no. 4 (Feb. 1900): 42.

76. Ken Champlin, "'Up the Flint': Neighborhood and Community in Fall River," *Spinner* 3 (1984): 153.

77. U.S. Census Office, *Twelfth Census,* vol. 2, *Population, Part 2,* 561; U.S. Census Office, *Report on the Social Statistics of Cities* (Washington, D.C.: GPO, 1886), pt. 1, p. 190.

78. U.S. Census Office, *Twelfth Census,* vol. 3, *Manufactures,* pt. 2, pp. 1040–94; Philip T. Silvia, *Victorian Vistas: Fall River, 1901–1911* (Fall River, Mass.: R. E. Smith, 1992), 1–30.

79. John Cumbler, "The Politics of Charity: Gender and Class in Late Nineteenth Century Charity Policy," *Journal of Social History* 14 (1980): 99–111; Associated Charities of

Fall River, District Conference 1, casework notes, 1888–90 (the casework records contain repeated calls to cut the city's payments to individual widows).

80. U.S. Census Office, *Twelfth Census,* vol. 2, *Population, Part 2,* 583.

81. Thomas Bell, *Out of This Furnace* (Pittsburgh: University of Pittsburgh Press, 1976 [1941]).

82. Kleinberg, *Shadow of the Mills,* 27–39.

83. U.S. Census Office, *Social Statistics,* pt. 2, p. 10. On Baltimore's status as a southern city, see Blaine A. Brownell and David R. Goldfield, "Southern Urban History," in *The City in Southern History: The Growth of Urban Civilization in the South,* ed. Brownell and Goldfield, 5–23 (Port Washington, N.Y.: Kennikat, 1977).

84. Lewis Hine, photographs at Central Millwork Company and J. S. Farrand Packing Company, repr. in Mame Warren and Marion E. Warren, *Maryland: Time Exposures, 1840–1940* (Baltimore, Md.: Johns Hopkins University Press, 1984), 143–45; Charles Hirschfeld, *Baltimore, 1870–1900: Studies in Social History* (Baltimore, Md.: Johns Hopkins University Press, 1941), 107.

85. Roderick N. Ryon, "'Human Creatures' Lives': Baltimore Women and Work in Factories, 1880–1917," *Maryland Historical Magazine* 83 (1988): 346–64; Patricia A. MacDonald, "Baltimore Women, 1870–1900" (Ph.D. diss., University of Maryland, 1976), 36.

86. Cynthia Neverdon-Morton, *Afro-American Women of the South and the Advancement of the Race, 1895–1925* (Knoxville: University of Tennessee Press, 1989), 176–77; Diane Batts Morrow, *Persons of Color and Religious at the Same Time: The Oblate Sisters of Providence, 1828–1860* (Chapel Hill: University of North Carolina Press, 2002).

87. See, e.g., Ofman, "Rural View."

88. Timothy A. Hacsi, *Second Home: Orphan Asylums and Poor Families in America* (Cambridge, Mass.: Harvard University Press, 1998), 49–51; Matthew A. Crenson, *Building the Invisible Orphanage: A Prehistory of the American Welfare System* (Cambridge, Mass.: Harvard University Press, 1998), 261–63.

89. Claudia Goldin documents a wide range of economic activities for widows in the early national era in *Understanding the Gender Gap* (Oxford: Oxford University Press, 1990), 48–49.

90. Lee J. Alston and Joseph P. Ferrie attempt to quantify the relationship between economic change and social and political structures but neglect African American women's employment and migration patterns; see their book *Southern Paternalism and the American Welfare State: Economics, Politics, and Institutions in the South, 1865–1965* (Cambridge: Cambridge University Press, 1999).

91. S. J. Kleinberg, "Widows' Welfare in the Great Depression," in *The Roosevelt Years,* ed. Robert A. Garson and Stuart S. Kidd, 72–90 (Edinburgh: Edinburgh University Press, 1999).

92. Axel Schafer, *American Progressives and German Social Reform, 1875–1920* (Stuttgart: Franz Steiner Verlag, 2000), 25.

Chapter 1: Widows

1. Manuscript census, Fall River, 1880. All names are fictional.

2. Manuscript census, Pittsburgh, 1920.

3. Susan Strasser, *Never Done: A History of American Housework* (New York: Pantheon, 1982); Glenna Matthews, *Just a Housewife: The Rise and Fall of Domesticity in America* (New York: Oxford University Press, 1987); Ruth Schwartz Cowan, *More Work for Mother: The Ironies of Household Technology from the Open Hearth to the Microwave* (New York: Basic Books, 1983) (these three works document the decreased labor entailed in housework); S. J. Kleinberg, "Technology and Women's Work: The Lives of Working Class Women, Pittsburgh, 1870–1900," *Labor History* 17 (1976): 58–72, focuses specifically on household labor in poorer families.

4. Manuscript census, Baltimore, 1920.

5. Manuscript census, Pittsburgh, 1900.

6. Alliance of Charitable and Social Agencies of Baltimore, *Poverty in Baltimore, 1916–1917* (Baltimore: Alliance of Charitable and Social Agencies, 1917), 32.

7. Samuel P. Hays viewed the Progressive Era as a response to industrialism; see his *Response to Industrialism* (Chicago: University of Chicago Press, 1957). I extend his analysis specifically to encompass families and social welfare.

8. Joan M. Jensen, *Loosening the Bonds: Mid-Atlantic Farm Women, 1750–1850* (New Haven, Conn.: Yale University Press, 1986), documents rural women's money earning efforts and their displacement by larger-scale enterprises. Claudia Goldin concludes that the children of different ethnic groups contributed from 28 to 46 percent of total family income in 1880, indicating the extent to which urban families relied on child labor; see Goldin, "Family Strategies and the Family Economy in the Late Nineteenth Century: The Role of Secondary Workers" in *Philadelphia,* ed. Theodore Hershberg, 277–310 (New York: Oxford University Press, 1981), 284.

9. Helena Znaniecki Lopata, *Widowhood in an American City* (Cambridge, Mass.: Schenkman, 1973), 8.

10. Elizabeth Rose, *A Mother's Job: The History of Day Care, 1890–1960* (Oxford: Oxford University Press, 1999), 71.

11. Lemuel Shattuck, *Report of the Committee of the City Council Appointed to Obtain the Census of Boston for the Year 1845* (Boston: John H. Eastvern, 1846), 130; U.S. Bureau of the Census, *Historical Statistics of the United States, Colonial Times to 1970* (Washington, D.C.: GPO, 1975), pt. 1, pp. 20–21. Widowers were fractionally more likely to reside in the countryside.

12. Joanne L. Goodwin describes this process in Chicago in *Gender and the Politics of Welfare Reform* (Chicago: University of Chicago Press, 1997), 64.

13. U.S. Bureau of the Census, *Fourteenth Census,* vol. 2, *Population 1920: General Report and Analytical Tables* (Washington, D.C.: GPO, 1923), 387; U.S. Bureau of the Census, *Fifteenth Census: Population* (Washington, D.C.: GPO, 1933), vol. 3, *Reports by States,* pt. 1, *Alabama–Missouri* (Washington, D.C.: GPO, 1932), 19; Clara Jackson, qtd. in Clyde Vernon Kiser, *Sea Island to City: A Study of St. Helena Islanders in Harlem and Other Urban Centers,* with a new preface by Joseph S. Himes (New York: Atheneum, 1969 [1932]), 119.

14. Manuscript census, Pittsburgh, 1900. Some African American women succeeded against the odds (see James Weldon Johnson, *Black Manhattan,* with a new preface by Allan H. Spear [New York: Atheneum, 1972 (1930)], 154). Maggie Lena Walker, the daughter of a widowed laundress, managed to complete a Normal School education, became a teacher, and subsequently became the first woman bank president in the United States

(see Gertrude W. Marlowe, "Maggie Lena Walker," in *Black Women in American History,* ed. Darlene Clark Hine, 1214–19 [New York: Carlton, 1990]).

15. Jacqueline Jones, *Labor of Love, Labor of Sorrow: Black Women, Work, and the Family from Slavery to the Present* (New York: Basic Books, 1985), 92.

16. Kiser, *Sea Island,* 119 (Hannah Pinkney's circumstances), 131 (quotation from "Lilly" ["Case No. 16"]).

17. Joan Jensen, *With These Hands: Women Working on the Land* (Old Westbury, N.Y.: Feminist Press, 1981), 122.

18. Eileen Boris, "The Power of Motherhood: Black and White Activist Women Redefine the 'Political,'" in *Mothers of a New World: Maternalist Politics and the Origins of Welfare States,* ed. Seth Koven and Sonya Michel, 213–45 (London: Routledge, 1993), 215 (Boris observes that motherhood frequently meant white mothers only in this era); Dorothy Salem, *To Better Our World: Black Women in Organized Reform 1890–1920* (New York: Carlson, 1990), 7–8.

19. Elizabeth H. Pleck, *Black Migration and Poverty: Boston, 1865–1900* (New York: Academic, 1979), 169–71; Linda Gordon and Sarah McLanahan, "Single Parenthood in 1900," *Journal of Family History* 16 (1991): 106 (one consequence of the higher levels of illegitimacy would be a greater dependence on the maternal family for assistance in supporting the child). Carroll D. Wright, *A Report on Marriage and Divorce in the United States, 1867 to 1886* (Washington, D.C.: GPO, 1889), contains one of the first systematic studies of marriage and divorce. Even if some African American women lied to census takers about being widows, as W. E. B. Du Bois claimed in *Philadelphia Negro* (New York: Schocken, 1967 [1899], 68), they were still women bringing up children on their own.

20. Robert V. Wells, *Revolutions in American Lives: A Demographic Perspective on the History of Americans, Their Families, and Their Society* (Westport, Conn.: Greenwood, 1982), 126–27; manuscript census, Pittsburgh and Baltimore, 1880, 1900, 1920.

21. Alexander Keyssar, "Widowhood in Eighteenth-Century Massachusetts: A Problem in the History of the Family," *Perspectives in American History* 8 (1974): 87–88; Wells, *Revolutions,* 43; Jack Ericson Eblen, "New Estimates of the Vital Rates of the United States Black Population during the Nineteenth Century," *Demography* 11, no. 2 (May 1974): 301–19; Daniel Scott Smith, Michel Dahlin, and Mark Friedberger, "The Family Structure of the Older Black Population in the American South in 1880 and 1900," *Sociology and Social Research* 63 (1979): 552–53; Peter R. Uhlenberg, "A Study of Cohort Life Cycles: Cohorts of Native Born Massachusetts Women, 1830–1920," in *Studies in American Historical Demography,* ed. Maris A. Vinovskis, 507–21 (New York: Academic, 1979).

22. U.S. Bureau of the Census, *Historical Statistics,* pt. 1, p. 49; Steven Ruggles et al., *Integrated Public Use Microdata Series: Version 3.0* (Minneapolis: Minnesota Population Center, 2004), census microdata set, 1880 and 1920 (I am grateful to David Ryden for undertaking these calculations).

23. Carole Haber and Brian Gratton discuss the decline of the extended family in *Old Age and the Search for Security: An American Social History* (Bloomington: Indiana University Press, 1994), 36–42. Cheryl Elman and Peter Uhlenberg found that employed older women or those with economic assets were less likely to live with a child ("Early-Twentieth Century Coresidence: Elderly U.S. Women and Their Children," *Population Studies* 49 [1998]: 509). Thus the slight rise in employment of older widows seem to have resulted in a decline in coresidence. Frances E. Kobrin has examined extension, household

size, and changing composition; see her article "The Fall in Household Size and the Rise of the Primary Individual in the United States," *Demography* 13 (1976): 127–38.

24. Manuscript census, Fall River, 1880.

25. Manuscript census, Baltimore and Pittsburgh, 1920. For discussions of life-course transitions, see also Howard Chudacoff and Tamara K. Hareven, "From the Empty Nest to Family Dissolution: Life Course Transitions into Older Age," *Journal of Family History* 4 (1979): 69–83; Glen H. Elder Jr., "Family History and the Life Course," in *Transitions: The Family and the Life Course in Historical Perspective,* ed. Tamara K. Hareven, 17–64 (New York: Academic, 1978); Maris A. Vinovskis, "From Household Size to the Life Course: Some Observations on Recent Trends in Family History," *American Behavioral Scientist* 21 (1977): 263–87.

26. There were a few private facilities open to African American women in Baltimore, such as the Shelter for Aged and Infirm Colored Persons, which opened in the 1880s, but these accommodated only a handful of the needy population.

27. Manuscript census, Baltimore, Pittsburgh, and Fall River, 1880 and 1920; Sandra M. O'Donnell, "The Care of Dependent African-American Children in Chicago: The Struggle between Black Self-Help and Professionalism," *Journal of Social History* 7 (1994): 763–76.

28. Manuscript census, Baltimore, Pittsburgh, and Fall River, 1880, 1900, 1920; Paul C. Glick, *American Families* (New York, 1957), 45; White House Conference on Child Health and Protection, *The Adolescent in the Family,* ed. Ernest Burgess (New York: Appleton-Century, 1934), 324.

29. Hermione Rondeau to Children's Bureau, 21 March 1918, Children's Bureau Papers, National Archives, Record Group 102, box 209, folder 7310.

30. Linda Gordon, *Pitied but Not Entitled: Single Mothers and the History of Welfare* (New York: Free Press, 1994), 19.

31. Children's homes housed a disproportionate number of widowers' children (St. Vincent's Home, Fall River, Boys' Register, 1886–1920; Nurith Zmora, *Orphanages Reconsidered: Child Care Institutions in Progressive Era Baltimore* [Phildelphia: Temple University Press, 1994], 50–57).

32. S. J. Kleinberg, *Shadow of the Mills: Working-Class Families in Pittsburgh, 1870–1907* (Pittsburgh, Pa.: University of Pittsburgh Press, 1989), 202–7; Susan Grigg, "Toward a Theory of Remarriage: A Case Study of Newburyport at the Beginning of the Nineteenth Century," *Journal of Interdisciplinary History* 8 (Autumn 1977): 183–220 (Grigg both reviewed the literature on remarriage and analyzed the data for Newburyport); Geraldine Mineau, "Utah Widowhood: A Demographic Profile," in *On Their Own: Widows and Widowhood in the American Southwest, 1848–1939,* ed. Arlene Scadron, 140–65 (Urbana: University of Illinois Press, 1988), 151–53. The U.S. Bureau of the Census stated simply that "men remarry more often than women" (*Statistics of Women at Work: Based on Unpublished Information Derived from the Schedules of the Twelfth Census: 1900* [Washington, D.C.: GPO, 1907], 27).

33. Stewart Tolnay, "The Great Migration and Changes to the Northern Black Family, 1940–1990," *Social Forces* 75 (1997): 1213–37; Jo Ann Manfra and Robert Dykstra, "Serial Marriage and the Origins of the Black Stepfamily: The Rowantry Evidence," *Journal of American History* 72 (1985): 18–44.

34. Cheryl Elman and Andrew S. London, "Sociohistorical and Demographic Perspec-

tives on U.S. Remarriage in 1910," *Social Science History* 26 (2002): 199–241. Lopata (*Widowhood,* 81) found remarriage more prevalent among blacks than whites in the 1960s.

35. Carole Haber, *Beyond Sixty-Five: The Dilemma of Old Age in America's Past* (Cambridge: Cambridge University Press, 1983), 86.

36. Associated Charities of Fall River, *Tenth Annual Report, 1898* (Fall River, 1898), 5.

37. Mrs. Frances White to Mayor William F. Browning, 1931, in Browning papers, Baltimore City Archives (Baltimore, Md.), Record Group 9, box 186. Mrs. White was not eligible for city aid because the minimum age for aid had been set at seventy.

38. Abraham Epstein, *The Challenge of the Aged* (New York: Vanguard, 1928), 41–42.

39. Manuscript census, Baltimore, Pittsburgh, and Fall River, 1900.

40. Steven Ruggles, "The Origins of African-American Family Structure," *American Sociological Review* 59 (1994): 139.

41. Marvin B. Sussman, "The Help Pattern in the Middle Class Family, *American Sociological Review* 18 (1953): 22–28; Eugene Litwak, "Geographical Mobility and Extended Family Cohesion," in *Social Structure and the Family: Generational Relations,* ed. Ethel Shanas and Gordon R. Streib, 290–325 (Englewood Cliffs, N.J.: Prentice Hall, 1963).

42. S. J. Kleinberg, "Gendered Space: Housing, Privacy, and Domesticity in the Nineteenth Century United States," in *Reading the Nineteenth Century Domestic Space,* ed. Janet Floyd and Inge Bryden, 142–61 (Manchester: Manchester University Press, 1998) (in this work I analyze class determination in the use of domestic space); David Katzman, *Seven Days a Week: Women and Domestic Service in Industrializing America* (Oxford: Oxford University Press, 1978), 262; Phyllis Palmer, *Domesticity and Dirt* (Philadelphia: Temple University Press, 1989); John Modell and Tamara K. Hareven, "Urbanization and the Malleable Household: An Examination of Boarding and Lodging in American Families," *Journal of Marriage and the Family* 35 (1973): 467–79.

43. Manuscript census, Pittsburgh, Fall River, and Baltimore, 1900 and 1920; U.S. Bureau of the Census, *Women at Work, 1900,* 27; Eli Zaretsky, "The Place of the Family in the Origins of the Welfare State," in *Rethinking the Family: Some Feminist Questions,* ed. Barrie Thorne, 168–224 (New York: Longman, 1992); Thomas A. Arcury, "Rural Elderly Household Life-Course Transitions, 1900 and 1980 Compared," *Journal of Family History* 11 (1986): 90 (Arcury maintains that "females in 1900 were perilously near to losing their independence in a household"); Howard Chudacoff and Tamara K. Hareven hypothesized that increased coresidence indicates mutual support, not growing dependency, among the elderly and that household composition depended on societal and economic contexts as well as on the internal condition of the family ("Family Transitions into Old Age," in *Transitions,* ed. Hareven, 218–19). Elman and London found that in 1910 one-fifth of widowed and divorced women across the United States lived in their parents' or adult children's households ("Sociohistorical and Demographic Perspectives," 224).

44. N. Sue Weiler, "Family Security or Social Security? The Family and the Elderly in New York State during the 1920s," *Journal of Family History* 11 (1986): 77–95.

45. William H. Matthews, *What Happened to 115 Widows and Their 470 Children* (New York: New York Association for the Improvement of the Poor, 1924), 5.

46. U.S. Bureau of the Census, *Women at Work, 1900,* 202–6.

47. Robert Griswold has explored the difficulties men encountered trying to work, run a home, and look after their children (*Fatherhood in America: A History* [New York: Basic Books, 1993]). Joanne L. Goodwin discovered that widows in Chicago also had high rates

of employment ("An American Experiment in Paid Motherhood: The Implementation of Mothers' Pensions in Early Twentieth Century Chicago," *Gender and History* 4 [1992]: 331–33).

48. Associated Charities of Fall River (ACFR), District Conference 1, Minute Book, 25 February 1889 (16 July 1888, case of Mr. Moore, a hod carrier; 29 October 1889, case of Patrick Reynolds, a carder with four children), manuscript in possession of the Family Services Association of Fall River; ibid. (16 July 1888, 29 Oct. 1888, 3 Dec. 1888, 7 Jan. 1889, 21 Jan. 1889).

49. St. Vincent's Home, Fall River, Boys' Register, 1886–1920; Children's Temporary Home, Pittsburgh, *Annual Report, 1890* (Pittsburgh, 1890); Florence Lattimore, "Pittsburgh as a Foster Mother," in *The Pittsburgh District: The Civic Frontage*, ed. Paul U. Kellogg, 377–439 (New York: Survey Associates, 1914), 384. Timothy A. Hacsi notes that many orphanages did not specify the surviving parent as father or mother (*Second Home: Orphan Asylums and Poor Families in America* [Cambridge, Mass.: Harvard University Press, 1998], 114).

50. Manuscript census, Baltimore, 1920; Barry W. Poulson, "The Family and the State: A Theoretical Framework," in *The American Family and the State*, ed. Joseph R. Peden and Fred R. Glahe, 49–80 (San Francisco: Pacific Research Institute for Public Policy, 1986), 79.

51. Manuscript census, Baltimore, 1920.

52. Manuscript census, Baltimore, Pittsburgh, and Fall River, 1900, 1920.

53. For a discussion of working-class and immigrant attitudes toward home ownership, see S. J. Kleinberg, "Success and the Working Class," in *Onward and Upward: Essays on the Self-Made American*, ed. Thomas D. Clark, 123–38 (Bowling Green, Ohio: Bowling Green University Popular Press, 1979); Francis Walsh, "Lace Curtain Literature: Changing Perception of Irish American Success," in *Onward and Upward*, ed. Clark, 139–46.

54. Manuscript census, Baltimore, Pittsburgh, and Fall River, 1920 (this discussion is limited to 1900 and 1920 since the census did not inquire about home ownership in 1880). Haber noted that "only" 34 percent of elderly female household heads were homeowners in 1900 (*Beyond Sixty-Five*, 31), but the census samples drawn for this research show that this figure was not appreciably lower than the level of male home ownership at the same time.

55. Manuscript census, Pittsburgh, 1900.

56. Manuscript census, Baltimore, 1920.

57. For more on the complex process of African American migration, women's experiences, and the interaction between family relationships and the migration process, see Joe William Trotter Jr., ed., *The Great Migration in Historical Perspective: New Dimensions of Race, Class, and Gender* (Bloomington: Indiana University Press, 1991); Carole Marks, *Farewell, We're Good and Gone: The Great Black Migration* (Bloomington: Indiana University Press, 1993); Peter Gottlieb, *Making Their Own Way: Southern Blacks' Migration to Pittsburgh, 1916–1930* (Urbana: University of Illinois Press, 1987).

58. U.S. Bureau of the Census, *Fifteenth Census: Population*, vol. 5, *General Report on Occupations* (Washington, D.C.: GPO, 1933), 272; idem, *Sixteenth Census: Population*, vol. 3, *The Labor Force, Employment, and Family Characteristics of Women* (Washington, D.C.: GPO, 1943).

59. Inconsistencies in the enumerations of 1910 and 1920 might have affected the pro-

portion of women considered to be in the labor force. For a discussion of the validity of the enumeration, see Robert W. Smuts, "The Female Labor Force: A Case Study in the Interpretation of Historical Statistics," *Journal of the American Statistical Association* 55 (Mar. 1960): 71–79; Valerie Oppenheimer, *The Female Labor Force in the United States* (Berkeley: University of California Press, 1970), 2–6.

60. S. J. Kleinberg, "The Economic Origins of the Welfare State, 1870–1939," in *Social and Secure? Politics and the Culture of the Welfare State: A Comparative Inquiry,* ed. Hans Bak, Frits van Holthoon, and Hans Krabbendam, 94–116 (Amsterdam: VU Press, 1996). Some cities and states limited aid to citizens, and private charities found it difficult to communicate with non-English-speaking individuals (ACFR, District Conference 1, Minute Book, 1888–89). The Pittsburgh Association for the Improvement of the Poor, too, gave relatively little assistance to the foreign born (see Pittsburgh Association for the Improvement of the Poor, *Annual Report,* for years 1880–96).

61. Mary Elizabeth Poole concludes that the Social Security Act incorporated a racialized, gender hierarchy instead of being explicitly racist ("Securing Race and Ensuring Dependence: The Social Security Act of 1935" [Ph.D. diss., Rutgers University, 2000]). Nevertheless, it widened the distinctions between the races.

62. Manuscript census, Baltimore, 1920; Katherine Anthony, *Mothers Who Must Earn* (New York: Russell Sage Survey Research Associates, 1914), 62. Orville Vernon Burton describes the African American passion for education and the setbacks it endured once Reconstruction ended (*In My Father's House Are Many Mansions* [Chapel Hill: University of North Carolina Press, 1985], 253). Pleck (*Black Migration,* 140) states that black educational rates were higher than those of Irish immigrants in 1880.

63. Darline Clark Hine, "Black Migration to the Urban Midwest: The Gender Dimension, 1915–1945," in *The Great Migration in Historical Perspective: New Dimensions of Race, Class, and Gender,* ed. Joe William Trotter, 127–46 (Bloomington: Indiana University Press, 1991).

64. Tamara K. Hareven, *Family Time and Industrial Time: The Relationship between the Family and Work in a New England Industrial Town* (Cambridge: Cambridge University Press, 1982), 172, 214–16; Mary White Ovington, *Half a Man: The Status of the Negro in New York* (New York, 1969 [1911]), 77–79. For a comparison of women's employment along ethnic and racial lines, see Teresa L. Amott and Julie A. Matthaei, *Gender, Race, and Work: A Multicultural Economic History of Women in the United States* (Boston: South End, 1991).

65. U.S. Department of Labor, Women's Bureau, *Women Workers in Their Family Environment* (Washington, D.C.: GPO, 1941); U.S. Bureau of the Census, *Women at Work, 1900,* 170–74; idem, *Fifteenth Census: Population,* vol. 5, *Occupations,* 273.

66. Manuscript census, Pittsburgh, 1880; Pittsburgh Association for the Improvement of the Poor, casework records, 1880 (the Pittsburgh Association for the Improvement of the Poor merged with the Child Abuse Prevention Center in 1986; its papers are now held by Family Resources of Pittsburgh, the successor organization).

67. Claudia Goldin, *Understanding the Gender Gap* (Oxford: Oxford University Press, 1990), 28–37. The higher the employment rate for single women, the greater the probability that women would work after marriage. Joanne J. Meyerowitz analyses women's employment by marital status in *Women Adrift: Independent Wage Earners in Chicago, 1880–1930* (Chicago: University of Chicago Press, 1988); she emphasizes single women but

mentions widows as well. See also Lois Scharf, *To Work and to Wed: Female Employment, Feminism, and the Great Depression* (Westport, Conn.: Greenwood, 1980); Susan Ware, *Holding Their Own: American Women in the 1930s* (Boston: Twayne, 1982).

68. Manuscript census, Baltimore, 1920; John Martin, qtd. in Gwendolyn Hughes, *Mothers in Industry: Wage Earning by Mothers in Philadelphia* (New York: New Republic Press, 1925), 2.

69. Jones, *Labor of Love,* 200–202; Darlene Clark Hine, *Black Women in White: Racial Conflict and Cooperation in the Nursing Profession, 1890–1950* (Bloomington: Indiana University Press, 1989); Louis R. Harlan, *Separate and Unequal: Public School Campaigns and Racism in the Southern Seaboard States, 1901–1915* (New York: Atheneum, 1968). For a comparison with white women, see Margaret Jarman Hagood, *Mothers of the South: Portraiture of the White Tenant Farm Woman,* intro. Anne Firor Scott (New York: Norton, 1977 [1939]).

70. U.S. Bureau of the Census, *Women at Work, 1900,* 171–72; U.S. Bureau of the Census, *Fifteenth Census: Population,* vol. 5, *Occupations,* 273.

71. Mrs. Mary Brewer to Children's Bureau, 12 June 1922, Children's Bureau Papers, Record Group 102, box 209, folder 7311. The Children's Bureau devoted so much time to answering similar inquiries that the librarian wrote to the bureau's head, Julia Lathrop, suggesting the preparation of a booklet on alternatives to institutionalizing children (see Laura Thompson to Julia Lathrop, 11 November 1913, Children's Bureau Papers, Record Group 102, box 188, folder 8641). Mink points out that "maternalist reformers nevertheless resisted measures that would have reconciled wage work and motherhood" (*Wages of Motherhood,* 47). There were various sorts of nurseries, but these were limited in number and opening times.

72. Eileen Boris emphasizes that despite the exploitative piece rates, women chose (and choose) to work at home because it enabled them to combine their domestic, nurturing, and wage-earning roles (*Home to Work: Motherhood and the Politics of Industrial Homework in the United States* [Cambridge: Cambridge University Press, 1994], 194).

73. Elizabeth Clark-Lewis, "'This Work Had a End': African American Domestic Workers in Washington, D.C., 1910–1940," in *"To Toil the Livelong Day": America's Women at Work, 1780–1980,* ed. Carol Groneman and Mary Beth Norton, 196–212 (Ithaca, N.Y.: Cornell University Press, 1987), 202; Gerda Lerner, *Black Women in White America: A Documentary History* (New York: Pantheon Books, 1972), 226–28.

74. Women's Bureau Papers, National Archives, Record Group 86, box 11; Elizabeth Butler, *Women and the Trades: Pittsburgh, 1907–1908,* intro. Maurine Weiner Greenwald (Pittsburgh, Pa.: University of Pittsburgh Press, 1984 [1909]) (chaps. 9–11 describe the physically arduous nature of the steam laundries); U.S. Congress, 61st Congress, 2d sess., *Condition of Women and Child Wage-Earners: Employment of Women in Laundries,* Senate documents no. 97 (Washington, D.C.: GPO, 1911), 39–118.

75. Daniel Sutherland, *Americans and Their Servants: Domestic Service in the United States from 1800 to 1920* (Baton Rouge: Louisiana State University Press, 1981), 55.

76. A Negro nurse, "More Slavery at the South," *The Independent* 72, no. 3295 (25 Jan. 1912): 196–200, qtd. in Lerner, *Black Women,* 229. Tera W. Hunter discusses the situation of washerwomen in the South in *To 'Joy My Freedom: Southern Black Women's Lives and Labors after the Civil War* (Cambridge, Mass.: Harvard University Press, 1997).

77. Charlotte Keeble, "African American Domestic Servants in Pittsburgh during the Great Depression" (Ph.D. diss., Brunel University, U.K., 2000).

78. U.S. Census Office, *Report on the Social Statistics of Cities* (Washington, D.C.: GPO, 1886); U.S. Bureau of the Census, *Women at Work*, 1900, 219–23, 244–45, 287–89. In 1900, 46 percent of all working widows in Baltimore were of African ancestry, whereas only 15 percent in Pittsburgh and none in Fall River were. The percentage of those taking in boarders is derived from the manuscript census, since the printed census included boarding only if it was carried on at a commercial level; hence, boardinghouse keepers are not included in table 7.

79. Lucy Larcom, *A New England Girlhood* (Boston: Houghton Mifflin, 1889) (Larcom describes going into the mills earlier in the century to help support her family); Carroll D. Wright, *The Working Girls of Boston: From the Fifteenth Annual Report of the Massachusetts Bureau of Statistics of Labor for 1884* (New York: Arno/New York Times, 1969 [1889]); Claudia Goldin and Kenneth Sokoloff, "Women, Children, and Industrialization in the Early Republic: Evidence from the Manufacturing Censuses," *Journal of Economic History* 42 (1982): 742–44.

80. Factors governing child labor will be explored further in the next chapter.

81. Manuscript census, Fall River, 1880. On the general structure of employment in Fall River, see John Cumbler, *Working-Class Community in Industrial America: Work, Leisure, and Struggle in Two Industrial Cities, 1880–1930* (Westport, Conn.: Greenwood, 1979).

82. Butler (*Women and the Trades*) describes the occupations open to Pittsburgh women in this era but excludes domestic servants and professionals, who in 1900 constituted 42 and 7 percent of the female labor force, respectively.

83. Manuscript census, Baltimore, 1920.

84. Interview with Miss Thomas, in charge of "Colored YWCA Employment Bureau," 29 June 1916, Children's Bureau Papers, Record Group 102, box 134; Hunter, *To 'Joy My Freedom*, 78–83.

85. Pleck (*Black Migration*, 104) found that northern-born blacks had better job prospects than migrants did at the turn of the century.

86. Northern cities averaged between 100 and 200 domestic servants per 1,000 families in 1880, declining to 40–74 per 1,000 families by 1920. In the South there were 200–324 servants and 80–200 laundresses per 1,000 families in 1880, falling to about half that level by 1920 (Hunter, *To 'Joy My Freedom*, 243).

87. Elizabeth Clark-Lewis, *Living in, Living Out: African American Domestics in Washington, D.C., 1910–1940* (New York: Prentice Hall, 1994).

88. Palmer, *Domesticity and Dirt*, 68.

89. Women who took in boarders also enjoyed more control over their working environment than did those doing domestic work in another's household; at the same time, they did lose some privacy, a situation of which reformers disapproved (S. J. Kleinberg, "Gendered Space").

90. Manuscript census, Baltimore, Pittsburgh, and Fall River, 1880, 1900, 1920.

91. Margaret Byington, *Homestead: The Households of a Mill Town*, intro. Samuel P. Hays (Pittsburgh, Pa.: University Center for International Studies, 1975 [1910]), 142–48. John Bodnar, Roger Simon, and Michael Weber discuss the place of boarders in the family life

cycles of couples but omit widow-headed households (*Lives of Their Own: Blacks, Italians, and Poles in Pittsburgh, 1900–1960* [Urbana: University of Illinois Press, 1982], 102–6).

92. Crystal Eastman describes the families of accident victims in *Work Accidents and the Law* (New York: Charities Publications Committee, 1910), 132–43.

93. Meyerowitz, *Women Adrift,* 70–75; Bodnar, Simon, and Weber, *Lives,* 218.

94. Commonwealth of Pennsylvania, *Manual of the Mothers' Assistance Fund, 1927* (Harrisburg: n.p., 1927), 14.

95. I explore this theme in "Seeking the Meaning of Life: The Family in the Pittsburgh Survey," in *The Pittsburgh Survey Revisited,* ed. Maurine Greenwald, Margo Anderson, and Martin Bulmer, 88–105 (Pittsburgh: University of Pittsburgh Press, 1996). Also see Boris, *Home to Work,* on the place of the home in social thought and legislation.

96. Bodnar, Simon, and Weber (*Lives,* 234n10) find some tendency during the Depression to take in boarders as a means of supplementing low or poor wages.

97. Rose discusses reformers' motivations in establishing day nurseries in *A Mother's Job,* chap. 1.

98. Associated Charities of Fall River, District Conference 2, Minute Book (14 Aug. 1888, 4 Dec. 1888).

99. U.S. Congress, *Condition of Women,* 38–40; Kleinberg, *Shadow of the Mills,* 246–47.

100. Keeble, "African American Domestic Servants," 15–18.

101. Electric Sewing Machine Society, *Annual Report* (Baltimore, 1896), 1.

102. Maryland Bureau of Industrial Statistics, *First Biennial Report, 1884–85* (Baltimore: Guggenheimer, 1886), 87–89.

103. Lewis W. Hine, "Baltimore to Biloxi and Back," *Survey* 30 (3 May 1913): 172.

104. Butler, *Women and the Trades,* 137.

105. Jeanne Boydston explores the changing definition of work in the nineteenth century in *Home and Work: Housework, Wages, and the Ideology of Labor in the Early Republic* (Oxford: Oxford University Press, 1994).

106. Boris, *Home to Work.* Gosta Esping-Anderson analyzes the role of the state in the organization of social relations in *The Three Worlds of Welfare Capitalism* (Princeton, N.J.: Princeton University Press, 1990). Vivien Hart discusses the constitutional basis for regulating women's employment in *Bound by Our Constitution: Women, Workers, and the Minimum Wage* (Princeton, N.J.: Princeton University Press, 1994).

107. Sherri Broder, *Tramps, Unfit Mothers, and Neglected Children: Negotiating the Family in Nineteenth-Century Philadelphia* (Philadelphia: University of Pennsylvania Press, 2002), 38–40.

108. For the development of the Social Security Act's old-age provisions, see Roy Lubove, *The Struggle for Social Security, 1900–1935* (Cambridge, Mass.: Harvard University Press, 1968); W. Andrew Achenbaum, *Social Security: Visions and Revisions* (Cambridge: Cambridge University Press, 1986); Gordon, *Pitied;* Alice Kessler-Harris, "Designing Women and Old Fools: The Construction of the Social Security Amendments of 1939," in *U.S. History as Women's History: New Feminist Essays,* ed. Linda K. Kerber, Alice Kessler-Harris, and Kathryn Kish Sklar, 87–106 (Chapel Hill: University of North Carolina Press, 1995); Poole, "Securing Race."

Chapter 2: Widows' Children and the Cult of True Childhood

1. Stanley W. Lindberg, "Institutionalizing a Myth: The *McGuffey Readers* and the Self-Made Man," in *Onward and Upward: Essays on the Self-Made American*, ed. Thomas D. Clark, 71–82 (Bowling Green, Ohio: Bowling Green University Popular Press, 1979), 77. Katherine Deupre Lumpkin and Dorothy Wolff Douglas's *Child Workers in America* (New York: R. M. McBride, 1937) documents the arduous conditions facing most young workers.

2. Seth Luther, *Address to the Working-Men of New England* (Boston, 1832).

3. Steven Mintz and Susan Kellogg, *Domestic Revolutions: A Social History of American Family Life* (New York: Free Press, 1989), chap. 3; Clark Nardinelli, *Child Labor and the Industrial Revolution* (Bloomington: Indiana University Press, 1990).

4. Olwen H. Hufton, *The Poor of Eighteenth-Century France, 1750–1789* (Oxford: Oxford University Press, 1974), 69–127 (Hufton describes this an as "economy of makeshifts"). For an analysis of the household-strategy approach, see Laurence Fontaine and Jürgen Schlumbohm, "Household Strategies for Survival: An Introduction," in *Household Strategies for Survival 1600–2000: Fission, Faction and Cooperation,* ed. Fontaine and Schlumbohm, 1–18 (Cambridge: Cambridge University Press, 2000).

5. Pamela Barnhouse Walters and Philip J. O'Connell, "The Family Economy, Work, and Educational Participation in the United States, 1890–1940," *American Journal of Sociology* 93 (1988): 116–52.

6. Joseph E. Illick, *American Childhoods* (Philadelphia: University of Pennsylvania Press, 2002), chaps. 4 and 5.

7. Viviana Zelizer, *Pricing the Priceless Child: The Changing Social Value of Children* (New York: Basic Books, 1985); Barbara Welter, "The Cult of True Womanhood: 1820–1860," *American Quarterly* 18 (1966): 151–74.

8. Kathryn Kish Sklar notes that women used their homes as a base from which to launch political activity (*Catharine Beecher: A Study in American Domesticity* [New York: Norton, 1973], 134).

9. Christopher Lasch, *Haven in a Heartless World: The Family Besieged* (New York: Basic Books, 1977), 5. Susan Householder van Horn highlights the importance of women's close attention to their children as a factor in improving child health in her book *Women, Work, and Fertility, 1900–1986* (New York: New York University Press, 1988), 46–47.

10. Claudia Goldin, "Household and Market Production of Families in a Late Nineteenth Century American City," *Explorations in Economic History* 16 (1979): 124.

11. Robert Coit Chapin, among other early twentieth-century economists, estimated that children in poor families contributed a significant portion of total family income; see Chapin, *The Standard of Living of Workingmen's Families* (New York: Russell Sage Foundation, 1909), 64–65.

12. Patrick M. Horan and Peggy G. Hargis found that "neither wife's income nor income from boarders has a significant effect on the work or school activities of children" ("Children's Work and Schooling in the Late Nineteenth-Century Family Economy," *American Sociological Review* 56 [1991]: 590). Families preferred to employ children, whose labor could be spared from the household, rather than mothers, whose domestic responsibilities were all-consuming in this era.

13. National Conference of Charities and Correction, *Proceedings* (1903), 120, 114 (hereinafter *PNCCC*).

14. Qtd. in Robert H. Maucione, "Lewis Hine Exposes Child Abuse," unpublished paper in the possession of the Fall River Historical Society.

15. Walter Trattner provides an overview of the activities of the National Child Labor Committee in *Crusade for the Children: A History of the National Child Labor Committee and Child Labor Reform in America* (Chicago: Quadrangle Books, 1970). Judith Sealander updates and expands his coverage, with a focus on the federal government, in *The Failed Century of the Child: Governing America's Young in the Twentieth Century* (Cambridge: Cambridge University Press, 2003).

16. *PNCCC*, for years 1889–1915; Sophonisba P. Breckinridge, ed., *The Child in the City: A Series of Papers Presented at the Conferences Held during the Chicago Child Welfare Exhibit* (London: P. S. King and Sons, 1912).

17. Michael B. Katz, *Improving Poor People: The Welfare State, the "Underclass," and Urban Schools as History* (Princeton, N.J.: Princeton University Press, 1999); David Tyack and Larry Cuban, *Tinkering toward Utopia: A Century of Public School Reform* (Cambridge, Mass.: Harvard University Press, 1995). Lasch (*Haven,* 7) views arguments over child labor as part of the Progressive campaign to wean first-generation children away from the influence of their families.

18. William J. Reese, *The Origins of the American High School* (New Haven, Conn.: Yale University Press, 1995); Joel Spring, *Deculturalization and the Struggle for Equality: A Brief History of the Education of Dominated Cultures in the United States* (New York: McGraw Hill, 1994).

19. Kathryn Kish Sklar, "The Historical Foundations of Women's Power in the Creation of the American Welfare State, 1830–1930," in *Mothers of a New World: Maternalist Politics and the Origins of Welfare States,* ed. Seth Koven and Sonya Michel, 43–93 (London: Routledge, 1993).

20. Kriste Lindenmeyer, *"A Right to Childhood": The U.S. Children's Bureau and Child Welfare, 1912–1946* (Urbana: University of Illinois Press, 1997), 9–18. See also Molly Ladd-Taylor, *Mother-Work: Women, Child Welfare, and the State, 1890–1930* (Urbana: University of Illinois Press, 1994); Robyn L. Muncy, *Creating a Female Dominion in American Reform, 1890–1935* (Oxford: Oxford University Press, 1990).

21. Jane Addams, *The Spirit of Youth and the City Streets,* intro. Allen F. Davis (Urbana: University of Illinois Press, 1972 [1909]), 110.

22. Charlotte Perkins Gilman, *The Home: Its Work and Its Influence* (New York: McClure, Phillips, 1903), 165.

23. Dorothy Ross, *G. Stanley Hall: The Psychologist as Prophet* (Chicago: University of Chicago Press, 1972); Joseph Kett, *Rites of Passage: Adolescence in America, 1790 to the Present* (New York: Basic Books, 1977); John Modell, Frank F. Furstenberg Jr., and Theodore Hershberg, "Social Change and Transitions to Adulthood in Historical Perspective," in *Philadelphia: Work, Space, Family, and Group Experience in the 19th Century,* ed. Theodore Hershberg, 311–42 (Oxford: Oxford University Press, 1981).

24. In 1887 Alabama passed an ineffectual child labor statute that contained no enforcement provisions and was repealed once northern mill owners opened mills in the state

(Wilma King, *Stolen Childhood: Slave Youth in Nineteenth-Century America* [Bloomington: Indiana University Press, 1995], xx).

25. Michael Katz's book *A History of Compulsory Education Laws* (Bloomington: University of Indiana Press, 1976) offers an overview of state educational requirements.

26. John R. Sutton explores the growing regulation of children's behavior in *Stubborn Children: Controlling Delinquency in the United States, 1640–1981* (Berkeley: University of California Press, 1988). See also LeRoy Ashby, *Saving the Waifs: Reformers and Dependent Children, 1890–1917* (Philadelphia: Temple University Press, 1984); Susan Tiffin, *In Whose Best Interest? Child Welfare Reform in the Progressive Era* (Westport, Conn.: Greenwood, 1982); Robert H. Bremner, ed., *Children and Youth in America: A Documentary History,* vol. 1, *1600–1865* (Cambridge, Mass.: Harvard University Press, 1970), 260; Carl F. Kaestle and Maris A. Vinovskis, "From Fireside to Factory: School Entry and School Leaving in Nineteenth-Century Massachusetts," in *Transitions: The Family and the Life Course in Historical Perspective,* ed. Tamara K. Hareven, 135–86 (New York: Academic, 1978), 136.

27. Lora Sharple, "Fall River Movement Sparked Change in State Labor Laws," *Fall River Standard Times,* 23 January 1983.

28. Stephan Thernstrom, *Poverty and Progress: Social Mobility in a Nineteenth Century City* (New York: Atheneum, 1971), 22.

29. Sealander (*Failed Century,* 138–43) provides a sensitive discussion of the accuracy of child-labor statistics.

30. Society for the Protection of Children from Cruelty and Immorality of Baltimore City, *Annual Report, 1894* (Baltimore: John W. Kennedy, 1894), 5. Not only did the U.S. Census first delineate children's employments in 1870; in addition, many of the larger industrial states established labor bureaus around this time.

31. Hine's photographs illustrated the Pittsburgh Survey and appeared on National Child Labor Committee posters.

32. John Cumbler, *Working-Class Community in Industrial America: Work, Leisure, and Struggle in Two Industrial Cities, 1880–1930* (Westport, Conn.: Greenwood, 1979), 104.

33. *The Outlook,* qtd. in August Kohn, "Children in the Mills," in *Childhood in America,* ed. Paula S. Fass and Mary Ann Mason, 251–52 (New York: New York University Press, 2000). Kohn, a journalist, defended the employment of children in southern textile mills.

34. U.S. Department of Labor, Children's Bureau, *Child Labor Facts and Figures,* Bureau Publication no. 197 (Washington, D.C.: GPO, 1933), 5.

35. Massachusetts Child Labor Committee, *Annual Report on Child Labor in Massachusetts* (Boston: Massachusetts Child Labor Committee, 1914), 13.

36. Carolyn M. Moehling disagrees with the emphasis on child-labor legislation, stating that the minimum-age limits for manufacturing employment "had relatively little effect on the occupation choices of children at the turn of the century" ("State Child Labor Laws and the Decline of Child Labor," *Explorations in Economic History* 36 [1999]: 72–106 [quotation, 95]). R. A. Margo and T. A. Finegan, however, found that a combination of child labor and compulsory school attendance laws increased school attendance ("Compulsory Schooling Legislation and School Attendance in Turn of the Century America: A 'Natural Experiment' Approach," *Economics Letters* 53 [1996]: 103–10).

37. Paul Osterman, *Getting Started: The Youth Labor Market* (Cambridge: Cambridge University Press, 1980), 60–61.

38. U.S. Bureau of the Census, *Earnings of Factory Workers 1899 to 1927: An Analysis of Pay-Roll Statistics* (Washington, D.C.: GPO, 1929), 156.

39. Margaret Byington, *Homestead: The Households of a Mill Town*, intro. Samuel P. Hays (Pittsburgh, Pa.: University Center for International Studies, 1975 [1910]), 107.

40. All statistical data, unless otherwise attributed, are derived from the U.S. Census samples taken for Pittsburgh, Fall River, and Baltimore in 1880, 1900, and 1920.

41. U.S. Bureau of the Census, *Historical Statistics of the United States, Colonial Times to 1970* (Washington, D.C.: GPO, 1975), vol. 1, p. 133.

42. Manuscript census, Pittsburgh, 1900.

43. Manuscript census, Pittsburgh, Fall River, and Baltimore, 1900.

44. U.S. Bureau of the Census, *Fourteenth Census*, vol. 4, *Population 1920: Occupations* (Washington, D.C.: GPO, 1923), 478.

45. Anne Moody, *Coming of Age in Mississippi* (New York: Laurel, 1976), 45; Tera W. Hunter, *To 'Joy My Freedom: Southern Black Women's Lives and Labors after the Civil War* (Cambridge: Mass.: Harvard University Press, 1997), 33, 51; Joel Perlmann, *Ethnic Differences: Schooling and Social Structure among the Irish, Italians, Jews, and Blacks in an American City, 1880–1935* (Cambridge: Cambridge University Press, 1988), 297n15 (Perlmann found that no young blacks in Providence worked in factories); Pamela Barnhouse Walters and David R. James, "Schooling for Some: Child Labor and School Enrollment of Black and White Children in the Early Twentieth-Century South," *American Sociological Review*, 57 (1992): 636.

46. Joanne J. Meyerowitz analyzes the literary depiction of these women's backgrounds in *Women Adrift: Independent Wage Earners in Chicago, 1880–1930* (Chicago: University of Chicago Press, 1988), 55–64.

47. Florence Kelley, "Factory Inspection in Pittsburgh with Special Reference to the Conditions of Working Women and Children," in *Wage-Earning Pittsburgh*, ed. Paul U. Kellogg, 189–216 (New York: Survey Associates, 1914).

48. Mary Willcox Brown, "Compulsory Education Laws," *The Charities Record* 3, no. 3 (Dec. 1898): 75–76.

49. Elizabeth Beardsley Butler, "Sharpsburg: A Typical Waste of Childhood," in *Wage-Earning Pittsburgh*, ed. Kellog, 279–306 (quotation, 286).

50. Lila VerPlank North, "Pittsburgh Schools," in *The Pittsburgh District: The Civic Frontage*, ed. Paul U. Kellogg, 217–306 (New York: Survey Associates, 1914), 279.

51. U.S. Census Office, *Twelfth Census*, vol. 2, *Population, Part 2* (Washington, D.C.: GPO, 1902), 386–97. Walters and O'Connell found that blacks had lower overall school enrollment levels than whites did because of their concentration in rural areas ("The Family Economy," 1134). Perlmann documented high rates of school attendance among African Americans in Providence during this period (*Ethnic Differences*, 175).

52. Rev. Edward J. O'Brien, *Child Welfare Legislation in Maryland, 1634–1936* (Washington, D.C.: Catholic University of America, 1937), 178–86.

53. Diane Batts Morrow, *Persons of Color and Religious at the Same Time: The Oblate Sisters of Providence, 1828–1860* (Chapel Hill: University of North Carolina Press, 2002).

54. Lewis Hine, "Baltimore to Biloxi and Back," *Survey* 30 (3 May 1913): 172; Alexander J. McKelway, "Welfare, Work, and Child Labor in Southern Cotton Mills," *Charities and the Commons* 17, no. 6 (10 Nov. 1906): 480–81.

55. Rudolph Vecoli, "Introduction," in *A Century of European Migrations,* ed. Rudolph Vecoli and Suzanne M. Sinke, 1–14 (Urbana: University of Illinois Press, 1991).

56. *Fall River News,* 9 March 1882. Cumbler (*Working-Class Communities,* 123) considers workers' attitudes toward these laws.

57. Newspaper cutting in Fall River Children's Home file, Fall River Historical Association, n.d. (probably 1898).

58. Yukari Takai, "The Family Networks and Geographical Mobility of French Canadian Immigrants in Early Twentieth Century Lowell," *Journal of Family History* 26 (July 2001): 374–75.

59. Associated Charities of Fall River, District Conference 1, casework notes, 1888–1890.

60. Grace Abbott, ed., *The Child and the State: Legal Status in the Family, Apprenticeship, and Child Labor,* 2 vols. (Chicago: University of Chicago Press, 1938), 1:480–81; PNCCC (1903), 115.

61. *Laws of the State of Maryland Made and Passed at a Session of the General Assembly, 1902* (Baltimore: King Brothers, 1902), 821–22.

62. Charity Organization Society of Baltimore, *Twenty-Fourth Annual Report* (Baltimore, Md.: Charity Organization Society, 1905), 18.

63. State of Maryland, *Child Labor Laws of Maryland* (Baltimore: King Brothers, 1912), chap. 731:4–6.

64. Lewis C. Solmon and Michael Tierney concluded that the interaction of child labor and compulsory education laws reduced levels of youth employment ("Education," in *Encyclopedia of American Economic History,* ed. Glen Porter, 1012–27 [New York: Charles Scribner's Sons, 1980]). See also David John Hogan, *Class and Reform: School and Society in Chicago, 1880–1930* (Philadelphia: University of Pennsylvania Press, 1985).

65. Massachusetts Child Labor Committee, *Annual Report on Child Labor, 1914,* 7, 12.

66. Alice Channing, *Child Labor on Maryland Truck Farms,* U.S. Department of Labor, Children's Bureau Publication no. 123 (Washington, D.C.: GPO, 1923), 14; Family Welfare Association, *Baltimore Survey* (Baltimore, Md.: n.p., 1933), 2.

67. Manuscript census, Pittsburgh, 1900.

68. Tamara K. Hareven describes widows holding on to their children in Manchester, New Hampshire, in *Family Time and Industrial Time: The Relationship between the Family and Work in a New England Industrial Town* (Cambridge: Cambridge University Press, 1982), 177.

69. Sara A. Burstall describes poor families' efforts to keep their children in school in *Impressions of American Education in 1908* (London: Longmans, Green, 1909), 53. Ileen A. DeVault examines the courses taken by Pittsburgh high school students in *Sons and Daughters of Labor: Class and Clerical Work in Turn-of-the-Century Pittsburgh* (Ithaca, N.Y.: Cornell University Press, 1990). See also Paula S. Fass, *Outside In: Minorities and the Transformation of American Education* (Oxford: Oxford University Press, 1989).

70. John Bodnar, Roger Simon, and Michael Weber, *Lives of Their Own: Blacks, Italians, and Poles in Pittsburgh, 1900–1960* (Urbana: University of Illinois Press, 1982), 98–99.

71. Barbara Miller Solomon, *In the Company of Educated Women: A History of Women and Higher Education in America* (New Haven, Conn.: Yale University Press, 1985), 65, 68. As Solomon notes, college tuition could easily take the entire $250 per year that, on average, a teacher earned at the time.

72. Mark J. Stern found a direct correlation between children's school attendance levels and their father's social class in 1915, although the picture was less clear cut in 1870; see his *Society and Family Strategy: Erie County, New York, 1850–1920* (Albany: State University of New York Press, 1987), 101. Unfortunately, he did not consider the mother's class or, it seems, the children of widowed mothers.

73. Manuscript census, Fall River, 1880.

74. Teresa Amott and Julie Matthaei, *Race, Gender, and Work: A Multicultural Economic History of Women in the United States* (Boston: South End, 1991), 164–70.

75. William H. Matthews, *What Happened to 115 Widows and Their 470 Children* (New York: New York Association for Improving the Condition of the Poor, 1928), 28. Hilda was one of the lucky ones; a charity grant enabled her to spend two years in a commercial course and get a secretarial position.

76. Manuscript census, Pittsburgh, Fall River, and Baltimore, 1920.

77. Charity Organization Society of Baltimore, *Twenty-Fourth Annual Report*, 17.

78. William H. Slingerland, *Child Welfare Work in Pennsylvania: A Cooperative Study of Child-Helping Agencies and Institutions* (New York: Russell Sage Foundation, 1915), 4. New York had the most (531), followed by the District of Columbia (494) and California (372). The data are for the year nearest to 1912 for which information could be obtained.

79. Society for the Protection of Children from Cruelty and Immorality of Baltimore City, *Annual Report, 1893* (Baltimore: John W. Kennedy, 1893), 10; idem, *Annual Report, 1896* (Baltimore: John W. Kennedy, 1896), 11.

80. Raymond A. Mohl, *Poverty in New York, 1873–1825* (Oxford: Oxford University Press, 1971), 17, 25 (Timothy A. Hacsi, too, discusses indenture as a means of caring for orphaned children; see his *Second Home: Orphan Asylums and Poor Families in America* [Cambridge, Mass.: Harvard University Press, 1998], 14–17); David Rothman, *The Discovery of the Asylum: Social Order and Disorder in the New Republic* (Boston: Little, Brown, 1971), 207, 221; Robert S. Pickett, *House of Refuge: Origins of Juvenile Reform in New York State, 1815–1857* (Syracuse, N.Y.: Syracuse University Press, 1969); Susan Whitelaw Downs and Michael W. Sherraden, "The Orphan Asylum in the Nineteenth Century," *Social Service Review* 57 (June 1983): 273. In 1790, 17 percent of the institutionalized dependent children in the United States lived in orphanages, and the rest, in almshouses. By the early decades of the nineteenth century, that proportion had risen to 33 percent, and it had climbed to 84 percent by 1880. By 1910 virtually all institutionalized dependent children (97 percent) were in orphanages.

81. Bernard Wishy, *The Child and the Republic: The Dawn of Modern American Child Nurture* (Philadelphia: University of Pennsylvania Press, 1968), 81–82; Patrick J. Kelly, *Creating a National Home: Building the Veterans' Welfare State, 1860–1900* (Cambridge, Mass.: Harvard University Press, 1997), 4.

82. U.S. Bureau of the Census, *Benevolent Institutions, 1910* (Washington, D.C.: GPO, 1913), 122–35, 140–47.

83. Ibid., 109–12, 146–47.

84. St. Vincent's Home, Boy's Register, Fall River 1885–1921.

85. Trattner, *Crusade,* 98; U.S. Bureau of the Census, *Special Reports: Paupers in Almshouses, 1904* (Washington, D.C.: GPO, 1906), 30.

86. U.S. Bureau of the Census, *Benevolent Institutions, 1910,* 30; Marshall B. Jones, "Crisis of the American Orphanage," *Social Service Review* 63 (Dec. 1989): 613.

87. Richard A. Meckel, "Protecting the Innocents: Age Segregation and the Early Child Welfare Movement," *Social Service Review* 59 (Sept. 1985): 461–63; Marilyn Irvin Holt, *The Orphan Trains: Placing Out in America* (Lincoln: University of Nebraska Press, 1992), 74.

88. Qtd. in Henry W. Thurston, *The Dependent Child: A Story of Changing Aims and Methods in the Care of Dependent Children* (New York: Columbia University Press, 1930), 241.

89. Florence Lattimore, "Pittsburgh as a Foster Mother," in *The Pittsburgh District: The Civic Frontage,* ed. Paul U. Kellogg, 337–449 (New York: Survey Associates, 1914), 340–41.

90. Miriam Z. Langsom, *Children West: A History of the Placing Out System of the New York Children's Aid Society, 1853–1890* (Madison: Wisconsin State Historical Society, 1964), 3; Holt, *Orphan Trains,* 52, 65; Slingerland, *Child Welfare Work,* 127.

91. "Mrs W." to Henry Watson Children's Aid Society, letter reproduced in Watson Society, *Annual Report, 1893* (Baltimore, 1983), 5.

92. Linda Gordon, *The Great Arizona Orphan Abduction* (Cambridge, Mass.: Harvard University Press, 1999) (this work documents the racial, religious, and class conflicts of child placing in Arizona in 1904).

93. Nurith Zmora, *Orphanages Reconsidered: Child Care Institutions in Progressive Baltimore* (Philadelphia: Temple University Press, 1994), 15.

94. Henry Watson Children's Aid Society, *History of the Henry Watson Children's Aid Society* (Baltimore, 1898); idem, *Annual Report, 1895* (Baltimore, 1895) 3, 12; idem, *Annual Report, 1898* (Baltimore, 1898), 10.

95. Ashby, *Saving the Waifs,* 58.

96. Watson Society, *Annual Report, 1895,* 10; *PNCCC, 1909,* 50.

97. Pete Daniel, *The Shadow of Slavery: Peonage in the South, 1901–1969* (Oxford: Oxford University Press, 1973), 23.

98. Holt (*Orphan Trains,* 71) notes that there was no placing out of "colored" children from New York, but the Baltimore situation clearly was different. In *Fallen Women, Problem Girls: Unmarried Mothers and the Professionalization of Social Work, 1890–1945* (New Haven, Conn.: Yale University Press, 1993), Regina G. Kunzel describes the growing pressure placed on white mothers to give up children, particularly babies, for adoption.

99. Ruth Bloodgood, "Public Care of Dependent Children in Baltimore through Placement in Free Family Homes," in Family Welfare Association of America, *Baltimore Survey* (Baltimore, 1933), 5–8.

100. Ibid., 8–12.

101. Ibid., 2, 23–26, 33; Gordon analyzes the white community's response to the placement of white children with Mexican American families in *Arizona Orphan Abduction,* 113–15.

102. On the sectarian pattern of American children's institutions, see Andrew Billingsley

and Jeanne M. Giovannoni, *Children of the Storm: Black Children and American Child Welfare* (New York: Harcourt Brace Jovanovich, 1972); Joan Gittens, *Poor Relations: The Children of the State in Illinois, 1818–1990* (Urbana: University of Illinois Press, 1994); Dorothy M. Brown and Elizabeth McKeown, *The Poor Belong to Us: Catholic Charities and American Welfare* (Cambridge, Mass.: Harvard University Press, 1997); Peter C. Hollran: *Boston's Wayward Children: Social Services for Homeless Children, 1830–1930* (Cranbury, N.J.: Associated University Presses, 1989); Gary Edward Polster, *Looking Out: The Cleveland Jewish Orphan Asylum, 1868–1924* (Kent, Ohio: Kent State University Press, 1990); Zmora, *Orphanages Reconsidered;* John R. Sutton, "Bureaucrats and Entrepreneurs: Institutional Responses to Deviant Children in the United States, 1890s–1920s," *American Journal of Sociology* 95 (May 1990): 1367–1400.

103. Slingerland, *Child Welfare Work,* 206; U.S. Bureau of the Census, *Special Reports: Benevolent Institutions, 1904* (Washington, D.C.: GPO, 1905), 77–78.

104. *Fall River City Directory,* for years 1874, 1880, 1886 (Fall River, Mass.: Sampson, Murdock, 1874, 1880, 1886); St. Vincent's Home, Boy's Register, Fall River, 1885–1921.

105. Hebrew Orphan Asylum, *34th Annual Report* (Baltimore: Kohn and Pollack, 1906), 5; Zmora, *Orphanages Reconsidered,* 56–63.

106. Family Welfare Association of America, *Baltimore Survey;* U.S. Bureau of the Census, *Benevolent Institutions, 1904,* 78; Supervisor of City Charities, "Annual Report," 1906, Baltimore City Archives, Baltimore, Record Group 9, box 81. On African American orphanages, see Dorothy Salem, *To Better Ourselves: Black Women in Organized Reform, 1890–1920* (Brooklyn, N.Y.: Carlson, 1990), 82–84.

107. U.S. Bureau of the Census, *Benevolent Institutions, 1904,* 118, 144–45; Lattimore, "Pittsburgh," 342–44; *Pittsburgh City Directory, 1896* (Pittsburgh: J. F. Diffenbacher, 1896), 79.

108. St. Vincent's Home, Boys' Register, 1886–1920. Unfortunately, no comparable register for girls or for the 1920s–1930s is extant.

109. Baltimore Orphan Asylum, *Annual Report,* for years 1888–94 (Baltimore, 1888–94); Lattimore, "Pittsburgh," 378–80.

Chapter 3: The Transition from Charity to Widows' Pensions

1. Sharon Perlman Krefetz, *Welfare Policy Making and City Politics* (New York: Praeger, 1976), 1.

2. Molly Ladd-Taylor, *Mother-Work: Women, Child Welfare, and the State, 1890–1930* (Urbana: University of Illinois Press, 1994), 3; Nancy F. Cott, "What's in a Name? The Limits of 'Social Feminism,'" *Journal of American History* 76 (1989): 809–29; Theda Skocpol and Gretchen Ritter, "Gender and the Origins of Modern Social Policies in Britain and the United States," *Studies in American Political Development* 5 (1991): 26–93.

3. Charles Noble observes that "in the crucible of the Great Depression, maternalism would be dropped entirely" (*Welfare as We Knew It* [Oxford: Oxford University Press, 1997], 53).

4. Patricia Hill Collins, "The Meaning of Motherhood in Black Culture and Black Mother/Daughter Relationships," *Sage* 4 (Fall 1987): 3–9; Elsa Barkley Brown, "Womanist Consciousness: Maggie Lena Walker and the Independent Order of Saint Luke," *Signs* 14

(Spring 1989): 610–33; Joyce A. Hanson, *Mary McLeod Bethune and Black Women's Political Activism* (Columbia: University of Missouri Press, 2003).

5. Marjorie Spruill Wheeler, "Maternalism: Noblesse Oblige as a Motivator of White Women Reformers in the New South," paper presented at the Organization of American Historians, Atlanta, 1994. Susan M. Sterett contrasts the rationale for different types of pensions in *Public Pensions: Gender and Civic Service in the States, 1850–1937* (Ithaca, N.Y.: Cornell University Press, 2003).

6. *Fall River City Directory,* for years 1853, 1854, and 1868–82; H. A. DuBuque, *Le Guide Canadien-Français (ou Almanach des Adresses) de Fall River et Notes Historiques sur les Canadiens de Fall River* (Fall River: Edmond-F. LaMoureux, 1888); Anthony Coelho, "A Row of Nationalities: Life in a Working-Class Community: The Irish, English, and French-Canadians in Fall River, Massachusetts, 1850–1890" (Ph.D. diss., Brown University, 1980); Sister Florence Marie Chevalier, "The Role of French National Societies in the Sociocultural Evolution of the Franco-Americans of New England from 1860 to the Present: An Analytical Macro-Sociological Case Study in Ethnic Integration based on Current Social System Models" (Ph.D. diss., Catholic University of America, 1972); Margaret Russell Durfee Johnson, *Annals of the Church of the Ascension* (Fall River: Munroe, n.d.).

7. Mrs. William Carr, Mrs. Eli Thurston, and Mrs. Charles Holmes, "History of the Central Congregational Church, Fall River Massachusetts, 1842–1905," manuscript in possession of Fall River Historical Society; *History of the Ladies' Benevolent Society of the First Congregational Church, Fall River, Massachusetts, 1904* (Fall River: J. H. Franklin, 1904); John Cumbler, "The Politics of Charity: Gender and Class in Late Nineteenth Century Charity Policy," *Journal of Social History* 14 (1980): 102; *St. Mary's Cathedral Centennial Observance, 1838–1938* (Fall River: n.p., n.d.).

8. *Fall River City Directory, 1889,* 596; Associated Charities of Fall River, "District Conference No. 1 Case Work Record" (hereinafter abbreviated as ACFRR), 28 May 1888 (manuscripts in possession of Family Welfare Association of Fall River); Josephine Shaw Lowell, "The Evils of Investigation and Relief," *Charities* 1 (1898): 8–10.

9. Paul Boyer, *Urban Masses and Moral Order in America, 1820–1920* (Cambridge, Mass.: Harvard University Press, 1978), 143–61; Nancy Hewitt, "Varieties of Voluntarism: Class, Ethnicity, and Women's Activism in Tampa," in *Women, Politics, and Change,* ed. Louise A. Tilly and Patricia Gurin, 63–68 (New York: Russell Sage Foundation, 1992).

10. ACFRR, 9 July 1888.

11. Associated Charities of Fall River (hereinafter ACFR), *Seventh Annual Report* (Fall River, Mass., 1895), 11; idem, *Fourth Annual Report* (Fall River, Mass., 1891), 11; idem, *Sixth Annual Report* (Fall River, Mass., 1893), 15; ACFRR, 16 July 1888, 24 September 1888.

12. ACFRR, 28 May 1888; Association for Community Welfare in Fall River, *Annual Report, 1919–1920* (Fall River, Mass.: Riley, 1920), 8.

13. ACFRR, 12 and 19 November, 31 December 1888; Charles Verrill, "Infant Mortality and Its Relation to the Employment of Mothers in Fall River Massachusetts," *Transactions of the 15th International Congress on Hygiene and Demography,* 6 vols. (Washington, D.C.: GPO, 1913), 3:319–20; Mark Aldrich, "Determinants of Mortality among New England Cotton Mill Workers during the Progressive Era," *Journal of Economic History* 42 (1982): 847–63; Fall River District Nursing Association, *Annual Report, 1914* (Fall River, Mass., 1914), 8.

14. The Home for Aged People in Fall River, "One Hundred Years of Excellence" (1991; manuscript in possession of Fall River Public Library), 4.

15. U.S. Bureau of the Census, *Special Reports: Benevolent Institutions, 1904* (Washington, D.C.: GPO, 1905), 220–65; Ethel McClure, *More Than a Roof: The Development of Minnesota Poor Farms and Homes for the Aged* (St. Paul: Minnesota Historical Society, 1965); John Cumbler, *Working-Class Community in Industrial America: Work, Leisure, and Struggle in Two Industrial Cities, 1880–1930* (Westport, Conn.: Greenwood, 1979), 154; Tamara K. Hareven, *Family Time and Industrial Time: The Relationship between the Family and Work in a New England Industrial Town* (Cambridge: Cambridge University Press, 1982), 177.

16. Massachusetts State Board of Charity, *Annual Report, 1915* (Boston: Wright and Patter, 1915), 105.

17. Fall River, city treasurer's ledger, 1890–98 (manuscript in possession of Fall River Public Library); Massachusetts Board of Charity, *Annual Report, 1915*, 105; Massachusetts Commission on the Support of Dependent Minor Children of Widowed Mothers, *Report* (Boston: Wright and Potter, 1913), 124, 154 (hereinafter cited as *MCDMCR*); Cumbler, "Politics."

18. Joanne L. Goodwin, "An Experiment in Paid Motherhood: The Implementation of Mothers' Pensions in Early Twentieth Century Chicago," *Gender and History* 4 (1992): 329. Because the overseers of the poor recorded only total expenditure, it is not possible to determine the percentages of one- and two-parent families.

19. Statement from Elizabeth T. Colburn to Massachusetts Commission on the Support of Dependent Minor Children, *MCDMCR*, 87.

20. St. Vincent's Home, Boys' Register.

21. *MCDMCR*, 118.

22. The Fall River Children's Home charged $1.00 to $1.25 per week for board, while St. Vincent's charged $1.50 to $1.75, although many parents paid nothing at all to keep their children in the Catholic home. Elizabeth Rose describes the tensions between day nurseries and their clients in *A Mother's Job: The History of Day Care, 1890–1960* (Oxford: Oxford University Press, 1999), 55–69.

23. U.S. Bureau of the Census, *Benevolent Institutions, 1904*, 57–127.

24. Sonya Michel, "Limits of Maternalism: Polices toward American Wage Earning Mothers during the Progressive Era," in *Mothers of a New World: Maternalist Politics and the Origins of Welfare States*, ed. Seth Koven and Sonya Michel, 277–320 (London: Routledge, 1993).

25. *MCDMCR*, 141–47.

26. Ibid., 51, 11.

27. Samuel Thayer Rutherford, "The Department of Charities of the City of Pittsburgh, 1888–1923" (master's thesis, University of Pittsburgh, 1938), 10–14, 35; City of Pittsburgh, Department of Charities, *Annual Report, 1910* (Pittsburgh, 1910), 618–19; idem, *Annual Report, 1895* (Pittsburgh, 1895), 313.

28. Pittsburgh death certificates, 1870–1900 (City of Pittsburgh, Division of Biostatistics); S. J. Kleinberg, *The Shadow of the Mills: Working-Class Families in Pittsburgh, 1870–1907* (Pittsburgh, Pa.: University of Pittsburgh Press, 1989).

29. Pittsburgh Association for the Improvement of the Poor (hereinafter PAIP), *Fourth Annual Report* (Pittsburgh, 1879).

30. U.S. Bureau of the Census, *Earnings of Factory Workers* (Washington, D.C.: GPO, 1929), 113–14; Elizabeth Butler, *Women and the Trades: Pittsburgh, 1907–1908*, intro. Maurine Weiner Greenwald (Pittsburgh, Pa.: University of Pittsburgh Press, 1984 [1909]), 237, 408–9; Lila VerPlank North, "Pittsburgh Schools," in *The Pittsburgh District: The Civic Frontage*, ed. Paul U. Kellogg, 217–315 (New York: Survey Associates, 1914), 269.

31. Leland Baldwin, *Pittsburgh: The Story of a City* (Pittsburgh: University of Pittsburgh Press, 1938), 213; Women's Christian Association, *Seventh Annual Report* (Pittsburgh: Mills and Brother, 1875), 5, 10.

32. *Pittsburgh City Directory, 1886.*

33. PAIP, *Annual Report for 1879–80* (Pittsburgh, 1880), 13.

34. PAIP, *Annual Report for 1889–90* (Pittsburgh, 1890), 15; PAIP, "History" (typescript [1917] in possession of Family Resources of Pittsburgh); PAIP, *Annual Report, 1879–80,* 13; L. Margaretta Culver, "A History of the Baltimore Association for the Improvement of the Poor from Its Foundation in 1849 to Its Federation with the Charity Organization Society in 1902" (master's thesis, Johns Hopkins University, 1923), 41.

35. Charity Organization Society of Baltimore (hereinafter COSB), *Twenty-Second Annual Report* (Baltimore, 1903), 24; PAIP, *Annual Report,* (1879–90).

36. *Pittsburgh City Directory, 1896,* 79–90.

37. Ibid., 99; Pittsburgh and Allegheny Home for the Friendless, *Tenth Annual Report* (Pittsburgh: Sloan King, 1871), 6–8.

38. *Pittsburgh City Directory,* for years 1870, 1881, and 1896; Pennsylvania Board of Commissioners of Public Charities, *Third Annual Report* (Harrisburg: B. Singerly, 1873), 81.

39. John Newton Boucher, *A Century and a Half of Pittsburg* [*sic*] *and Her People,* 4 vols. (Pittsburgh: Lewis, 1908), 2:443 (other homes for mothers and children included Mercy House, which took widows with children as well as single women, and the Temporary Home for Destitute Women, founded in 1868, which also housed poor women with children); Pennsylvania State Board of Public Charities, *Second Annual Report* (Harrisburg: B. Singerly, 1872), 81, 85, 93; *Pittsburgh City Directory, 1896,* 101.

40. *Pittsburgh City Directory,* for years 1868–96.

41. Pittsburgh had a higher density of widows' homes than did most cities of comparable size (U.S. Bureau of the Census, *Benevolent Institutions, 1904,* 220–65). On the consequences for widows, see Crystal Eastman, *Work Accidents and the Law* (New York: Charities Publications Committee, 1910); Kleinberg, *Shadow of the Mills.*

42. *Baltimore Evening Sun,* 18 May 1937; *Baltimore American,* 18 July 1954; *Baltimore Sun,* 23 February 1959 (quoting an early report of the society); COSB, *Directory of Charitable and Benevolent Organizations for 1892* (Baltimore, 1892), 40. Comparable organizations included the Mariners' Family Asylum, which offered aid to the aged wives, widows, sisters, and daughters of seamen; this institution, located on Staten Island, New York, opened in 1803 (U.S. Bureau of the Census, *Benevolent Institutions, 1904,* 220–65).

43. Baltimore Association for Improving the Condition of the Poor (hereinafter BAICP), *Tenth Annual Report* (Baltimore, 1860), 2, 6; idem, *Report, 1850,* 19; idem, *Report, 1856–57,* 14; Charles Hirschfeld, *Baltimore, 1870–1900: Studies in Social History* (Baltimore, Md.: Johns Hopkins University Press, 1941).

44. U.S. Bureau of the Census, *Benevolent Institutions, 1904,* 232; R. B. Rosenburg, *Living Monuments: Confederate Soldiers' Homes in the New South* (Chapel Hill: University of

North Carolina Press, 1993); *Baltimore Sun,* 30 January 1925, 3 February 1925, 15 August 1925; COSB, *Directory, 1892,* 27, 40. See Theda Skocpol, *Protecting Soldiers and Mothers: The Political Origins of Social Policy in the United States* (Cambridge, Mass.: Belknap, 1992), on the significance of federal provision for union veterans and their dependents.

45. U.S. Census Office, *Compendium of the Eleventh Census* (Washington, D.C.: GPO, 1892–97), 583–86; idem, *Eleventh Census,* vol. 1, *Population* (Washington, D.C.: GPO, 1892), pt. 1, p. 881. Amy E. Holmes found that native-born white women benefited disproportionately from Civil War pensions; see her article "'Such Is the Price We Pay': American Widows and the Civil War Pension System," in *Toward a Social History of the American Civil War: Exploratory Essays,* ed. Maris A. Vinovskis, 171–95 (Cambridge: Cambridge University Press, 1990). Patrick J. Kelly analyzes veterans' experiences and the efforts to care for them in *Creating a National Home: Building the Veterans' Welfare State, 1860–1900* (Cambridge, Mass.: Harvard University Press, 1997).

46. Maris A. Vinovskis noted there were 189,000 African American soldiers out of a total of 2,000,000 Union soldiers ("Have Social Historians Lost the Civil War?" in *Toward a Social History,* ed. Vinovskis, 9).

47. Sherry Olson, *Baltimore: The Building of an American City* (Baltimore, Md.: Johns Hopkins University Press, 1980), 186.

48. BAICP, *Report, 1865;* idem, *Report, 1892;* COSB, *Directory,* for years 1885, 1892, and 1901.

49. Shelter for Aged and Infirm Colored Persons, *Annual Report of the Board of Managers,* for years 1888–99 (Baltimore: William K. Boyle and Son, 1888–99). There were 136 white and 6 black subscribers in 1889 (*Annual Report, 1894,* 9).

50. COSB, *Directory, 1892,* 135. Most of the city's welfare money went to the almshouse and care for the insane. Hospitals and dispensaries received the next largest appropriation, followed by reformatories and children's homes, with the appropriations for programs specifically for African American children being smaller than those earmarked for institutions serving whites. Hirschfeld (*Baltimore,* 152) discusses the increase in city expenditure on charity, noting that it rose 270 percent between 1880 and 1900, but most of this increase was devoted to hospitals and insane asylums.

51. COSB, *Directory, 1892,* 38. Nationwide, excluding almshouses, there were approximately two dozen homes for elderly African American men and women in 1904; there were about half that number for women only, and there was only one for men (U.S. Bureau of the Census, *Benevolent Institutions, 1904,* 220–654; Culver, "A History," 25).

52. *Greisenheim, Fifty Years of the General German Aged People's Home* (Baltimore, 1931); BAICP, *Annual Report,* for years 1849–1902); COSB, *Annual Report,* for years 1881–1900.

53. U.S. Bureau of the Census, *Benevolent Institutions, 1904,* 233–34.

54. Hebrew Benevolent Society, *Annual Report* (Baltimore, 1903), 17; COSB, *Directory, 1892,* 27; idem, *Directory, 1901,* 73; *Baltimore Sun,* 23 May 1943.

55. BAICP, *Report,* for years 1849–1902; COSB, *Annual Report,* for years 1891–1906; *The Charities Record* 3, no. 3 (Dec. 1895): 68.

56. *The Charities Record* 1, no. 3 (Dec. 1892): 3; Joan Waugh, *Unsentimental Reformer: The Life of Josephine Shaw Lowell* (Cambridge, Mass.: Harvard University Press, 1997), 163–65.

57. Zilphah D. Smith, "Needy Families in Their Homes," *PNCCC* (1901): 285.

58. Amos G. Warner, "The Charities of Baltimore," in COSB, *Report on Charities Conference* (Baltimore, 1887), 151–52.

59. Henry Watson Children's Aid Society, *Annual Report* (Baltimore, 1899); William Gibson, "A History of Family and Child Welfare Agencies in Baltimore, 1849–1943" (Ph. D. diss., Ohio State University, 1969), 59; *The Charities Record* 3, no. 3 (Dec. 1897): 25; Watson Society, *Annual Report, 1899.*

60. Miriam Cohen and Michael Hanagan analyze this issue for the early twentieth century in "The Politics of Gender and the Making of the Welfare State, 1900–1940: A Comparative Perspective," *Journal of Social History* 24 (1991): 269–84. For a discussion of the way social workers' scientific jargon reinforced gender norms, see Regina G. Kunzel, *Fallen Women, Problem Girls: Unmarried Mothers and the Professionalization of Social Work, 1890–1945* (New Haven, Conn.: Yale University Press, 1993).

61. Roy Lubove, *Twentieth Century Pittsburgh: Government Business and Environmental Change* (Pittsburgh: University of Pittsburgh Press, 1994), 25.

62. For the origins and development of mothers' pensions at the national level, see Leff, "Consensus for Reform"; Skocpol, *Protecting;* Roy Lubove, *The Struggle for Social Security, 1900–1935* (Cambridge, Mass.: Harvard University Press, 1968); Ladd-Taylor, *Mother-Work.*

63. Susan M. Sterett, *Public Pensions: Gender and Civic Service in the States, 1850–1937* (Ithaca, N.Y.: Cornell University Press, 2003), 107–8 (Sterett argues that the courts would have rejected an entitlement model); Vivien Hart, *Bound by Our Constitution: Women, Workers, and the Minimum Wage* (Princeton, N.J.: Princeton University Press, 1994), 110.

64. Skocpol, *Protecting,* 57; Leff, "Consensus for Reform," 397–417; manuscript census, Pittsburgh and Baltimore, 1880, 1900, 1920; Pennsylvania Department of Public Welfare, *Report of the Mothers' Assistance Fund, 1926* (Harrisburg, 1926), 36–37.

65. Linda Gordon, *Pitied but Not Entitled: Single Mothers and the History of Welfare* (New York: Free Press, 1994); Sterett, *Public Pensions,* chap. 6; Nancy F. Cott, "Giving Character to Our Whole Civil Polity: Marriage and the Public Order in the Late Nineteenth Century," in *U.S. History as Women's History: New Feminist Essays,* ed. Linda K. Kerber, Alice Kessler-Harris, and Kathryn Kish Sklar, 107–21 (Chapel Hill: University of North Carolina Press, 1995). See also Ann Vanderpol, "Dependent Children, Child Custody, and Mothers' Pensions: The Transformation of State-Family Relations in the Early 20th Century," *Social Problems* 29 (1982): 21–35.

66. Edith Abbott, "The Experimental Period of Widows' Pension Legislation," *Proceedings of the National Conference of Social Work* (1917): 163.

67. Ann Shola Orloff, "Gender in Early U.S. Social Policy," *Journal of Policy History* 3 (1991): 249–81; Theda Skocpol and John Ikenberry, "The Political Formation of the American Welfare State in Historical and Comparative Perspective," *Comparative Social Research* 6 (1983): 87–148; Eileen Boris, *Home to Work: Motherhood and the Politics of Industrial Homework in the United States* (Cambridge: Cambridge University Press, 1994), 115–16; Michel, "Limits of Maternalism," 277.

68. Krefetz, *Welfare Policy,* 9. Ofman regarded rural pensions as less restrictive and intrusive than urban ones.

69. Mothers' Pension League of Allegheny County (hereinafter MPLAC), *Report, 1929*

(Pittsburgh, 1929), 9–10; Commonwealth of Pennsylvania, State Board of Education, *Report of the Mothers' Assistance Fund* (Harrisburg, J. L. L. Kuhn, 1919), 3.

70. Helen Glenn Tyson, *The Mothers' Assistance Fund in Pennsylvania: A Brief Review of the Work of the Mothers' Assistance Fund with a Discussion of the Immediate Needs in This Field of Child Care* (Philadelphia: Public Charities Association of Pennsylvania, 1926), 4; Virginia Sapiro, "The Gender Basis of American Social Policy," in *Women, the State and Welfare*, ed. Linda Gordon, 36–54 (Madison: University of Wisconsin Press, 1990).

71. Emma Octavia Lundberg, "Progress of Mothers' Aid Administration," *Social Service Review* 2 (1928): 435–58; Bureau of Municipal Research, *Widows' Pension Legislation* (New York: Bureau of Municipal Research and Training School for Public Service, 1917), 24–31.

72. Tyson, *Mothers' Assistance Fund*, 4; Pennsylvania, *Mothers' Assistance Fund Report, 1918*; Amos Pinchot, "A Brutal Charity," handbill in Mayor James H. Preston's papers, Baltimore City Archives, Record Group 9, box 15.

73. Pennsylvania, *Mothers' Assistance Fund Report, 1919*, 3.

74. Edith Abbott and Sophonisba P. Breckinridge, *The Administration of the Aid-to-Mothers Law in Illinois*, Children's Bureau Publication no. 82 (Washington, D.C.: GPO, 1921), 90; Elizabeth L. Hall, *Mothers' Assistance in Philadelphia: Actual and Potential Costs: A Study of 1010 Families* (Hanover, N.H.: Dartmouth University Press, 1933), 12; Sterett, *Public Pensions*, 112–20.

75. Pennsylvania, *Mothers' Assistance Fund Report, 1920*, 60; Pamela B. Walters, Holly J. McCammon, and David R. James, "Schooling or Working? Public Education, Racial Politics and the Organization of Production in 1910," *Sociology of Education* 63 (1991): 1–26.

76. Massachusetts State Board of Charity (hereinafter MSBC), *Annual Report, 1914* (Boston: Wright and Potter, 1915), 107; Laura A Thompson, comp., *Laws Relating to Mothers' Pensions in the United Sates, Canada, Denmark, and New Zealand*, Children's Bureau Bulletin no. 63 (Washington, D.C.: GPO, 1919); Gordon, *Pitied*, 15–36; Mimi Abramovitz, *Regulating the Lives of Women* (Boston: South End, 1989), 181–206.

77. Mr. Justice Brewer, *Muller v. Oregon* (1908); Leo Kanowitz, *Sex Roles in Law and Society: Cases and Materials* (Albuquerque: University of New Mexico Press, 1973), 46–47. For a positive view of protective legislation, see Dianne Kirkby, *Alice Henry: The Power of Pen and Voice* (Cambridge: Cambridge University Press, 1991).

78. Boris, *Home to Work*, 113–16.

79. New York State Commission on Relief for Widowed Mothers, *Report* (Albany: J. B. Lyon, 1914), 8.

80. Annie Marion MacLean, *Wage-Earning Women* (New York: Macmillan, 1910), 178.

81. Pennsylvania, *Mothers' Assistance Fund Report, 1927*, 7.

82. Mrs. Marcus Spiro, "Address to the Second Annual Mothers' Day Meeting, May 9th, 1915," in MPLAC, *Report, 1915–1916* (Pittsburgh, 1916), unpaginated. Gordon (*Pitied*, 19) makes a similar generalization.

83. Florence Lattimore, "Pittsburgh as a Foster Mother," in *The Pittsburgh District: The Civic Frontage*, ed. Paul U. Kellogg, 337–452 (New York: Survey Associates, 1914), 378.

84. Robert Treat Paine, "Pauperism in Great Cities: Its Four Chief Causes," in *Children and Youth in America: A Documentary History*, 6 vols., ed. Robert Bremner (Cambridge,

Mass.: Harvard University Press, 1970), 2:348–49; Christian C. Carstens, *Public Pensions to Widows with Children: A Study of Their Administration in Several American Cities* (New York: Russell Sage Foundation, 1913), 5.

85. *Proceedings of the Conference on the Care of Dependent Children, Held at Washington, D.C., January 25, 1909* (Washington, D.C.: GPO, 1909), 9 (Roosevelt quotation), 193.

86. Edward Devine, "Pensions for Mothers," in *Selected Articles on Mothers' Pensions,* ed. Edna D. Bullock, 176–83 (White Plains, N.Y.: H. W. Wilson, 1915); Mary Richmond, "Pensions to Widows—discussion," *PNCCC* (1912): 492–93; Arthur W. Towne, "Recent Conferences," *The Survey* 25 (1910): 323. Roy Lubove details the Charity Organization Society's objections to mothers' pensions in *The Professional Altruist* (Cambridge, Mass.: Harvard University Press, 1965), 101–6.

87. New York Commission on Relief, *Report,* 3.

88. Towne, "Recent Conferences," 323 (quoting Hannah Einstein).

89. Sterett, *Public Pensions,* 128.

90. Because pensions were state rather than local, this discussion focuses on states.

91. MPLAC, *Report, 1915–16,* i (epigraph).

92. Ibid., 3.

93. "How Mothers' Pension Bill Became a Law," MPLAC, *Report, 1915–16.* Sterett (*Public Pensions,* 112–20) examines the role of "taxpayer" suits against mothers' pensions.

94. Pennsylvania, *Mothers' Assistance Fund Report, 1920,* 23, 82; William Graebner, *Coal-Mining Safety in the Progressive Period: The Political Economy of Reform* (Lexington: University of Kentucky Press, 1976), 148–52; MPLAC, *Report, 1915–16.*

95. Alfred W. Crosby, *America's Forgotten Pandemic: The Influenza of 1918* (Cambridge: Cambridge University Press, 1989); Pennsylvania, *Mothers' Assistance Fund Report, 1920,* 27; Abbott and Breckinridge, *Aid-to-Mothers Law,* 33; Thomas Bell's novel *Out of This Furnace* (Pittsburgh: University of Pittsburgh Press, 1976 [1941]) includes a fictionalized portrait of the spread of tuberculosis within steel mill families.

96. Elizabeth F. Moloney, "Subdivision of Mothers' Aid," in MSBC, *Annual Report, 1922* (Boston, 1923), 11; MSBC, *Annual Report, 1917* (Boston, 1918), 123; Mary F. Bogue, *The Administration of Mothers' Aid in Ten Localities with Special Reference to Health, Housing, Education and Recreation,* Children's Bureau Publication no. 184 (Washington, D.C.: GPO, 1928), 11–13.

97. Pennsylvania, *Mothers' Assistance Fund Report, 1918,* 14–15.

98. Tyson, *Mothers' Assistance Fund,* 4.

99. Pennsylvania, *Mothers' Assistance Fund Report, 1920,* 30; Ladd-Taylor, *Mother-Work,* 158.

100. Massachusetts Child Labor Committee, *Annual Report on Child Labor in Massachusetts, 1912* (Boston, 1912), 12; idem, *Report on Child Labor, 1919,* 19.

101. Massachusetts Commission on Dependent Children, *Report,* 9.

102. MSBC, *Annual Report, 1913* (Boston, 1914), 4; idem, *Annual Report, 1915* (Boston, 1916), 105.

103. Moloney, "Subdivision," 11.

104. Massachusetts Commission on Dependent Children, *Report,* 37; Sterett, *Public Pensions,* 169.

105. MSBC, *Annual Report, 1913,* 133; MSBC, *Annual Report, 1922,* 24.

106. Pennsylvania, *Mothers' Assistance Fund Report, 1919,* 7; idem, *Mothers' Assistance Fund Report, 1920,* 29.

107. MSBC, *Annual Report, 1917,* 123.

108. Municipal Research Bureau, *Widows' Pension Legislation,* (New York: Bureau of Municipal Research and Training School for Public Service, 1917), 14.

109. MSBC, *Annual Report, 1914,* 106.

110. MPLAC, *Report, 1916.* Mayor James H. Preston's papers, stored at the Baltimore City Archives, contain letters, petitions, and written protests over his actions.

111. Alan D. Anderson, *The Origin and Resolution of an Urban Crisis: Baltimore, 1890–1930* (Baltimore, Md.: Johns Hopkins University Press, 1977), 33–36; Olson, *Baltimore,* 190.

112. Children's Bureau, "History of Mothers' Pensions," typescript, Children's Bureau Papers, National Archives, Record Group 102, box 209; Maryland statute qtd. in Edward J. O'Brien, "Child Welfare Legislation in Maryland, 1634–1936" (Ph.D. diss., Catholic University of America, 1937), 76.

113. Mayor Preston, "Statement for the Afternoon Papers," October 1916, Mayor Preston's papers, Record Group 9, box 155.

114. Fanny Middleton to Mayor Preston, 29 July 1916, Mayor Preston's papers, Record Group 9, box 155; petition to Mayor Preston calling for a hearing on the ordinance placing mothers' pensions under the supervisors of city charities, Mayor Preston's papers, Record Group 9, box 155; *Baltimore City Directory, 1916.*

115. Matilda Weekes to Mayor Preston, 23 July 1916; Marie H. Heath to Mayor Preston, 24 July 1916; Natalie B. Ells to Mayor Preston, 12 August 1916; petition to Mayor Preston (all in Mayor Preston's papers, Record Group 9, box 155).

116. Emmet Wallace White, attorney-at-law, to Mayor James H. Preston, 9 October 1916, Mayor Preston's papers, Record Group 9, box 155.

117. James H. Preston, *Baltimore Sun,* 9 October 1916; Anderson, *Urban Crisis,* 27.

118. Henry Neil to Mayor Preston, Mayor Preston's papers, Record Group 9, box 155.

119. F. B. Lee to Mayor Preston, 27 August 1916; W. B. Smoot to Mayor Preston, 7 August 1916 (both in Mayor Preston's papers, Record Group 9, box 155).

120. E. Marriott to Mayor Preston, 10 October 1916, Mayor Preston's papers, Record Group 9, box 155; Howard N. Rabinowitz, "From Exclusion to Segregation: Health and Welfare Services for Southern Blacks, 1865–1890," *Social Service Review* 48:327–55; John Dittmer, *Black Georgia in the Progressive Era, 1900–1920* (Urbana: University of Illinois Press, 1980); Olson, *Baltimore,* 277. Not a single new school was built for blacks in this period, although their numbers expanded greatly.

121. Children's Bureau, *Mothers' Aid, 1931,* Children's Bureau Publication no. 220 (Washington, D.C.: GPO, 1933), 19.

122. African Americans retained suffrage despite efforts to introduce grandfather clauses in Maryland because foreign-born voters joined forces to defeat these measures (James B. Crooks, *Politics and Progress: The Rise of Urban Progressivism in Baltimore, 1895–1911* [Baton Rouge: Louisiana State University Press, 1968], 61).

123. Cynthia Neverdon-Morton, *Afro-American Women of the South and the Advancement of the Race, 1895–1925* (Knoxville: University of Tennessee Press, 1989), 188; *The*

Charities Record, 4 (1900): 42; Federated Charities of Baltimore, *Annual Report* (Baltimore, 1901), 89; Emma Lundberg to Mrs. Walter S. Ufford, n.d., Children's Bureau Papers, Record Group 86, box 209.

124. Baltimore Supervisors of City Charities, "Specimen Letter Confirming Mothers' Relief Grant," 29 October 1929, Baltimore City Archives.

125. Children's Bureau, *Mothers' Aid 1931,* 13, 26–27. Many cities and states did not report the race of pension families to the Children's Bureau. Pennsylvania data indicate that in 1920 about 1 percent of pensions went to African Americans. As African Americans urbanized, their numbers on the pension rolls rose.

126. Emma O. Lundberg, *Public Aid to Mothers with Dependent Children,* Children's Bureau Publication no. 62 (Washington, D.C.: GPO, 1926), 6.

127. Pennsylvania, *Mothers' Assistance Fund Report, 1920,* 25.

128. Children's Bureau, *Mothers' Aid 1931,* 27; Hall, *Mothers' Assistance,* 28. As late as 1931 Knoxville, Tennessee, was giving pensions to only three African American widows; Memphis, with its much larger black population, was giving none.

129. Skocpol, *Protecting,* 459; Rabinowitz, "From Exclusion to Segregation," 341; Olson, *Baltimore,* 186–87; Lee L. Dopkin, "Pension or Poorhouse," *Baltimore Evening Sun,* 13 March 1935.

130. Lundberg to Ufford.

131. Family Welfare Association of America, "Baltimore Survey" (1933), 16–18, typescript in Maryland Room, Enoch Pratt Free Library; Winifred Bell, *Aid to Dependent Children* (New York: Columbia University Press, 1965), 9–10.

132. Linda Gordon and Sarah McLanahan, "Single Parenthood in 1900," *Journal of Family History* 16 (1991): 106; Lundberg, *Public Aid,* 4–8; Bell, *Aid to Dependent Children,* 7.

133. Lundberg, "Progress," 435, 457.

Chapter 4: The Implementation of Widows' Pensions

1. Suzanne Mettler describes the central role of "states' rights" in welfare policy during and after the New Deal in *Dividing Citizens: Gender and Federalism in New Deal Public Policy* (Ithaca, N.Y.: Cornell University Press, 1998), 20.

2. Roy Lubove explicitly connects mothers' pensions and Social Security in *The Struggle for Social Security, 1900–1935* (Cambridge, Mass.: Harvard University Press, 1968), 110–12. For an overview of the Social Security system's origins and development, see W. Andrew Achenbaum, *Social Security: Visions and Revisions* (Cambridge: Cambridge University Press, 1986). Linda Gordon, in *Pitied but Not Entitled: Single Mothers and the History of Welfare* (New York: Free Press, 1994), focuses on the gender issues of the Social Security Act, with particular attention to matters of bureaucratic infighting in which the Children's Bureau lost out.

3. Commonwealth of Pennsylvania, Department of Welfare, *Report to the General Assembly of Pennsylvania of the Mothers' Assistance Fund* (Harrisburg, 1920), 75 (hereinafter *Pennsylvania Mothers' Assistance Fund*); Gwendolyn Mink, *The Wages of Motherhood: Inequality in the Welfare State, 1917–1942* (Ithaca, N.Y.: Cornell University Press, 1995), 43.

4. Emma Octavia Lundberg, *Public Aid to Mothers with Dependent Children,* Children's Bureau Publication no. 162 (Washington, D.C.: GPO, 1926), 16; Children's Bureau, *Mothers' Aid, 1931,* Bureau Publication no. 220 (Washington, D.C.: GPO, 1933), 7–10. The Children's Bureau listed Kentucky, Mississippi, North Carolina, Rhode Island, and the District of Columbia as proffering pensions between 1921 and 1931. To this must be added Maryland, although that state disbursed no pensions until 1929, when it finally enacted an effective pension law.

5. Ira DeA. Reid, in Children's Bureau, *White House Conference on Child Health and Protection of Dependent and Neglected Children* (Washington, D.C.: GPO, 1930), 303; Winifred Bell, *Aid to Dependent Children* (New York: Columbia University Press, 1965), 9–10; Elizabeth L. Hall, *Mothers' Assistance in Philadelphia: Actual and Potential Costs; a Study of 1010 Families* (Hanover, N.H.: Sociological Press, 1933), 28.

6. Mrs. Dora Datcher, qtd. in Bertha Keiningham, "An Informal History of Mothers' Relief" (1933), 9, typescript, Maryland Room, Enoch Pratt Free Library.

7. Children's Bureau, *Mothers' Aid, 1931,* 26–27; Andrew Billingsley and Jeanne M. Giovannoni, *Children of the Storm: Black Children and American Child Welfare* (New York: Harcourt Brace Jovanovich, 1972), 73–75; Children's Bureau, *White House Conference on Children in a Democracy* (Washington, D.C.: GPO, 1941), 54. Mink (*Wages of Motherhood,* 49–52) discusses inequality in funding mothers' assistance programs and the issues of reform across the color line.

8. Children's Bureau, *Mothers' Aid, 1931,* 26–27; idem, *White House Conference,* 302.

9. Children's Bureau, "Activities of the Children's Bureau in Furthering Administration of Mothers' Aid," typescript, Children's Bureau Papers, National Archives, Record Group 102, box 456; Bureau of Municipal Research, *Widows' Pension Legislation* (New York: Bureau of Municipal Research and Training School for Public Service, 1917), 30–31; Mrs. J. S. Hahan to Julia C. Lathrop, 23 September 1918, and Julia C. Lathrop to Mrs. J. S. Hahan, 29 October 1918, Children's Bureau Papers, Record Group 102, box 209, folder 7311.

10. Emma Octavia Lundberg, "The Progress of Mothers' Aid Administration," *Social Service Review* 3 (1928): 442; Kay Walters Ofman, "A Rural View of Mothers' Pensions: The Allegan County, Michigan, Mothers' Pension Program, 1913–1928," *Social Service Review* 70 (Mar. 1996): 105.

11. Mrs. Mary Brewer to Children's Bureau, 12 June 1922, Children's Bureau Papers, Record Group 102, box 209, folder 7311; Theda Skocpol, *Protecting Soldiers and Mothers: The Political Origins of Social Policy in the United States* (Cambridge, Mass.: Belknap, 1992), 472–73.

12. Lundberg, "Progress of Mothers' Aid," 442–43.

13. Helen Glenn Tyson, *The Mothers' Assistance Fund in Pennsylvania* (Philadelphia: Public Charities Association of Pennsylvania, 1926), 7; Edith Abbott and Sophonisba P. Breckinridge, *Administration of the Aid-to-Mothers Law in Illinois,* Children's Bureau Publication no. 82 (Washington, D.C.: GPO, 1921), 113; Joanne L. Goodwin, *Gender and the Politics of Welfare Reform* (Chicago: University of Chicago Press, 1997), 153, 18.

14. Emma Octavia Lundberg, "Aid to Mothers with Dependent Children," *Annals of the American Academy of Political and Social Science* 97 (1921): 98–99; Family Welfare Association, *Baltimore Survey* (Baltimore, Md.: n.p., 1933), 32.

15. Family Welfare Association, *Baltimore Survey*, 49.

16. Michigan State Welfare Department, *Mothers' Aid in Michigan* (Lansing: Michigan State Welfare Dept., 1934), 4, cited in Bell, *Aid to Dependent Children*, 9; Family Welfare Association, *Baltimore Survey*, 3.

17. Massachusetts State Board of Charity (hereinafter MSBC), *Annual Report, 1914* (Boston: Wright and Potter, 1915), 100–104.

18. MSBC, *Annual Report, 1915* (Boston: Wright and Potter, 1916), 162; idem, *Annual Report, 1924* (Boston: Wright and Potter, 1925), 8–9. Molly Ladd-Taylor found a similar situation in other jurisdictions (*Mother-Work: Women, Child Welfare, and the State, 1890–1930* [Urbana: University of Illinois Press, 1994], 149).

19. *Pennsylvania Mothers' Assistance Fund, 1926*, 22–24. The Pennsylvania Mothers' Assistance authorities compared their relief systems unfavorably with those in Massachusetts.

20. MSBC, *Annual Report, 1919* (Boston: Wright and Potter, 1920), 103.

21. MSBC, *Annual Report, 1914*, 102.

22. MSBC, *Annual Report, 1926* (Boston: Wright and Potter, 1927), 10–11. Mink (*Wages of Motherhood*, 54) describes the Americanization efforts of the Sheppard-Towner clinics.

23. MSBC, *Annual Report, 1914*, 108.

24. MSBC, *Annual Report*, for years 1920–30 (Boston: Wright and Potter, 1921–31).

25. MSBC, *Annual Report, 1935* (Boston: Wright and Potter, 1936), 9.

26. MSBC, *Annual Report, 1914*, 108.

27. MSBC, *Annual Report, 1929* (Boston: Wright and Potter, 1930), 9–10.

28. MSBC, *Annual Report, 1935*, 8–9.

29. MSBC, *Annual Report, 1922* (Boston: Wright and Potter, 1923), 12.

30. Joanne L. Goodwin, "An American Experiment in Paid Motherhood: The Implementation of Mothers' Pensions in Early Twentieth Century Chicago," *Gender and History* 4 (1992): 330.

31. MSBC, *Annual Report, 1920* (Boston: Wright and Potter, 1921), 81.

32. Data compiled from MSBC, *Annual Report*, for years 1913–39 (Boston: Wright and Potter, 1914–40); U.S. Bureau of the Census, *Fourteenth Census*, vol. 2, *Population 1920: General Report and Analytical Tables* (Washington, D.C.: GPO, 1922), 47.

33. Ibid.

34. U.S. Census Office, *Twelfth Census*, vol. 8, *Manufactures*, pt. 2, *States and Territories* (Washington, D.C.: GPO, 1902), 382, 389–90. Cotton accounted for nine-tenths of the manufacturing capital in Fall River and less than half in Lowell.

35. Mary H. Blewett, *Constant Turmoil: The Politics of Industrial Life in Nineteenth Century New England* (Amherst: University of Massachusetts Press, 2000), 162, 408–9; Sharon Perlman Krefetz, *Welfare Policy Making and City Politics* (New York: Praeger, 1976), 9. Martha Derthick concludes that the values and preferences of agency heads played a significant role in determining levels of generosity ("Intercity Differences in the Administration of the Public Assistance Program: The Case of Massachusetts," in *City Politics and Public Policy*, ed. James Q. Wilson, 243–66 [New York: John Wiley, 1968]).

36. *Fall River News*, 8 December 1885; Associated Charities of Fall River, casework notes, 1888–90 (manuscript in possession of the Family Welfare Association of Fall River).

37. Massachusetts Child Labor Committee, *Annual Report: Child Labor in Massachusetts* (Boston, 1912), 4.

38. MSBC, *Annual Report, 1921* (Boston: Wright and Potter, 1922), 22; idem, *Annual Report, 1925* (Boston: Wright and Potter, 1926), 11.

39. Data compiled from MSBC, *Annual Report,* for years 1913–39 (Boston: Wright and Potter, 1914–1940); idem, *Annual Report, 1929,* 9–10.

40. Commonwealth of Pennsylvania, *Laws,* act of 29 April 1913, no. 80; Edith Miller Tufts, *Family Welfare and Relief Activities in Pittsburgh and Allegheny County, 1920–1931* (Pittsburgh: Federation of Social Agencies of Pittsburgh and Allegheny County, 1932), 20. Assistance to the wives of the insane was granted in 1926.

41. *Pennsylvania Mothers' Assistance Fund, 1922,* 7.

42. *Pennsylvania Mothers' Assistance Fund, 1920,* 23.

43. Hall, *Mothers' Assistance,* 4; *Pennsylvania Mothers' Assistance Fund, 1918* (Harrisburg, 1919), 6; Mary F. Bogue, in *Pennsylvania Mothers' Assistance Fund, 1924,* 12.

44. Mrs. Marcus T. Spiro, qtd. in *Report of the Mothers' Pension League of Allegheny County* (Pittsburgh, 1916), unpaginated.

45. Children's Bureau, *Mothers' Aid, 1931,* 27.

46. *Pennsylvania Mothers' Assistance Fund, 1926,* 14–15.

47. *Pennsylvania Mothers' Assistance Fund, 1920,* 23; *Pennsylvania Mothers' Assistance Fund, 1926,* 25, 36–38.

48. "Summary of a Study of the Adequacy of Relief to Fatherless Families in Philadelphia Aided under the Mothers' Assistance Fund Law of Pennsylvania," in *Pennsylvania Mothers' Assistance Fund, 1926,* 61. This survey estimated that the actual annual contribution was less than $250 per year owing to unemployment and slack time.

49. *Pennsylvania Mothers' Assistance Fund, 1926,* 57; David T. Beito, *From Mutual Aid to the Welfare State: Fraternal Societies and Social Services, 1890–1967* (Chapel Hill: University of North Carolina Press, 2000).

50. Mary F. Bogue, *The Administration of Mothers' Aid in Ten Localities with Special Reference to Health, Housing, Education and Recreation,* Children's Bureau Publication no. 184 (Washington, D.C.: GPO, 1928), 29.

51. Hall, *Mothers' Assistance,* 36.

52. Manuscript census, Pittsburgh, 1920.

53. Eileen Boris, "Power of Motherhood: Black and White Activist Women Redefine the 'Political,'" in *Mothers of a New World: Maternalist Politics and the Origins of Welfare States,* ed. Seth Koven and Sonya Michel, 213–45 (London: Routledge, 1993), 231.

54. *Pennsylvania Mothers' Assistance Fund, 1922,* 10.

55. Ibid., 58.

56. *Pennsylvania Mothers' Assistance Fund, 1926,* 41–42.

57. Bell, *Aid to Dependent Children,* 9.

58. Gordon, *Pitied,* 212. Grassroots organizations wrote to the House Ways and Means Committee to support ADC; see Mrs. George Gellhorn, Chairman, Joint Committee in Support of Wagner-Lewis Social Security Bill of the League of Women Voters, St. Louis, to Hon. Robert L. Doughton, Chairman, House Ways and Means Committee, 16 April 1935, in Committee on Economic Security Papers, National Archives, Record Group 128.

59. Keiningham, "Informal History," 3; Edward J. O'Brien, "Child Welfare Legislation in Maryland, 1634–1936" (Ph.D. diss., Catholic University of America, 1937), 79; Family Welfare Association, *Baltimore Survey,* 61.

60. Transcript of radio program on child welfare by Bertha Keiningham, 13 October 1932, WFBR radio (Baltimore), in Keiningham, "Informal History," 37.

61. Family Welfare Association, *Baltimore Survey,* 10–12; Ruth Bloodgood, "Public Care of Dependent Children in Baltimore through Placement in Free Family Homes," in Family Welfare Association, *Baltimore Survey,* 5.

62. Family Welfare Association, *Baltimore Survey,* 8.

63. Bloodgood, "Public Care," 5.

64. Keiningham, "Informal History," newspaper clipping attached to typescript dated 1930.

65. Family Welfare Association, *Baltimore Survey,* 10–12; Agnes Hanna, Director of Social Services, to Mrs. William Robertson, 7 June 1932, Children's Bureau Papers, Record Group 102, box 61.

66. Family Welfare Association, *Baltimore Survey,* 17; *Mothers' Aid, 1931,* 28.

67. U.S. Bureau of the Census, *Fifteenth Census: Population,* vol. 3, *Reports by States,* pt. 1, *Alabama–Missouri* (Washington, D.C.: GPO, 1932), 1084; Cynthia Neverdon-Morton, *Afro-American Women of the South and the Advancement of the Race, 1895–1925* (Knoxville: University of Tennessee Press, 1989), 188–89.

68. The black population increased by 30 percent in the 1920s.

69. James B. Crooks, *Politics and Progress: The Rise of Urban Progressivism in Baltimore, 1895–1911* (Baton Rouge: Louisiana State University Press, 1968), 61; Family Welfare Association, *Baltimore Survey,* 18.

70. Neverdon-Morton, *Afro-American Women,* 177; Keiningham, "Informal History."

71. Laura A. Thompson, *Laws Relating to Mothers' Pensions in the United States, Canada, Denmark, and New Zealand* (Washington, D.C.: GPO, 1919), 18.

72. Mrs. Louise Wilson Schwarz to Mayor Preston, 25 August 1916, in Mayor Preston's papers, Baltimore City Archives, Record Group 9, box 15 (Schwarz here specifically compares widows to veterans, stating that neither would accept a pension they thought to be charity); Ramsey County, Minnesota, Mothers' Aid Department, family arrangements, 1926, Women's Bureau Papers, National Archives, Record Group 86, Box 5; Pennsylvania, "Report of the Mothers' Assistance Fund, 1918," typescript, Women's Bureau Papers, Record Group 86, box 5. Mimi Abramovitz discusses pensions in these terms in *Regulating the Lives of Women* (Boston: South End, 1989), 183–205. Also see Ladd-Taylor, *Mother-Work,* 152–56; Lubove, *Struggle,* 108–9.

73. Baltimore Supervisors of City Charities, "Specimen Letter Confirming Mothers' Relief Grant," 29 October 1929, Baltimore City Archives.

74. Ibid.

75. Family Welfare Association, *Baltimore Survey,* 6.

76. Bogue, *Administration of Mothers' Aid,* 7; Lundberg, *Public Aid,* 8.

77. U.S. Bureau of the Census, *Children under Institutional Care and in Foster Homes, 1933* (Washington, D.C.: GPO, 1935), 4; Marshall B. Jones, "Crisis of the American Orphanage, 1931–1940," *Social Service Review* 63 (1989): 613–29. On orphanages during the Great Depression, see Jones, "Crisis," 613–25; Marian J. Morton, "Surviving the Great

Depression: Orphanages and Orphans in Cleveland," *Journal of Urban History* 26 (2000): 438–55; Howard Goldstein, *The Home on Gorham Street and the Voices of Its Children* (Tuscaloosa: University of Alabama Press, 1955); Kenneth Cmiel, *A Home of Another Kind: One Chicago Orphanage and the Tangle of Child Welfare* (Chicago: University of Chicago Press, 1995).

78. Baltimore Supervisors of City Charities, letter confirming mothers' relief grant, 1929, in Mayor Browning's papers, Baltimore City Archives, Record Group 9, box 50.

79. Bell, *Aid to Dependent Children*, 15; White House Conference on Child Health and Protection, *Addresses and Abstracts of Committee Reports* (New York, 1931), 194–95; Bogue, *Administration of Mothers' Aid*, 7 (quotation).

80. U.S. Bureau of the Census, *Historical Statistics of the United States, Colonial Times to 1970* (Washington, D.C.: GPO, 1975), pt. 1, p. 133; idem, *Statistics of Women at Work: Based on Unpublished Information Derived from the Schedules of the Twelfth Census: 1900* (Washington, D.C.: GPO, 1907), 14; idem, *Fifteenth Census: Population*, vol. 5, *General Report on Occupations* (Washington, D.C.: GPO, 1932), 275.

81. Brenda Gray, *Black Female Domestics during the Depression in New York City, 1930–1940* (New York: Garland, 1993).

82. James D. Anderson, *The Education of Blacks in the South, 1860–1935* (Chapel Hill: University of North Carolina Press, 1988), 150–52. Pamela Barnhouse Walters and David R. James found that in the South, African American children, as well as poor whites, had limited opportunities for public education ("Schooling for Some: Child Labor and School Enrollment of Black and White Children in the Early Twentieth-Century South," *American Sociological Review* 57 [1992]: 635–50).

83. Bogue, *Administration of Mothers' Aid*, 152; Viola I. Paradise, *Child Labor and the Work of Mothers in Oyster and Shrimp Canning Communities on the Gulf Coast*, Children's Bureau Publication no. 98 (Washington, D.C.: GPO, 1922), 14; Paul Osterman, *Getting Started: The Youth Labor Market* (Cambridge: Cambridge University Press, 1980), 60–61.

84. U.S. Bureau of the Census, *Historical Statistics*, pt. 1, pp. 20–21. In 1890, 59 percent of women aged sixty-five and over were widows, the figure falling to 57 percent by 1940 (Maryland Commissioner of Labor and Statistics, *The Older Worker in Maryland* [N.p.: n.p., 1930], 47–49).

85. Baltimore Humane and Impartial Society and Aged Woman's Home, *Annual Report, 1880* (Baltimore: James Young, 1881), 23; Daniel Scott Smith, Michel Dahlin, and Mark Friedberger, "The Family Structure of the Older Black Population in the American South in 1880 and 1900," *Sociology and Social Research* 63 (1979): 552–53; Mrs. Lizzie Chris to Mrs. Enoch Rauh, director, Department of Charities, City of Pittsburgh, 3 August 1922, in Archives of Industrial Society, University of Pittsburgh.

86. Massachusetts State Board of Charity, *Annual Report, 1934* (Boston: Wright and Potter, 1935), 9; Earl S. Bellman, *A Study of the Care of the Needy Aged in Maryland Counties* (Baltimore: Christian Social Justice Fund, 1933); Achenbaum, *Social Security*, 14–15.

87. Pennsylvania Commission on Old Age Pensions, *Report* (Harrisburg: J. L. L. Kuhn, 1919), 12.

88. Ann Shola Orloff, "The Political Origins of America's Belated Welfare State," in *The Politics of Social Policy in the United States*, ed. Margaret Weir, Ann Shola Orloff, and

Theda Skocpol, 37–80 (Princeton, N.J.: Princeton University Press, 1988). For a comparative perspective, see Peter Flora and Arnold J. Heidenheimer, eds., *The Development of Welfare States in Europe and America* (New Brunswick, N.J.: Transaction, 1981); Gaston V. Rimlinger, *Welfare Policy and Industrialization in Europe, America, and Russia* (New York: John Wiley, 1971); Ann Shola Orloff and Theda Skocpol, "Why Not Equal Protection? Explaining the Politics of Public Social Spending in Britain, 1900–1911, and the United States, 1880s–1920," *American Sociological Review* 49 (1984): 726–50; Jill Quadagno, "From Poor Laws to Pensions: The Evolution of Economic Support for the Aged in England and America," *Milbank Memorial Fund Quarterly* 62 (1984): 45.

89. Skocpol, *Protecting*, 532–53; William Graebner, *A History of Retirement: The Meaning of an American Institution, 1885–1978* (New Haven, Conn.: Yale University Press, 1980). M. Rubinow (*Social Insurance* [New York: Henry Holt, 1913]) and Abraham Epstein (*The Problem of Old Age Pensions in Industry* [Harrisburg: Pennsylvania Old Age Commission, 1926]) offer differing estimates of the number of men receiving old-age pensions, but they agree that pension coverage increased in industry and commerce.

90. Carole Haber and Brian Gratton discuss wealth holding among the elderly and analyze unemployment in old age in *Old Age and the Search for Security: An American Social History* (Bloomington: Indiana University Press, 1994).

91. Thelma Du Vinage, *A Study of Old Age Dependency in the City of Baltimore* (Baltimore: Saturday Night Club, 1930), 16.

92. Jill Quadagno, *The Transformation of Old Age: Class and Politics in the American Welfare State* (Chicago: University of Chicago Press, 1988), 70–71, 81–83. Quadagno believes that manufacturers provided pensions as a means of pacifying workers, enhancing loyalty, and decreasing the attractiveness of labor unions. There were far fewer pension schemes inaugurated in the textile and food industries between 1905 and 1932 than in iron and steel, paper, printing, chemicals, metals, and machinery (28 and 143, respectively).

93. "Fire Department Pensions," in Mayor Jackson's papers, Baltimore City Archives, Record Group 9, sect. 17, box 185; Isaac S. Field, president, board of school commissioners, to Mayor Howard W. Jackson, 19 December 1925, Mayor Jackson's papers, Record Group 9, sect. 17, box 185 (Mr. Field objected to raising the retirement age to seventy-five because he felt that would reduce operational efficiency in the schools).

94. Theda Skocpol and John Ikenberry, "The Political Formation of the American Welfare State in Historical and Comparative Perspective," *Comparative Social Research* 6 (1983): 87–148; Orloff and Skocpol, "Equal Protection," 728–50.

95. Family Welfare Association, *Baltimore Survey: Old Age Pensions* (Baltimore, 1933), 2; U.S. Bureau of the Census, *Paupers in Almshouses: 1923* (Washington, D.C.: GPO, 1925). Carole Haber discusses the institutionalization of the elderly in chapter 5 of *Beyond Sixty-Five: The Dilemma of Old Age in America's Past* (Cambridge: Cambridge University Press, 1983).

96. Lora B. Pine, "Old Age Assistance Recipients Living in Institutions for the Aged in Allegheny County," *The Federator* 13 (Apr. 1938): 91; Home for Aged People in Fall River, "One Hundred Years of Excellence" (1991), typescript in possession of Fall River Public Library; Du Vinage, *Old Age Dependency*, 5.

97. Jacob Fisher, *The Response of Social Work to the Depression* (Rochester, Vt.: Schenkman Books, 1980) (Fisher describes the programs and their implementation on a firsthand

basis); Emma A. Winslow, *Trends in Different Types of Public and Private Relief in Urban Areas, 1929–1935,* Children's Bureau Publication no. 237 (Washington, D.C.: GPO, 1937), 10–11.

98. U.S. Children's Bureau, "Amount Expended for Mothers' Aid, Old-Age Relief, and Aid for the Blind in March, 1933 in Specified Cities," typescript, Children's Bureau Papers, Record Group 102, box 611; Agnes Hanna, Director of Social Services, to Mrs. A. H. Turney of Kansas League of Women Voters, 30 June 1931, Children's Bureau Papers, Record Group 102, box 403; Winslow, *Trends,* 39–43.

99. *Fall River Herald News,* 14 July 1936; Family Welfare Association, *Old Age Pensions,* 7.

100. Family Welfare Association, *Baltimore Survey,* 7.

101. Ibid., 3, 8.

102. Brian Gratton, *Urban Elders: Family Work and Welfare among Boston's Aged, 1890–1950* (Philadelphia: Temple University Press, 1986), 87–94 (Gratton discusses the increase in elderly women's employment during the Depression, finding it to be part of the long-term increase in women's participation in the labor force); Family Welfare Association, *Baltimore Survey,* "Pension Investigations," case 163.

103. Susan Ware believes that the balance of evidence suggests stronger family ties during the Depression (*Holding Their Own: American Women in the 1930s* [Boston: Twayne, 1982]).

104. Harriet A. Byrne, *The Effects of the Depression on Wage Earners' Families: A Second Survey of South Bend,* Women's Bureau Bulletin no. 108 (Washington, D.C.: GPO, 1936), 4.

105. Personal interview with Dr. Jack S. Berger, Mahwah, N.J., 18 August 1993. Dr. Berger recalled that his uncles fell out after a bitter argument over contributions to support his widowed grandmother during the Depression. Any money given to the older generation deprived cash-starved families of resources needed for their own survival.

106. Family Welfare Association of Fall River, "Returns from Appeals" and "Record of Income and Expenses from 1929 to 1944," typescripts in possession of Family Services Association of Fall River; these documents record a small increase in receipts in the first two years of the Depression and then a sharp drop.

107. There are several excellent works on women's experiences during the Depression and on the policy debates framing the Social Security Act. See, in particular, Lois Scharf, *To Work and to Wed: Female Employment, Feminism, and the Great Depression* (Westport, Conn.: Greenwood, 1980); Ware, *Holding Their Own;* Jeane Westin, *Making Do: How Women Survived the '30s* (Chicago: Follett, 1976); Winifred Wandersee, *Women's Work and Family Values, 1920–1940* (Cambridge, Mass.: Harvard University Press, 1981); Julia Kirk Blackwelder, "Women in the Workforce: Atlanta, New Orleans, and San Antonio, 1930 to 1940," *Journal of Urban History* 4 (1978): 331–62; Donna J. Guy, "The Economics of Widowhood in Arizona, 1880–1940," in *On Their Own: Widows and Widowhood in the American Southwest,* ed. Arlene Scadron, 216–18 (Urbana: University of Illinois Press, 1988). See also Martha Oehmke Loustaunau, "Hispanic Widows and Their Support Systems in the Mesilla Valley of Southern new Mexico, 1910–1940," in *On Their Own,* ed. Scadron, 91–116.

108. Family Welfare Association, *Baltimore Survey,* 2.

109. Sybil Lipschultz makes a similar point based on Supreme Court decisions in *Muller v. Oregon* (1908) and *Adkins v. Children's Hospital* (1923) ("Social Feminism and Legal Discourse: 1898–1923," *Yale Journal of Law and Feminism* 2 [1989]: 131–60).

110. Linda Gordon argues that the programs designed by women for women supported them when men failed ("Social Insurance and Public Assistance: The Influence of Gender in Welfare Thought in the United States, 1890–1935," *American Historical Review* 97 [1992]: 49).

111. Abramovitz, *Regulating*, 235.

112. Lynn Y. Weiner, *From Working Girl to Working Mother: The Female Labor Force in the United States, 1820–1980* (Chapel Hill: University of North Carolina Press, 1985), 89.

Chapter 5: Widows and Orphans First?

1. These themes are explored in the following works: Alice Kessler-Harris, "Designing Women and Old Fools: The Construction of the Social Security Amendments of 1939," in *U.S. History as Women's History: New Feminist Essays,* ed. Linda K. Kerber, Alice Kessler-Harris, and Kathryn Kish Sklar, 63–86 (Chapel Hill: University of North Carolina Press, 1995); Linda Gordon, *Pitied but Not Entitled: Single Mothers and the History of Welfare* (New York: Free Press, 1994); Suzanne Mettler, *Dividing Citizens: Gender and Federalism in New Deal Public Policy* (Ithaca, N.Y.: Cornell University Press, 1998); Gwendolyn Mink, *The Wages of Motherhood: Inequality in the Welfare State, 1917–1942* (Ithaca, N.Y.: Cornell University Press, 1995); Robyn Muncy, *Creating a Female Dominion in American Reform, 1890–1935* (Oxford: Oxford University Press, 1990); Susan Ware, *Beyond Suffrage: Women in the New Deal* (Cambridge, Mass.: Harvard University Press, 1981); Mary Poole, "Securing Race and Ensuring Dependence: The Social Security Act of 1935" (Ph.D. diss., Rutgers University, 2000). Edward Berkowitz and Kim McQuaid provide a succinct review of the act's passage and the reasons for local control over many of its programs in "Social Security and the American Welfare State," *Research in Economic History,* supp. 6 (1991): 169–90.

2. Mettler, *Dividing Citizens,* 23.

3. Poole, "Securing Race," 3–4. For explorations of the racial values encoded in local welfare provision, see Michael K. Brown, *Race, Money, and the American Welfare States* (Ithaca, N.Y.: Cornell University Press, 1999); Martin Gilens, *Why Americans Hate Welfare: Race, Media, and the Politics of Antipoverty Policy* (Chicago: University of Chicago Press, 1999).

4. Frances Fox Piven and Richard Cloward, *Regulating the Poor: The Functions of Public Welfare* (New York: Vintage Books, 1971), 141n27. According to Piven and Cloward (272), the Great Society welfare programs greatly expanded access to public assistance as part of the process of integrating African Americans into the political system. Chistopher Howard concludes that age and disability account for what he labels the upper tier of welfare provision with uniform benefits across the states ("The American Welfare State, or States?" *Political Research Quarterly* 52 [1999]: 421–42).

5. Grace Abbott, *From Relief to Social Security* (New York: Beard Books, 1966 [1941]), 211. Both Mink (*Wages of Motherhood*) and Poole ("Securing Race") discuss the role of the Children's Bureau in the development of the Social Security Act. See Muncy, *Creat-*

ing a Female Dominion (158–59), on the interlocking institutional nexus of maternalist reformers.

6. E. Stina Lyon provides a critical overview of the scholarship on race and welfare benefits in "Race and the American Welfare State," *Ethnic and Racial Studies* 24 (2001): 125–30.

7. Alice Kessler-Harris, *In Pursuit of Equity: Women, Men, and the Quest for Economic Citizenship in Twentieth-Century America* (New York: Oxford University Press, 2001), 75–77.

8. U.S. Bureau of the Census, *Historical Statistics of the United States, Colonial Times to 1970* (Washington, D.C.: GPO, 1975), vol. 1, p. 133. The proportion of employed single women declined from 51 to 46 percent, most probably as a result of the altered age interval.

9. Susan Ware, *Holding Their Own: American Women in the 1930s* (Boston: Twayne, 1982), 21; U.S. Bureau of the Census, *Fifteenth Census: Population,* vol. 5, *General Report on Occupations* (Washington, D.C.: GPO, 1933), 273; idem, *Sixteenth Census: Population,* vol. 3, *The Labor Force,* pt. 1, *U.S. Summary* (Washington, D.C.: GPO, 1943), 111.

10. For information on the way organized labor benefited from the New Deal, see Patrick Renshaw, "The Labour Movement," in *Nothing Else to Fear: New Perspectives on America in the Thirties,* ed. Stephen Baskerville and Ralph Willett, 214–36 (Manchester, U.K.: Manchester University Press, 1985).

11. Between 1930 and 1940, the number of single working women declined from 5,734,825 to 5,335,155 (U.S. Bureau of the Census, *Fifteenth Census: Population,* vol. 5, p. 273; idem, *Sixteenth Census: Population,* vol. 3, pt. 1, pp. 111, 115).

12. A. J. Badger, *The New Deal: The Depression Years, 1933–1940* (Basingstoke, U.K.: Macmillan 1989), chap. 3.

13. Mettler, *Dividing Citizens,* 58–60; House Committee on Ways and Means, *A Bill to Alleviate the Hazards of Old Age, Unemployment, Illness, and Dependency, to Establish a Social Insurance Board in the Department of Labor, to Raise Revenue, and for Other Purposes: Hearings on H.R. 4120,* 74th Cong., 1st sess, 13 May 1935 (Washington, D.C.: GPO, 1935), 950 (hereinafter *Hearings, 1935*); William Graebner, *A History of Retirement: The Meaning and Function of an American Institution* (New Haven, Conn.: Yale University Press, 1980).

14. Ralph Carr Fletcher, Katharine A. Biehl, and Joseph L. Zarefsky, *Direct and Work Relief and Federal Work Programs in Allegheny County, 1920–1941* (Pittsburgh, Pa.: Federation of Social Agencies, 1942), 11; Nancy K. Cauthen and Edwin Amenta, "Not for Widows Only: Institutional Politics and the Formative Years of Aid to Dependent Children," *American Sociological Review* 61 (1996): 434.

15. Gordon, *Pitied,* 291–92.

16. Kessler-Harris describes the common assumptions of New Dealers in the "advocacy of democratic social order reflected in the traditional family" and shows the extent to which they incorporated the values of organized labor into their legislation (*Pursuit of Equity,* 76).

17. Mark Leff ("Taxing the 'Forgotten Man': The Politics of Social Security Finance in the New Deal," *Journal of American History* 70 [1983]: 359–83) explores the financial underpinnings of the act and the president's determination that its old-age pension sections should "not become a dole through the mingling of insurance and relief" (366).

18. Berkowitz and McQuaid, "Social Security," 172–73.

19. Mettler, *Dividing Citizens*, 126–28.

20. Ruth Milkman, "Women's Work and the Economic Crisis: Some Lessons from the Great Depression," in *A Heritage of Her Own*, ed. Nancy F. Cott and Elizabeth H. Pleck, 507–41 (New York: Simon and Schuster, 1979) (Milkman believes that official statistics understated female unemployment, but I suggest that official statistics simply missed the unknown but clearly large number of women who shifted from their normal employments into lesser jobs, such as domestic work); Badger, *New Deal*, 23–29; Harriet A. Byrne, *The Effects of the Depression on Wage Earners' Families: A Second Survey of South Bend*, Women's Bureau Bulletin no. 108 (Washington, D.C.: GPO, 1936), 17.

21. U.S. Bureau of the Census, *Fifteenth Census: Population*, vol. 5, p. 276; idem, *Sixteenth Census: Population*, vol. 3, pt. 1, p. 111.

22. Raymond Wolters, *Negroes and the Great Depression* (Westport, Conn.: Greenwood, 1970), 21–56 (Wolters discusses agriculture generally but says little about black women); Gunnar Myrdal, *An American Dilemma: The Negro Problem and Modern Democracy*, 2 vols. (New York: Harper Torchbooks, 1962), 1:254.

23. Jacqueline Jones, *Labor of Love, Labor of Sorrow: Black Women, Work, and the Family from Slavery to the Present* (New York: Basic Books, 1985), 200–202; U.S. Bureau of the Census, *Sixteenth Census: Population*, vol. 5, *Characteristics of Persons Not in the Labor Force 14 Years Old and Over* (Washington, D.C.: GPO, 1943), 10–11.

24. Federal Emergency Relief Administration (hereinafter FERA), *Bulletin* no. 5054; "Women Who Are Heads of Families on Relief, July, 1935," typescript, Women's Bureau Papers, National Archives, Record Group 86, box 6.

25. Margaret Hagood, *Mothers of the South: Portraiture of the White Tenant Farm Woman* (New York: W. W. Norton, 1977 [1939]), 168.

26. FERA, "Women in the Urban Relief Population, October, 1935," FERA Release no. 6572, Women's Bureau Papers, Record Group 86, box 6; Mary Ellen Pidgeon, *Women in the Economy of the United States of America: A Summary Report*, Women's Bureau Bulletin no. 155 (Washington, D.C.: GPO, 1937), 37.

27. Pidgeon, *Women in the Economy*, 37; U.S. Bureau of the Census, *Sixteenth Census: Population*, vol. 5, p. 11.

28. Elisabeth D. Benham, *The Woman Wage Earner: Her Situation Today*, Women's Bureau Bulletin no. 172 (Washington, D.C.: GPO, 1939), 48.

29. Robert Lieberman discusses these omissions in *Shifting the Color Line: Race and the American Welfare State* (Cambridge, Mass.: Harvard University Press, 1998), 39–48. Gareth Davies describes this as a move to demonstrate the actuarial soundness of the act's Old Age Insurance provisions ("The Unsuspected Radicalism of the Social Security Act," in *The Roosevelt Years*, ed. Robert A. Garson and Stuart S. Kidd, 56–71 [Edinburgh: Edinburgh University Press, 1999], 63).

30. Julia Kirk Blackwelder, "Women in the Work Force: Atlanta, New Orleans, and San Antonio, 1930 to 1940," *Journal of Urban History* 4 (May 1978): 350; Jo Ann E. Argersinger, *Toward a New Deal in Baltimore: People and Government in the Great Depression* (Chapel Hill: University of North Carolina Press, 1988); Elizabeth Clark-Lewis, "'This Work Had a End': African American Domestic Workers in Washington, D.C., 1910–1940," in *"To Toil the Livelong Day": America's Women at Work, 1870–1980*, ed. Carol Groneman and Mary

Beth Norton, 196–212 (Ithaca, N.Y.: Cornell University Press, 1987); Brenda Clegg Gray, *Black Female Domestics during the Depression in New York City, 1930–1940* (New York: Garland, 1993). Andor Skotnes describes one attempt on the part of African Americans to overcome the pervasive discrimination they faced in Baltimore's Depression labor market ("'Buy Where You Can Work': Boycotting for Jobs in African American Baltimore, 1933–1934," *Journal of Social History* 27 [1994]: 735–62).

31. U.S. Bureau of the Census, *Sixteenth Census: Population,* vol. 3, pt. 1, p. 124; Gray, *Black Female Domestics,* 57; Jean Collier Brown, *The Negro Woman Worker,* Women's Bureau Bulletin no. 165 (Washington, D.C.: GPO, 1938), 3; Pidgeon, *Women in the Economy,* 70, 82.

32. Women's Bureau, "The Effect of Migrating Industries upon Women's Opportunities for Employment," typescript, Women's Bureau Papers, Record Group 86, box 6; Mary Anderson, *Women's Place in Industry in Ten Southern States* (Washington, D.C.: GPO, 1931), 7.

33. Badger, *New Deal,* 87.

34. Dolores Janiewski, "Flawed Victories: The Experiences of Black and White Women Workers in Durham during the 1930s," in *Decades of Discontent,* ed. Lois Scharf and Joan Jensen, 90–92 (Westport, Conn.: Greenwood, 1983); Benham, *Woman Wage Earner,* 49; Nancy Gabin, *Feminism in the Labor Movement: Women and the United Auto Workers, 1935–1975* (Ithaca, N.Y.: Cornell University Press, 1990), 8–46 (Gabin describes the mechanisms by which unionized men in heavy industry protected their own jobs at the expense of women workers); U.S. Bureau of the Census, *Sixteenth Census: Population,* vol. 3, pt. 1, p. 115.

35. Children's Bureau, *White House Conference on Children, 1941* (Washington, D.C.: GPO, 1941), 226–27; Walter Trattner, *Crusade for the Children: A History of the National Child Labor Committee and Child Labor Reform in America* (Chicago: Quadrangle Books, 1970), 216, 301. The altered basis for enumerating child workers in 1940 makes it impossible to compare the employment of ten to thirteen year olds.

36. U.S. Bureau of the Census, *Historical Statistics,* 132.

37. Glen Elder Jr., *Children of the Great Depression: Social Change in Life Experience* (Chicago: University of Chicago Press, 1974), 65.

38. Lizbeth Cohen found that relief agencies in Chicago required children to contribute their entire earnings to their families and maintains that they were better able to get jobs than their fathers were (*Making a New Deal: Industrial Workers in Chicago, 1919–1939* [Cambridge: Cambridge University Press, 1990], 247).

39. Qtd. in John A. Garraty, *The Great Depression* (New York: Anchor Doubleday, 1987), 189; Garraty contrasts the CCC and the Hitler Youth.

40. Fletcher, Biehl, and Zarefsky, *Direct and Work Relief,* 25.

41. Massachusetts Department of Public Welfare, *Annual Report, 1931* (Boston, 1931), 9; Fletcher, Biehl, and Zarefsky, *Direct and Work Relief,* 19–20; Ways and Means Committee, *Hearings on H.R. 4120,* 80.

42. Emma A. Winslow, *Trends in Different Types of Public and Private Relief in Urban Areas, 1929–1935,* Children's Bureau Publication no. 237 (Washington, D.C.: GPO, 1937), 39–43.

43. Ways and Means Committee, *Hearings on H.R. 4120,* 80. Andrew Billingsley and

Jeanne M. Giovannoni, *Children of the Storm: Black Children and American Child Welfare* (New York: Harcourt Brace Jovanovich, 1972), 78–79; Miss Margaret Wead, Family Welfare Association of New York, 18 February 1932, Children's Bureau Papers, National Archives, Record Group 102, box 441.

44. White caseworker, "The Southern Negro and Depression," *The Churchman,* 10 Sept. 1932, clipping, Children's Bureau Papers, Record Group 102, box 546.

45. Maya Angelou, *I Know Why the Caged Bird Sings* (New York: Random House, 1970), 40.

46. Mr. W. A. Hill, caseworker at the Cook County Bureau of Public Welfare, to Miss Alida Bowler, Children's Bureau, 16 September 1932, Children's Bureau Papers, Record Group 102, box 418. (Bowler attached a memo to Hill's letter before passing it to her research assistant, Mary Milburn; in the memo she wrote, "I wonder if you could help me by listing for me the material which we have that you think this gentleman needs. He is a colored worker who impressed me as being quite an effective person.") Darlene Clark Hine suggests that women's migration patterns may have differed from men's but also that many African American women left behind their children to forge an economic beachhead in the North ("Black Migration to the Urban Midwest: The Gender Dimension, 1915–1945," in *The Great Migration in Historical Perspective: New Dimensions of Race, Class, and Gender,* ed. Joe William Trotter, 127–46 [Bloomington: Indiana University Press, 1991]).

47. *New York Times,* 1 December 1932; Agnes K. Hanna to Caroline Degener of the Child Welfare Committee of America, 22 December 1932, Children's Bureau Papers, Record Group 102, box 403; Emily Rienby, an Arkansas widow, to the Children's Bureau, 22 July 1935, Children's Bureau Papers, Record Group 102, box 546 (Rienly stated that her relief had been curtailed because of a lack of funds); Fletcher, Biehl, and Zarefsky, *Direct and Work Relief,* 60–63.

48. Fall River Family Welfare Association, scrapbook, 1929–1939; Family Service Association of Fall River, "History," typescript; Fall River Family Welfare Association, "Highlights, 1934," typescript (all three documents in possession of the Family Service Association of Fall River). "Twenty-fourth Annual Neediest Cases Appeal," *New York Times,* 8 December 1935, emphasizes worn-out mothers and older children who had been helped to find employment.

49. Hopkins, qtd. in Bonnie Fox Schwartz, *The Civil Works Administration, 1933–1934: The Business of Emergency Employment in the New Deal* (Princeton, N.J.: Princeton University Press, 1984), 179.

50. Ware, *Beyond Suffrage,* 54. Women increased their share of government jobs, but this did not carry over into government programs or employment generally.

51. Barbara Melosh, "Manly Work: Public Art and Masculinity in Depression America," in *Gender and American History since 1890,* ed. Barbara Melosh, 155–81 (London: Routledge, 1993), 173 (Melosh writes specifically about the paucity of depictions of working women in New Deal public art but also refers to the "insistent gendering of work" [174] in both murals and the national psyche); Winifred Wandersee, *Women's Work and Family Values, 1920–1940* (Cambridge, Mass.: Harvard University Press, 9180); Lois Scharf, *To Work and to Wed: Female Employment, Feminism, and the Great Depression* (Westport, Conn.: Greenwood Press, 1980).

52. Laura Hapke, *Daughters of the Great Depression: Women, Work, and Fiction in the*

American 1930s (Athens: University of Georgia Press, 1995). Elizabeth Faue examines the iconography of the labor movement during the Depression in *Community of Suffering and Struggle: Women, Men, and the Labor Movement in Minneapolis, 1915–1945* (Chapel Hill: University of North Carolina Press, 1991).

53. Contemporary scholarship emphasized employment's role in preserving masculine self-respect but ignored women entirely. See, among others, Mirra Komarovsky, *The Unemployed Man and His Family* (New York: Octagon Books, 1970 [1940]).

54. Fletcher, Biehl, and Zarefsky, *Direct and Work Relief,* 65; Mary Ruth Colby to Miss Hutsinpillar, memorandum, 22 September 1932, Children's Bureau Papers, Record Group 102, box 404.

55. Gene D. L. Jones, "The Chicago Catholic Charities, the Great Depression, and Public Moneys," *Illinois Historical Journal* 83 (1990): 13–30. Peter Fearon describes the mechanisms by which relief was distributed in "Kansas Poor Relief: The Influence of the Great Depression" (unpublished paper, 1995). Ralph Carr Fletcher and Katherine A. Biehl ("Trends in Direct Relief Expenditures in Allegheny County, 1920–1937," *The Federator* 13 [1938]: 69) indicate that mothers' assistance in Allegheny County increased in the mid-1920s, dropped at the start of the Depression, and rose steadily thereafter. Gordon (*Pitied,* 189) estimates that relief expenditures for single mothers and children were three and a half times higher on federal funds than on mothers' assistance.

56. Mrs. Elizabeth Gilroy, Scranton Pennsylvania, letter forwarded to the Children's Bureau, Children's Bureau Papers, Record Group 102, box 546; Mrs. Elizabeth Budde to Children's Bureau, 19 March 1934, Children's Bureau Papers, Record Group 102, box 544 (Mrs. Budde was referred to the New Jersey State Board of Charities).

57. Ralph Carr Fletcher and Katherine A. Biehl, "Source of Income of Mothers' Assistance Fund Families," *The Federator* 12 (1937): 208.

58. Susan Ware, *Partner and I: Molly Dewson, Feminism, and New Deal Politics* (New Haven, Conn.: Yale University Press, 1987), chap. 12.

59. FERA, "Women on Relief and Their Employment," FERA Release 7369, Women's Bureau Papers, Record Group 86, box 68.

60. Argersinger, *Toward a New Deal,* 72; FERA Release no. 5439, Women's Bureau Papers, Record Group 86, box 68.

61. Hagood, *Mothers of the South,* 168; "Women Who Are Heads of Families on Relief, July, 1935," typescript, Women's Bureau Papers, Record Group 86, box 6; Works Progess Administration, *Research Bulletin,* ser. 4, no. 2 (Washington, D.C.: GPO, 1937); "Employment of Women on Works Progress Administration Projects," typescript, Women's Bureau Papers, Record Group 86, box 68; Federal Works Agency, *Report on the Progress of the WPA Program,* (Washington, D.C.: GPO, 1941), 51.

62. Scharf, *To Work and to Wed,* 124.

63. Ralph Carr Fletcher, "Work Relief and Work Programs in Allegheny County, 1920–1937," *Federator* 13 (May 1938): 121–26; "Economic Problems of Women," typescript, Women's Bureau Papers, Record Group 86, box 68.

64. Works Progress Administration, *Research Bulletin,* ser. 4, no. 2; "Employment of Women."

65. U.S. Bureau of the Census, *Sixteenth Census: Population,* vol. 3, pt. 1, p. 358; "Employment of Women."

66. Federal Works Agency, *Final Report on the WPA Program, 1935–1943* (Washington, D.C.: GPO, 1947), 45; Richard Sterner, *The Negro's Share* (New York: Harper and Brothers, 1943), 245–46.

67. Wolters, *Negroes,* 206; Donald S. Howard, *The WPA and Federal Relief Policy* (New York: Russell Sage Foundation, 1943), 292; Argersinger, *Toward a New Deal,* 75–78. Myrdal (*American Dilemma,* 1:1087) describes training programs for African American domestics. Mary V. Robinson notes older women's preferences for live-out domestic services (*Domestic Workers and Their Employment Relations: A Study Based on the Records of the Domestic Efficiency Association of Baltimore, Maryland,* Women's Bureau Publication no. 39 [Washington, D.C.: GPO, 1924], 32).

68. U.S. Bureau of the Census, *Sixteenth Census: Population,* vol. 3, pt. 3, pp. 358, 451; idem, *Sixteenth Census: Population,* vol. 3, *The Labor Force,* pt. 5, *Pennsylvania–Wyoming* (Washington, D.C.: GPO, 1943), 12.

69. Argersinger and William R. Brock both describe the distinctive approach to welfare and the New Deal adopted in Maryland, especially by Mayor Jackson. See Argersinger, *Toward a New Deal,* 207; Brock, *Welfare, Democracy, and the New Deal* (Cambridge: Cambridge University Press, 1988), 154–59.

70. Gareth Davies and Martha Derthick, "Race and Social Welfare Policy: The Social Security Act of 1935," *Political Science Quarterly* 112 (1997): 226.

71. William E. Leuchtenburg, *Franklin D. Roosevelt and the New Deal, 1932–1940* (New York: Harper and Row, 1963), 132 (Leuchtenburg, however, condemns the act as fiscally inept); Roy Lubove, *Struggle for Social Security, 1900–1935* (Cambridge, Mass.: Harvard University Press, 1968), 179; Leonard Krieger, "The Idea of the Welfare State in Europe and the United States," *Journal of the History of Ideas* 24 (1963): 553–68 (Krieger traces the development of the welfare state to the nation's first stages; the authors of the Articles of Confederation, for example, included in the document a desire to "promote the general welfare"). Mary Nolan reviews Seymour Martin Lipset's *American Exceptionalism: A Double-Edged Sword* (New York: Norton, 1996) and rejects his exceptionalist claims about the American welfare state (see Nolan, "Against Exceptionalisms," *American Historical Review* 102 [1997]: 769–74). See also Gisela Bock and Pat Thane, eds., *Maternity and Gender Policies: Women and the Rise of the European Welfare States, 1880s-1950s* (New York: Routledge, 1986), and Koven and Michel, *Mothers.*

72. Theda Skocpol, *Protecting Soldiers and Mothers: The Political Origins of Social Policy in the United States* (Cambridge, Mass.: Belknap, 1992), 536.

73. Davies, "Unsuspected Radicalism," 56–71; Edward D. Berkowitz, *America's Welfare State: From Roosevelt to Reagan* (Baltimore, Md.: Johns Hopkins University Press, 1991), 2.

74. Kessler-Harris, "Designing Women," 89.

75. Mimi Abramovitz, *Regulating the Lives of Women* (Boston: South End, 1989), 216. See also Michael Katz, *Poverty and Policy in American History* (New York: Academic Press, 1983), 235. Carole Haber and Brian Gratton argue that Social Security (as amended in 1937) benefits women because they receive pensions based on their husbands' contribution records (*Old Age and the Search for Security: An American Social History* [Bloomington: Indiana University Press, 1994], 85).

76. Edwin E. Witte, *The Development of the Social Security Act* (Madison: University of Wisconsin Press, 1963), 152–56.

77. Paul H. Douglas, *Social Security in the United States* (New York: Whittlesey House, 1936), 100–101; testmony of Charles H. Houston, in *Hearings, 1935, 796.*

78. Kessler-Harris discusses the rationale for excluding part-time workers and wives in *Pursuit of Equity,* 117–18.

79. Abramovitz, *Regulating,* 250.

80. Davies and Derthick, "Race and Social Welfare," 217–35.

81. Lieberman, *Shifting the Color Line,* 30; Jill Quadagno, *The Transformation of Old Age Security: Class and Politics in the American Welfare State* (Chicago: University of Chicago Press, 1988), 116.

82. *Reminiscences of Barbara Nachtrieb Armstrong,* cited in Mettler, *Dividing Citizens,* 65.

83. *Hearings, 1935.*

84. Franklin D. Roosevelt, "Message from the President to the Congress of the United States in Support of the Economic Security Act," in *Hearings, 1935,* 47–48.

85. Edwin E. Witte, in *Hearings, 1935,* 161.

86. Jennifer Mittelstadt discusses the caretaker amendment in "The Dilemmas of the Liberal Welfare State, 1945–1964: Gender, Race and Aid to Dependent Children" (Ph.D. diss., University of Michigan, 2000).

87. Witte, *Development of Social Security,* 163; Gordon, *Pitied,* 264–72; Skocpol, *Protecting,* 534–35 (Skocpol discusses the Children's Bureau's waning influence, as does Kriste Lindenmeyer in *"A Right to Childhood": The U.S. Children's Bureau and Child Welfare, 1912–1946* [Urbana: University of Illinois Press, 1997]); House Committee on Ways and Means, *Amendments to the Social Security Act: Hearings on H.R. 5710,* 76th Cong., 1st sess., 3 March 1939, 3 vols. (Washington, D.C.: GPO, 1939), 1:295, 501, 794 (hereinafter *Hearings, 1939*). Blanche Coll also described ADC as "an orphan program" and observed that lobbying on behalf of children was "miniscule" (*Safety Net: Welfare and Social Security, 1929–1979* [New Brunswick, N.J.: Rutgers University Press, 1995], 103).

88. Poole gives a full account of this battle ("Securing Race," 270–79).

89. Witte, *Development of Social Security,* 162–63.

90. Abraham Epstein, in *Hearings, 1939,* 2:1012.

91. Walter Graebner, *A History of Retirement* (New Haven, Conn.: Yale University Press, 1980); Edwin Amenta and Yvonne Zylan, "It Happened Here: Political Opportunity, the New Institutionalism, and the Townsend Movement," *American Sociological Review* 56 (1991): 250–65; Edwin Amenta and Bruce G. Carruthers, "The Formative Years of U.S. Social Spending Policies: Theories of the Welfare State and the American States during the Great Depression," *American Sociological Review* 53 (1988): 661–78 (see Alan Brinkley, *Voices of Protest: Huey Long, Father Coughlin and the Great Depression* [New York: Random House, 1988], for information on other radical pressure groups); Andrew Achenbaum, *Social Security: Visions and Revisions* (Cambridge: Cambridge University Press, 1986), 23; James T. Patterson, *America's Struggle against Poverty,* 1900–1980 (Cambridge, Mass.: Harvard University Press), 74–75.

92. Theda Skocpol analyzes the rhetorical and policy implications that had followed from this approach and were still present at the millennium in *The Missing Middle: Working Families and the Future of American Social Policy* (New York: W. W. Norton, 2000).

93. The 1990s debate over Social Security, Medicare, and AFDC carried these biases into the late twentieth century.

94. Berkowitz and McQuaid, "Social Security," 172–73.

95. In *Hearing, 1935*, 263.

96. Coll, *Safety Net*, 52. Subsequently, commodity-surplus programs and food stamps restored some of the in-kind provisions that ADC initially rejected.

97. Charles H. Houston, in *Hearings, 1935*, 796. Howard (*The WPA*, 437) found that state income and racial composition had a greater impact on the amount spent on AFDC benefits than on unemployment insurance.

98. *Hearings, 1935*, 976 (statements of the Hon. Howard W. Smith), 977 (statements of Rep. Jenkins); Piven and Cloward, *Regulating the Poor*, 116. Myrdal (*American Dilemma*, chap. 22) discusses the southern political scene and the methods used to keep whites in power. Rep. John L. McClellan, from Arkansas, protested that his state would be unable to raise tax revenues in order to fund the requirements of the act (*Hearings, 1935*, 1127).

99. *Hearings, 1935*, 590, 600, 796.

100. Howard, *The WPA*, 437. The same did not hold for unemployment compensation.

101. Map of approved plans for Social Security, 8 December 1936, Children's Bureau Papers, Record Group 102, box 546; Scharf, *To Work and to Wed*, 129–30.

102. *Hearings, 1939*, 1:14.

103. Testimony of Millard W. Rice, legislative representative Veterans of Foreign Wars, in *Hearings, 1939*, 2:1071.

104. Mary S. Larabee, "Unmarried Parenthood under the Social Security Act," *Proceedings of the National Conference of Social Work* (1939): 447–9.

105. Myrdal, *American Dilemma*, 359; Berkowitz, *America's Welfare State*, 102.

106. This transition occurred for fourteen- to thirty-four year-old women between the 1930 and 1940 censuses (U.S. Bureau of the Census, *Historical Statistics*, 20); *Hearings, 1939*, 2:1071; Coll, *Safety Net*, 105.

107. Abramovitz, *Regulating*, 317.

108. A. G. Thomas to Francis A. Staten, cited in Mettler, 165.

109. Fall River, Aid to Dependent Children Register, 15 Sept. 1937 and 15 Dec. 1939; *Fall River City Directory*, for years 1920–39 (these documents are in the possession of the Fall River Library). I traced recipients back through the city directories until I located their late husbands' occupations.

110. Pennsylvania Department of Public Charities, "Public Asistance in Pennsylvania, December 1, 1938," unpublished leaflet (1938); Fletcher, Biehl, and Zarefsky, *Direct and Work Relief*, 17.

111. Children's Bureau, unpublished map, Children's Bureau Papers, Record Group 102, box 546; Argersinger, *Toward a New Deal*, 46; Baltimore, Department of Public Welfare, *Annual Statistical Report* (Baltimore: n.p., 1937); testimony of D. S. Howard, in *Hearings, 1939*, 2:1328–29.

112. *Hearings, 1939*, 1:6, 14.

113. Ibid., 3:2199 (testimony of A. J. Altmeyer).

114. Ibid., 2:1134 (testimony of Marion B. Folsom).

115. Ibid., 2:1221 (testimony of Dr. J. Douglas Brown).

116. Patricia Huckle, *Tish Sommers, Activist, and the Founding of the Older Women's League* (Knoxville: University of Tennessee Press, 1991).

117. *Hearings, 1939,* 1:6.

118. Ibid., 3:2164, 2299 (testimony of A. J. Altmeyer).

119. Ibid., 1:32; Abramovitz, *Regulating,* 320–27.

120. Ibid., 2:1316 (testimony of Paul T. Beisser), 1377 (statement of Mrs. Harris T. Waldwin).

121. D. B. Eppley, "Decline in the Number of AFDC Orphans," *Welfare in Review,* Sept.–Oct. 1968, pp. 1–7; Rickie Solinger, *Wake Up Little Susie: Single Pregnancy and Race before Roe v. Wade* (London: Routledge, 1992), 37.

122. Berkowitz, *America's Welfare State,* 103.

123. Myrdal, *American Dilemma,* 359.

124. George E. Haynes, executive secretary of the Department of Race Relations of the Federal Council of Churches of Christ in America, in *Hearings, 1935,* 590.

125. Joanne Goodwin, "'Employable Mothers' and 'Suitable Work': A Re-Evaluation of Welfare and Wage-Earning for Women in the Twentieth-Century United States," *Journal of Social History* 29 (Winter 1995): 259.

126. These anomalies led in the 1970s and 1980s to the campaigns for displaced homemakers and for divorced women's pension rights and eventually to pension sharing. See Berkowitz, *America's Welfare State,* chap. 6, for a cogent formulation of welfare issues and race in the postwar era.

127. Foster Hailey, "Newburgh Faces a Crisis over Relief," *New York Times,* 11 June 1961 (the city manager of Newburgh, New York, imposed a set of welfare rules on AFDC recipients that strictly regulated recipients' behavior); Gilbert Y. Steiner, *Social Insecurity: The Politics of Welfare* (Chicago: Rand McNally), 110–12; Coll, *Safety Net,* 210–16.

128. For a discussion of postwar masculinist and racist filters on ADC, see Ruth Feldstein, *Motherhood in Black and White: Race and Sex in American Liberalism, 1930–1965* (Ithaca, N.Y.: Cornell University Press, 2000), 66–71. In *Weinburger v. Wiesenfeld* (1975) the Supreme Court decided that men and widowers' children were entitled to survivors' benefits on the same basis as women and widows' offspring.

129. Elizabeth Alling and Agnes Leisy observe that "censure of the parents" became part of the welfare process ("Aid to Dependent Children in a Postwar Year," *Social Security Bulletin* 13 [1950]: 13). Piven and Cloward (*Regulating the Poor,* 205–6) document this process in Mississippi.

130. Haber and Gratton, *Old Age,* 84. In 1940 nearly three-fifths of all older widows resided with their children (either as household heads or dependents); by 1970 half as many did so. See Frances E. Kobrin, "The Fall in Household Size and the Rise of the Primary Individual in the United States," *Demography* 13 (1976): 127–38; Helena Znaniecki Lopata, *Widowhood in an American City* (Cambridge, Mass.: Schenkman, 1973), 33–34.

131. Linda Gordon, "Black and White Visions of Welfare: Women's Welfare Activism, 1890–1945," *Journal of American History* 78 (1991): 559–90.

Index

S. J. KLEINBERG is a professor of American history at Brunel University, London. Her many publications include *The Shadow of the Mills: Working-Class Families in Pittsburgh, 1870–1907* and *Women in the United States, 1830–1945*. She is the editor of the *Journal of American Studies* and a member of both the executive committee of the British Association for American Studies and the American Studies Association International Committee.

Women in American History

The University of Illinois Press
is a founding member of the
Association of American University Presses.

———————————————————————

Composed in 10.5/13 Adobe Minion
by Jim Proefrock
at the University of Illinois Press
Manufactured by Thomson-Shore, Inc.

University of Illinois Press
1325 South Oak Street
Champaign, IL 61820-6903
www.press.uillinois.edu